Palgrave Studies in Classical Liberalism

Series Editors
David Hardwick
Vancouver, BC, Canada

Leslie Marsh
Department of Pathology and Laboratory Medicine
Faculty of Medicine
University of British Columbia
Vancouver, BC, Canada

This series offers a forum to writers concerned that the central presuppositions of the liberal tradition have been severely corroded, neglected, or misappropriated by overly rationalistic and constructivist approaches. The hardest-won achievement of the liberal tradition has been the wrestling of epistemic independence from overwhelming concentrations of power, monopolies and capricious zealotries. The very precondition of knowledge is the exploitation of the epistemic virtues accorded by society's situated and distributed manifold of spontaneous orders, the DNA of the modern civil condition. With the confluence of interest in situated and distributed liberalism emanating from the Scottish tradition, Austrian and behavioral economics, non-Cartesian philosophy and moral psychology, the editors are soliciting proposals that speak to this multidisciplinary constituency. Sole or joint authorship submissions are welcome as are edited collections, broadly theoretical or topical in nature.

More information about this series at
http://www.palgrave.com/gp/series/15722

Kevin Currie-Knight

Education in the Marketplace

An Intellectual History of Pro-Market
Libertarian Visions for Education
in Twentieth Century America

Kevin Currie-Knight
East Carolina University
Greenville, NC, USA

Palgrave Studies in Classical Liberalism
ISBN 978-3-030-11777-1   ISBN 978-3-030-11778-8   (eBook)
https://doi.org/10.1007/978-3-030-11778-8

Library of Congress Control Number: 2019932115

© The Editor(s) (if applicable) and The Author(s) 2019
This work is subject to copyright. All rights are solely and exclusively licensed by the Publisher, whether the whole or part of the material is concerned, specifically the rights of translation, reprinting, reuse of illustrations, recitation, broadcasting, reproduction on microfilms or in any other physical way, and transmission or information storage and retrieval, electronic adaptation, computer software, or by similar or dissimilar methodology now known or hereafter developed.
The use of general descriptive names, registered names, trademarks, service marks, etc. in this publication does not imply, even in the absence of a specific statement, that such names are exempt from the relevant protective laws and regulations and therefore free for general use.
The publisher, the authors and the editors are safe to assume that the advice and information in this book are believed to be true and accurate at the date of publication. Neither the publisher nor the authors or the editors give a warranty, express or implied, with respect to the material contained herein or for any errors or omissions that may have been made. The publisher remains neutral with regard to jurisdictional claims in published maps and institutional affiliations.

Cover illustration: Pattadis Walarput/Alamy Stock Photo

This Palgrave Macmillan imprint is published by the registered company Springer Nature Switzerland AG
The registered company address is: Gewerbestrasse 11, 6330 Cham, Switzerland

Acknowledgements

The journey in writing this book has been as fascinating as it has been long. First, I have to thank those closest to me for their support along the way: my parents Rob and Lynne, my wife Tricia, and our son Lachlan.

The research that became this book started with my dissertation research at the University of Delaware. I have to thank my dissertation committee—Robert Hampel, Eugene Matusov, Jan Blits, and Matt Zwolinski—for their advice and intellectual support. There are many others who've given advice, support, and encouragement along the way. In no particular order (other than alphabetical), they are: Nigel Ashford, John "Jack" Coons, Stephen Davies, Bill Glod, Daniel Keuhn, William Kline, Geoffrey Lea, Phil Magness, Leslie Marsh Matt McCaffrey, Michael Valdez Moses, and Stephen Sugarman. I also wish to thank the librarians at East Carolina University's Joyner Library for their help tracking down rare books, helping me track down challenging details for research, and other detective work. Lastly, I want to acknowledge a debt to the amazing open-access online book libraries provided by Liberty Fund and the Ludwig von Mises Institute. While libertarian ideologies are often caricatured as being about selfishness and the profit motive, these two institutes have created treasure troves of freely accessible online books in a variety of formats. Without these libraries, I just can't imagine how much more onerous my research would have been.

Contents

1 Introduction   1

2 Albert Jay Nock: Pessimism About Education by State or Market   23

3 Frank Chodorov: Consumer Sovereignty, Markets in Education, and "A School on Every Corner"   41

4 Ayn Rand: Isabel Paterson, Private Education for a Free Society, and Education for Galt's Gulch   59

5 Murray Rothbard: Separating Education and the State Beyond Left and Right   77

6 Milton (and Rose) Friedman: Education Vouchers and State Financing of Private Education   99

7 Myron Lieberman: Education Without Romance, Public Choice Economics, and Markets in Education   127

8 "Other Conceptions, Both Powerful and Exotic":
   School Choice Visions from Voices from the Political Left   155

9 Conclusion   179

Bibliography   191

Index   205

1

Introduction

In his 1973 book *For a New Liberty*, libertarian economist Murray Rothbard describes a thought experiment. He analogized the American system of public education with a hypothetical American system of government news.

> What then would we think of a proposal for the government, federal or state, to use the taxpayers' money to set up a nationwide chain of public magazines or newspapers, and then to compel all people, or all children, to read them? Further, what would we think of the government outlawing all other newspapers and magazines, or at the very least outlawing all newspapers or magazines that do not come up to certain "standards" of what a government commission thinks children ought to read?[1]

Rothbard used this thought experiment to argue a point: that a government institution retaining a monopoly over the press not only would likely invoke a public outcry about individual liberty and freedom of the press. It would also let the government control the dissemination of infor-

---

[1] Murray Rothbard, *For a New Liberty* (Auburn, AL: Ludwig von Mises Institute, 1973), 157.

© The Author(s) 2019
K. Currie-Knight, *Education in the Marketplace*,
Palgrave Studies in Classical Liberalism,
https://doi.org/10.1007/978-3-030-11778-8_1

mation in dangerous ways. Yet the structure of his thought experiment, he argued, is virtually the same as the structure of American public schooling, where governments create their own tax-funded schools to which all students must go unless their family can pay private tuition to one of the few private schools the government certifies as meeting its own regulatory standards. "In fact," argued Rothbard, "the suppression of free schooling should be regarded with even greater horror than the suppression of a free press, since here the tender and unformed minds of children are more directly involved."[2]

Perhaps we can see, in Rothbard's analogy, a larger point: while the government's quasi-monopoly over the schooling of the young *should* be seen as a more serious blow to individual liberty than its establishment of a news monopoly, the very real school system doesn't seem to evoke as much outcry as the hypothetical (yet similar) "public news system." In other words, Rothbard's thought experiment denaturalizes the rules of the American (and most other) school system(s) by applying those rules to a very different situation, in order to take a fresh look at familiar issues. *If the fictitious scenario of a monopolistic government news service seems objectionable, why don't the same concerns apply to the monopolistic public school system objectionable?*

Of course, to Rothbard, this would have been a purely rhetorical question. A government quasi-monopoly on news would violate the same individual liberty by denying individual choice, and invite the same abuse by the monopolists as our quasi-monopolistic system of public education does.

What was the preferred alternative? What would restore individual liberty to the people (by giving them choice) and reduce or eliminate the potential for abuse and inefficiency that monopolies carry? Like all of the libertarian subjects in this work, Rothbard supported free markets in education services (the possible exception being Albert Jay Nock, who was skeptical of both government-provided and market-provided education). Like the current system of news delivery, where people can choose the private news service that best suits their needs within a competitive market, Rothbard argued that people should be able to choose the schooling

---

[2] Rothbard, *For a New Liberty*, 157.

they thought best for their children and that schools should compete for business the same way news services do.

This is a history of pro-market arguments about American education—the idea that we should reject the current public education system and replace it with a market in educational services that allows producers to offer competing schooling options and consumers to choose those that work best for them. The intellectuals I profile in this history vary in their opinions of the roles the government should play in this market; Rothbard, an anarchist, left no room for government in education markets, where Milton Friedman and Myron Lieberman (the subjects of the final two chapters) wanted governments to provide people with vouchers with which to purchase schooling and possibly set some minimal standards. Despite these differences (and others, such as the differing rationale each had for supporting markets in education), each intellectual profiled in these pages argued that the then-current public education system (for various reasons) was dangerous and markets in education were a potential solution.

The subjects in this book are what I will call *market libertarians*. I use the term *market libertarian* in reference to those who hold a political position that goods and services should be bought and sold in free markets as opposed to being provided by governments. Libertarian philosopher Jason Brennan describes the basics of the libertarian position this way: "Libertarians believe respect for individual liberty is the central requirement of justice. They believe human relationships should be based on mutual consent. Libertarians advocate a free society of cooperation, tolerance, and mutual respect."[3] Because of this respect for individual liberty—defined in its "negative" sense where people have liberty to the extent that others are not coercing them[4]—libertarians believe that government should be constrained only to functions that cannot arise in other, voluntary, ways.[5] In seeking to minimize government authority, libertarians look to markets

---

[3] Jason Brennan, *Libertarianism: What Everyone Needs to Know* (New York: Oxford University Press, 2012), 17.
[4] Isaiah Berlin, "Two Concepts of Liberty," in *The Proper Study of Mankind*, ed. Henry Hardy (New York: Farrar, Strauss & Giroux, 1997), 191–242.
[5] Some libertarians, like anarchist Murray Rothbard, argued that government was not necessary at all, and that all important social functions could be provided by private initiative. More commonly, libertarians like Ayn Rand and Milton Friedman argued that such things as national defense and a

of buyers and sellers as a more effective way to allocate goods and services between people, largely because markets are voluntary and allow individuals to make choices about their own lives. "Libertarians," says Brennan, "believe economic freedom is necessary if people are to be authors of their own lives."[6]

While libertarians vary in degree, libertarians agree that governments should leave markets as free *as possible*, avoiding regulations on production and consumption and redistribution of wealth within markets. Libertarians are also concerned that governments do not usurp markets by producing goods and services the market can provide. Schooling is one such area of concern for many libertarians. Libertarians, as we will see, have consistently argued that education is essentially a private affair and that, for various reasons and in various ways, markets of private producers will do a much better job than governments at producing education in a way that is responsive to "consumer" demand.

Given that school choice has been advocated at various times by those of various political stripes—libertarians being only one—why write a history focusing primarily on market libertarian arguments? There are several reasons. First, in today's political climate, "school choice" has become more and more associated with a conservative position and, according to its opponents, to a segregationist position. In a recent op-ed, the President of the American Federation of Teachers Randi Weingarten was able to admonish us to recognize the segregationist history of school choice: "make no mistake: The real "pioneers" of private school choice were the white politicians who resisted school integration."[7] Similarly, historian of education Diane Ravitch writes that:

> During the 1950's and 1960's, the term "school choice" was stigmatized as a dodge, invented to permit white students to escape to all-white public schools or to all-white segregated academies. For someone like me, raised in the south and opposed to racism and segregation, the word "choice" and

---

legal system were legitimate government functions that are necessary for a functioning society but could not be performed solely by private action.

[6] Brennan, *Libertarianism*, 96.

[7] Randi Weingarten, "School Choice—Past and Present," American Federation of Teachers, July 22, 2017, https://www.aft.org/column/school-choice-past-and-present.

the phrase "freedom of choice," became tainted. We knew they were being used as a conscious strategy to maintain state-sponsored segregation.[8]

Likewise, legal scholar James Forman (who has written a history school choice's roots in progressive politics) complains that "choice is associated with free-market economist Milton Friedman, attempts to defy *Brown* [*vs. Board of Education*] wealthy conservative philanthropists, and the attacks on the public school bureaucracy by Ronald Reagan and George W. Bush."[9]

To be sure, school choice—specifically in the form of vouchers families can use to attend the school of their choice—played a significant part in segregationist attempts to obviate *Brown vs. Board* and the forced integration of public schools. Several Southern states and counties sought to close public schools and replace them with vouchers parents can use to attend (segregated, it was hoped) private schools.[10]

One reason, then, to focus this history specifically on market libertarian arguments for school choice is that libertarian advocacy of school choice predates these massive resistance and segregationist plans, and are generally quite devoid of appeals to racism and segregation. Instead, they appeal to philosophical and economic arguments about the superiority of a market system to a public system. One could, of course, suggest that racism or segregation might have covertly motivated these libertarian arguments, but neither the arguments not the history of their authors, as we shall see, supports such an uncharitable reading. Looking at these market libertarian arguments for school choice, then, should complicate the arguably dominant cultural story that school choice has its roots bound up in segregationists' desire to avoid public school integration.

Another reason to examine these market libertarian arguments for school choice is that while libertarians have always been a political minority in the United States, they have arguably had a larger impact than their numbers suggest. Several libertarian figures in this book, for

---

[8] Diane Ravitch, *The Death and Life of the Great American School System: How Testing and Choice Are Undermining Education* (New York: Basic Books, 2010).
[9] James Forman, "The Secret History of School Choice: How Progressives Got There First," *Georgetown Law Journal* 93, no. 4 (2005): 1287–1319.
[10] Jim Carl, *Freedom of Choice: Vouchers in American Education* (Santa Barbara, CA: Praeger, 2011).

instance—from perhaps the most famous school choice advocate Milton Friedman to economists James Buchanan and Friedrich Hayek—have won Nobel prizes in economics. (Ludwig von Mises, the libertarian economist who influenced Frank Chodorov—the subject of one of our chapters—never won a Nobel, but is consistently seen as an important figure in the history of economics.) While libertarians have never been a major force in American politics—the Libertarian Party was started only in 1971 and has never successfully placed a candidate into national office—based on polling data, philosopher Jason Brennan suggests that in 2012, "Somewhere between one-tenth and one-third of Americans are libertarian."[11] (This estimate is based not on the labels with which people self-identify, but a survey of their general policy stances "such as whether we should have more or less government control of the economy or whether we should be more or less tolerant of others with different lifestyles and moral beliefs."[12]) Libertarianism, while a minority position, is worth taking seriously.

Lastly, in my own judgment, the libertarian arguments (and plans) for school choice are worth grappling with for their sheer strength. Even if one ultimately disagrees with market libertarians' philosophical and economic objections to markets being kept out of K–12 educational spaces, the arguments themselves offer serious challenges to the culturally dominant idea that unlike most other areas of goods and services, education should be delivered primarily by governments rather than markets. These market libertarians remind us that government-run public education entails the coercion of some to support others, takes away the arguably natural rights of families to control the education of their children, suffers from all of the inefficiencies that plague other state monopolies, and other potential problems. Even those who ultimately disagree with the libertarian position on markets in education will arguably benefit from considering the arguments of the libertarians who saw things very differently.

In this book, I am especially interested in how market libertarian arguments against government provision of education have changed over time, from a socially conservative defense of private education in a *laissez-faire* economy to current voucher proposals that see government's role as pro-

---

[11] Brennan, *Libertarianism*, 172.
[12] Brennan, *Libertarianism*, 172.

viding citizens funding for education, while keeping the provision of education private. In other words, I want to explore how and why libertarian arguments regarding education have changed over the twentieth century. To do this, I will spend each chapter exploring the thought of a prominent market libertarian intellectual, analyzing their educational writings. I will focus on how each intellectual crafted his or her argument against state education, for markets in education, and how each imagined the proper role (if any) for governments and private actors in markets in schooling. The intellectuals I will examine are:

1. **Albert Jay Nock** (1870–1945): Nock was a news magazine writer and social critic who wrote, among other things, a book called *Theory of Education in the United States*. For Nock, an anarchist who favored laissez-faire capitalism in the vein of philosopher Herbert Spencer, state education was an impermissible intrusion on individual liberty less suited to true education than to training good workers. Unlike other figures in this book, while Nock entertained private schools providing education through markets, he was ultimately skeptical that markets could provide quality education, largely because he feared that consumer sovereignty would lead people to prefer inferior and easy educational experiences.
2. **Frank Chodorov** (1887–1966): Chodorov was also a news magazine writer and editor. A professed protégé of Nock's, Chodorov's libertarian political philosophy resembled Nock's in every area except Chodorov's optimism toward markets in education. This difference, I argue, was likely due to his familiarity with economists unfamiliar to Nock who stressed the importance of consumer sovereignty and hesitated to infuse their analysis of what consumers prefer with a philosophical discussion of what consumers *should* prefer. Chodorov ideally preferred no role for government in education, but compromised to support the minimal government function of giving individuals tax deductions/credits for money spent purchasing private education.
3. **Ayn Rand** (1905–1982): Rand was a successful novelist, social critic, and philosopher. An immigrant to America from Soviet Russia, Rand produced several successful libertarian-themed novels and created a philosophy called Objectivism, which placed primacy on the use of human reason as well as individual liberty, achieved through laissez-faire

capitalism. Her educational writings stressed that, as a state enterprise, public education was ill-equipped to teach the kind of individualism and rational thinking on which a free society depends. Private markets in education were preferred, among other reasons, because they were thought more likely to equip individuals for a market-driven society. For similar reasons as Chodorov, Rand supported a role for government in education limited to giving tax credits to individuals for the purchase of education.

4. **Murray Rothbard** (1926–1995): Rothbard was an anarchist economist who believed the market could replace *all* social functions currently supplied by governments, including law and security. Rothbard viewed the state as an agency that sought to obtain and retain power over citizens; state education was an instrument toward this goal. He argued that markets in educational services were justified because markets avoided coercion against individuals as well as forced standardization of instruction for all. Rothbard believed there was no role the state should play in education.

5. **Milton Friedman** (1912–2006): Friedman was an economist who wrote well-known defenses of markets like *Capitalism and Freedom* and *Free to Choose* (with his wife, Rose). His defense of markets was largely consequentialist; markets, he argued, were justified because (and insofar as) they produce more desirable consequences (namely, increases in human well-being) than state intervention. While Friedman believed that there were "public goods" reasons why the state-funded education, state provision of education was unnecessary and produced schools that were inflexible and unresponsive to consumer demand. He preferred a voucher system where the state provides educational funding to families but did not maintain schools (even though his voucher plans allowed for the existence of public schools as options in education markets).

6. **Myron Lieberman** (1919–2013): Lieberman was a public school teacher and teachers' union negotiator turned professor of education. Like Friedman, Lieberman lamented the inflexibility and bureaucracy of the public school system, which, he believed, stemmed from the public school bureaucracy's operation outside of competitive markets and market pressures. Lieberman argued not only that models of school choice (whether vouchers or charters) could alleviate this situation but

also that good school-choice plans should allow and encourage for-profit schools to compete in the educational marketplace.
7. **Assorted advocates for choice from non-libertarian positions**: In this chapter, for purposes of contrast, I review in some detail arguments for school choice made from decidedly non-market-libertarian positions, with focus on advocates on the political left. As James Forman notes, the conventional account that school choice is primarily a right wing issue is "incomplete," and, by Forman's appraisal, leaves out "the left's substantial ... contribution to the development of school choice."[13] This chapter will not be so much a survey of that contribution as an in-depth exploration of three particular arguments for and visions of school choice from advocates on the political left. Theodore Sizer (1932–2009) advocated for school choice as a way to potentially assuage persisting racial and economic inequities that seemed to persist in a non-competitive system where most students are residentially zoned into public schools as well as for reasons of pedagogical pluralism. John "Jack" Coons (1929–) and Stephen Sugarman (1942–) were, like Sizer, primarily concerned with school choice as a vehicle to combat racial and economic inequity in the way schools are financed. In the wake of several California Supreme Court decisions finding that funding public schools primarily through local property taxes unconstitutional, Sugarman and Coons thought a voucher plan where the state distributed money directly to families a more equitable solution. Lastly, John Holt (1923–1985), who considered himself a "small 'l' libertarian," objected to the cultural dominance of formal schooling, finding it a largely ineffective way for most children to learn. He supported school choice largely as a way to attack this cultural dominance and introduce educational pluralism (as choice would extend not just to competing schools, but the choice to learn without school). Not being market libertarians, none of these choice advocates had aversions to introducing government interventions into the market, such as allowing different levels of funding to go to different students to encourage more equitable outcomes, a large role in accreditation of schools in the market,

---

[13] Forman, "The Secret History of School Choice," 1288.

or a government role in collecting and distributing information about schools to parents to aid their ability to choose.

My criteria for the scope of this project necessarily and unfortunately means that I must leave out some very worthy figures. In limiting myself to figures who favored markets in education over state education, I am excluding some familiar libertarian thinkers who were critical of state education but did not argue for markets in education like children's rights advocate Paul Goodman and "unschooling" advocate John Holt.[14] In limiting myself to American market libertarians, I must exclude British market libertarians who focused on education like E.G. West and James Tooley.[15] Lastly, as the focus of this work is market libertarians who wrote at least a fair amount in defense of markets in education, many prominent defenders of market libertarianism as a broad political theory (but not applied to education) like Robert Nozick and James Buchanan will be excluded.

Also, while several of my choices may seem obvious given my criteria, I should elaborate on two that may not appear obvious: Albert Jay Nock and Myron Lieberman. Albert Jay Nock did not necessarily defend markets in education; although he entertained them as an alternative to state education, he was unconvinced that private schools would be less flawed than state schools. So, why choose Nock for the first chapter of a history chronicling libertarian defenses of markets in education? In all honesty, I originally chose Nock in error: having read many of Nock's work defending markets and several essays of his criticizing state education, I *assumed* from these that his solution to the ills of state education would be markets in education. Further research revealed Nock to be as much a skeptic of markets in education as a critic of state education. Yet this itself makes for an interesting reason to start a project like this with an exploration of Albert Jay Nock. Particularly as Nock's libertarian thought was such an influence on Frank Chodorov—the second intellectual I examine—there

---

[14] Paul Goodman, *Compulsory Mis-Education, and the Community of Scholars* (New York: Vintage Books, 1964); John C. Holt, *Escape from Childhood* (Cambridge, MA: Holt Associates, 2013), Kindle ebook ed.

[15] E. G. West, *Education and the State: A Study in Political Economy* (Indianapolis: Liberty Fund, 1994); James Tooley, *Education Without the State* (London: Institute of Economic Affairs, 1998).

is an interesting story to tell about why, for all his libertarianism, Nock did not support markets in education the same way as in other areas, while Chodorov did.

Next, it could be argued that Myron Lieberman is one of several recent libertarian defenders of markets I could have chosen. Others might have chosen Terry Moe or John Chubb, authors of several high-profile defenses of markets in education and critiques of public education.[16] Chubb or Moe (or both) would have been worthwhile candidates for inclusion. My interest in Lieberman has to do with the philosophical coherence of his analysis over time that is well suited for an intellectual history like this one. Not only does Lieberman use a particular economic methodology (public choice economics) to analyze the shortcomings of public education and private alternatives, but he also offers an interesting argument specifically for the allowance (and potential superiority) of for-profit schools in markets for education.

While historical stories are never perfectly linear, there is an overall "shape" to the gradual change in how markets in education have been defended over time. Broadly, the trend has been from defending something like a pure laissez-faire model (where the state has little or no role in education) to something of a "mixed-economy" model of vouchers (where government distributes funding for education, but schooling is produced by private actors). Earlier market libertarians—in order, Frank Chodorov, Ayn Rand, and Murray Rothbard—envisioned either government's educational role relegated to providing tax credits to individuals for the purchase of private education (Chodorov, Rand) or no role for government at all (Rothbard). The remaining two intellectuals—Milton Friedman and Myron Lieberman—saw valid reason for governments to play a relatively strong role in redistributing tax funds for people's purchase of education and even something of a role in regulating/accrediting to determine what schools were eligible to receive vouchers. Yet both still criticized government administration of schooling, largely on grounds that

---

[16]John E. Chubb and Terry M. Moe, *Politics Markets and Americas Schools* (Washington, DC: Brookings Institution Press, 1990); Terry M. Moe, *Schools, Vouchers, and the American Public*, 1st ed. (Washington, DC: Brookings Institution Press, 2001); Terry M. Moe and John E. Chubb, *Liberating Learning: Technology, Politics, and the Future of American Education* (San Francisco: Jossey-Bass, 2009); and Terry M. Moe, *Special Interest: Teachers Unions and America's Public Schools* (Washington, DC: Brookings Institution Press, 2011).

monopolies, and especially government monopolies, were inefficient and unresponsive to consumer preference.

Some Notes on Terminology

I use the term *market libertarian* rather than simply *libertarian* because the latter term can be used in at least two other ways, from which my usage differs. Particularly outside the United States, the term *libertarian* has often been used to refer to political positions that seek to liberate individuals not only from dependence on the state but also from dependence on market forces and their possible consequences.[17] Moreover, in the field of education, *libertarian* is often a word describing any system of education where the child has maximum freedom to direct her educational trajectory and experience (as opposed to a system where the teacher or school leads the student).[18]

In contrast to these latter two uses, I analyze the educational arguments of "market libertarians," rather than "left-libertarians" or "educational libertarians." While the market libertarians I will study all put forward slightly different arguments, they are united in opposition to government production of education and favor private provision of education via market competition.

One last note on my use of terminology: while I use the term *libertarian* (and specifically *market libertarian*) to label the subjects in this history, it should be noted that not all of those "libertarians" profiled used the term to classify their own thought. Murray Rothbard, Milton Friedman, and Frank Chodorov used the term to describe their social views (though the latter two used the term with a bit of reservation, Chodorov preferring the term *individualism* and Friedman preferring the term *liberalism* in its "clas-

---

[17] For an example of this usage, see David Goodway, *Anarchist Seeds Beneath the Snow: Left-Libertarian Thought and British Writers from William Morris to Colin Ward* (Liverpool, UK: Liverpool University Press, 2006).

[18] For an example, see Michael P. Smith, *The Libertarians in Education* (Boston: Allen & Unwin, 1983).

sical" sense[19]). Albert Jay Nock did not use the term to describe his own positions, likely because the term hadn't come into vogue yet to describe pro-market positions. Ayn Rand disavowed the "libertarian" label largely because, while her belief in individual liberty and support for markets over state action accorded nicely with libertarians like Rothbard, she believed that libertarians were often nihilistic regarding moral theory in a way that conflicted with her own normative philosophy of "Objectivism."[20] Lastly, while Myron Lieberman frequently wrote for the libertarian CATO Institute think-tank and clearly preferred free-market policies in education, there is no evidence that he referred to his own thought as libertarian (though this may be because Lieberman's work focuses exclusively on the economics and politics of education, rather than advocating any particular political viewpoint).

For my purposes, it is less important whether the figures chosen for this history used the *libertarian* moniker to describe their own thought than whether their thought (particularly regarding the structure of education in society) fits with an overall market libertarian position. Each of the figures in this book (save for the final chapter of non-market-libertarian advocates of choice) fits that criterion, as they all argue against a state quasi-monopoly on education and for a free market in education services as a viable alternative.

Setting the Historical Stage

As our first chapter will start with Albert Jay Nock in the 1930s, we might briefly survey the history he and others were responding to—the rise of (and controversy around) state-administered public schooling in

---

[19] Frank Chodorov, "About Me: An Editorial," *The Freeman*, July 1954; Brian Doherty, "Best of Both Worlds," *Reason Magazine*, June 1996, 3, http://reason.com/archives/1995/06/01/best-of-both-worlds.

[20] For an example of an "Objectivist" take on libertarianism, see Peter Schwartz, "Libertarianism: The Perversion of Liberty," in *The Voice of Reason: Essays in Objectivist Thought*, ed. Leonard Peikoff (New York: New America Library, 1988), 311–33. While the essay is written by Peter Schwartz, Schwartz was a student of Ayn Rand's, and the essay appears as a supplement in a collection of essays written by Ayn Rand, presumably because it approximates Rand's own thought on the differences between Objectivism and libertarianism.

the nineteenth century. Admittedly, the history I will tell here is selective, emphasizing the ascendance of public schooling over private schooling and the centralization and expansion of public schooling in American history. This selective telling of American educational history is deliberate, as my goal is to tell the history in a way that highlights the trends libertarians in the following chapters might have been concerned by and been responding to.

Arguably, the United States was a country premised on (what we would now call) libertarian values of skepticism toward government power and respect for the rights of individuals from state coercion. Few, perhaps, were more concerned with maintaining individual liberties over state coercion than Thomas Jefferson. In his inauguration speech as the third president of the United States, Jefferson argued for this very libertarian vision of government "which shall restrain men from injuring one another, which shall leave them otherwise free to regulate their own pursuits of industry and improvement, and shall not take from the mouth of labor the bread it has earned. This is the sum of good government."[21] On this view, government-administered education would be hard to reconcile with "good government." Though Jefferson (twenty-two years before he won the presidency) would propose an education system in the state of Virginia where all students could receive (if they chose) free education for three years (and more if they paid for it), the bill failed to pass the Virginia legislature several times. "Virginia did not implement anything like a universal system of education for white—let alone black children—for another 100 years."[22]

While several other American political elites—Benjamin Rush, George Washington, Benjamin Franklin—either proposed statewide public education plans or expounded on the importance of a government role in schooling, "support had not yet developed for a strong state role in directing education" among the general population of the thirteen states in the late eighteenth and early nineteenth centuries.[23]

---

[21] Thomas Jefferson, "First Inaugural Address," 1801, http://avalon.law.yale.edu/19th_century/jefinau1.asp.
[22] Charles L. Glenn, *The American Model of State and School: An Historical Inquiry* (New York: Continuum, 2012).
[23] Glenn, *The American Model of State and School*, 47.

While locally controlled district schools existed in some regions (more common in the northeastern states, "funded in a variety of ways," often involving at least some charge to parents in the form of "rate bills"),[24] education in many other localities was regarded as a private affair. Children might gain apprenticeships to learn basic skills and a trade, attend "dame" schools taught by a neighborhood woman in her own home, attend charity schools, or (for those who could afford it) attend private academies. As a historian of education Carl Kaestle writes, "The proliferation of private-venture schools in rural areas was a response to popular demand. Provincial America's informal, unsystematic, local mode of schooling resulted in a relatively high level of elementary education and proved capable of expansion."[25]

As for education in the cities, Kaestle suggests that most city children attended schools in private tuition-charging schools. While public school existed in the cities of Philadelphia and New York in the early 1800s, "attended almost exclusively by paupers and 'charity' cases," the majority of students attended private schools in one form or another.[26]

Several states, like New York and Pennsylvania, provided financial support for those who could not afford education, leaving the provision of education largely in private hands.

> For decades in Pennsylvania state authorities sought to meet their constitutional obligation to provide for the schooling of those whose parents could not afford to pay tuition by providing what we would now call "vouchers" enabling them to attend existing non-public schools and academies, including church schools. This practice continued well into the 1840s.[27]

Yet it was precisely this "informal, unsystematic, local mode of schooling" Carl Kaestle referred to above that led reformers like Horace Mann in Massachusetts and Henry Barnard in Connecticut, starting in the late

---

[24] Carl Kaestle, *Pillars of the Republic: Common Schools and American Society, 1780–1860* (New York: Hill and Wang, 1983), 3.
[25] Kaestle, *Pillars of the Republic*, 4.
[26] David Nasaw, *Schooled to Order: A Social History of Public Schooling in the United States* (New York: Oxford University Press, 1979), 34.
[27] Glenn, *The American Model of State and School*, 138. See also E. G. West, "The Political Economy of American Public School Legislation," *Journal of Law and Economics* 10 (1967): 101–28.

1830s, to push for a larger state role in education, creating a more standardized system of "common" schools where all could be educated in common. "In a decisive shift of focus, the 1830s and 1840s saw legislation that proposed and sometimes adopted in state after state that strengthened considerably the oversight of state government over local schools."[28]

In response to attempts in Massachusetts to extend authority to its newly created Board of Education over the schools of the state (and in effect, hamper private schools' ability to compete with common schools), the Massachusetts legislature entertained a bill to abolish the recently created Board of Education. Though the bill ultimately failed, it was fiercely debated.

Orastes Brownson, a prominent New England public intellectual, was one of the most outspoken critics not only of Horace Mann's efforts but also of any efforts to expand the state's role in education. Brownson worried that increased government oversight over, or administration of, schooling was incompatible with the freedom of people to control their own educations and, hence, belief.

> Government is not in this country, and cannot be, the educator of the people. In education, as in religion, we must rely mainly on the voluntary system. ... Government here must be restricted to material interests and forbidden to concern itself with what belongs to the spiritual culture of the community. It has of right no control over our opinion, literary, moral, political, philosophical, or religious.[29]

While not advocating for markets in education per se, Brownson allowed for government to subsidize education, but he wanted it to stop shy of dictating or even influencing the forms and content of schooling that people could choose. He proposed that government "may fund and endow schools, and pay the teachers, but it can not [sic] dictate or interfere with the education or discipline of the school."[30]

In other states, similar proposals for an increase in state power to create and expand state-administered education as well as regulate private edu-

---

[28] Glenn, *The American Model of State and School*, 143.
[29] Orastes Brownson, as quoted in Glenn, *The American Model of State and School*, 147.
[30] Glenn, *The American Model of State and School*, 146.

cation met with resistance. In 1825, the Illinois legislature enacted a law calling for free public school funded entirely by tax dollars (rather than "rate bills" paid by attendees' families), but "public reaction had been so negative that the following session abandoned the requirement." Only in 1855 did Illinois succeed in enacting a law calling for tax-supported common schools.[31] In 1849, New York proposed a similar law; to replace the "rate bill" system, where 80% of school costs were paid by families who had children in the school (and thus, could remove their children and money from the school if or when they saw fit), New York reformers moved to create a system of public schools funded by property tax. In the words of historian David Nasaw, "The most violent and organized opposition to the state's action occurred after the law had passed."[32] The opposition was fierce enough that the legislature, judging that it could not raise tax rates for this project but still wanting to create a tax-funded school system, reduced operating costs by reducing the school year in existing common schools from eight months to five.[33] In 1840 the Connecticut legislature successfully abolished the position of state superintendent of schools held by Henry Barnard, though the position was reinstated in 1845.[34]

Nasaw suggests that these reformers in New York (and elsewhere), though they "were not overjoyed at the thought of paying higher taxes," objected more to the "element of state dictation" over schooling that used to be a local, if not a personal or familial, affair. In discussing the "individualists" who opposed state-expanding reforms in education, historian Henry J. Perkinson concurs: "The individualist education reformers wanted only state support, not state control."[35] While individualists like Brownson did not oppose the state subsidizing education for those who could not otherwise afford it (nor even governments creating schools that people could attend by paying tuition) they opposed any sort of state monopoly of education where funds were paid by taxes. This not only meant that the taxed had no choice as to whether or not to support the local schools but

---

[31] Glenn, *The American Model of State and School*, 88.
[32] Nasaw, *Schooled to Order*, 5.
[33] Ibid., 57.
[34] Glenn, *The American Model of State and School*, 149.
[35] Henry J. Perkinson, *The Imperfect Panacea: American Faith in Education* (Boston: McGraw Hill, 1995), 21.

also gave public schools an unfair advantage of not having their funding tied to providing a service that individuals chose to pay for, as their private school counterparts did.[36]

Other opponents of expansion of state power over schooling—a small minority, to be sure—argued that the state had no business in schooling whatsoever, whether administering public schools or subsidizing private schools. Intellectual descendants of laissez-faire philosophers Herbert Spencer and Auberon Herbert, these self-proclaimed "voluntaryists"—often anarchists in worldview—argued that the state was always and everywhere a purveyor of injustice and that state schooling was a contrivance to create obedience to the state.[37] Politician (serving in Congress as a member of the short-lived Free Soil Party) and activist Gerrit Smith epitomized this voluntaryist position when he wrote, "Let government restore to them their land, and what other rights they have been robbed of, and they will then be able to pay for themselves—to pay their school masters as well as their parsons."[38] While the voluntaryists were a vocal minority who published in several small journals like *Liberty* and attempted to establish several private schools on voluntaryist principles, they were never influential in the politics of American education.

> Most political battles centered not on whether the state should educate at all, but on whether state aid should go to sectarian schools, whether attendance should be compulsory and so forth. Voluntaryism—consistent opposition to all state aid and interference—never achieved the dimensions of a national movement in America.[39]

Though opposition sometimes forced state legislatures and reform efforts to stall, ultimately, states were gradually able to abolish rate bill systems and, in so doing, create state quasi-monopolies on education.

---

[36] Perkinson, *The Imperfect Panacea*, 21–22.
[37] For Auberon Herbert's views on education, see: Auberon Herbert, "State Education: A Help or Hindrance?" in *The Right and Wrong of Compulsion by the State, and Other Essays*, ed. Eric Mack (Indianapolis: Liberty Fund, 1978), 53–80.
[38] Gerrit Smith, quoted in George H. Smith, "Nineteenth Century Opponents of State Education: Prophets of Modern Revisionism," In *The Public School Monopoly*, 109–44 (Cambridge, MA: Ballinger Publishing Company, 1982), 113.
[39] Smith, "Nineteenth Century Opponents of State Education," 113.

Once schools became "free" (in the sense that tax funding meant that parents no longer had to pay public schools tuition as they did with private schools), public schools now had a distinct advantage.

> By 1860, Americans had decided that schooling was a public good. The quasi-private [privately operated, but subsidized directly or indirectly by government] and quasi-public [publicly operated on a rate bill system] school that had grown up in the first quarter of a century had given way to public schools: schools open to all, free for all, publicly supported and publicly controlled.[40]

The common school movement (which we might say "ended" around 1860[41]) may have given birth to tax-supported public schools and a marked decline in private schooling in the United States. Yet by the end of the common school movement, the United States was still largely "a nation of small schools," where even as late as the 1930s many districts still employed only one teacher.[42] It was the ensuing progressive movement that centralized school districts, created larger schools, and increased the power of those schools in American society.

It was primarily in the progressive era that education was made compulsory in all states of the Union. Massachusetts was the first state to make education compulsory in 1852. By 1900, thirty-one states had compulsory education laws. In 1918, Mississippi became the last state in the Union to make education compulsory. If allowing public schools to be tax funded could be seen as putting private schools at an unfair disadvantage by guaranteeing financial support to public schools, compulsory education laws could justly be accused of compounding this effect. If parents must send their children to a (state-approved) school, then only parents who could afford to "pay twice" for schooling (in taxes and tuition) would send their children to private schools. All other parents *must*, in effect, send their children to "free" public schools. As Ethan Hutt notes, compulsory education laws led to pressure from the courts (in cases where

---

[40] Perkinson, *The Imperfect Panacea*, 32.
[41] Kaestle, *Pillars of the Republic*.
[42] Christopher Berry, "School Inflation: Did the 20th-Century Growth in School Size Improve Education?" *Education Next* 4, no. 4 (January 2004): 58.

parents challenged the state's right to force school attendance) to equate education with schooling. When school attendance was recognized as voluntary, the courts "began ... with a view of the aims of education as being synonymous with learning, only to end [in the age of compulsory education] with a view of education as being synonymous with attendance at school."[43] Instead of choosing what kind of education is best for one's children and proving to the state that the child is educated, one must now prove that one's child is attending a school approved by the state for a proscribed number of years.

In the early 1900s, progressive reformers (often called "administrative progressives" for their focus on administrative, rather than pedagogical, reforms) sought to consolidate school districts from a locally controlled (and largely amateur) systems of local wards to larger school districts of professional administrators who were, allegedly, "above politics."[44] For these reformers, "putting schools in the hands of professional educators was seen as a cure for both the corruption of urban school system and the parochialism of rural systems," as well as making schooling more cost-efficient by taking advantage of economies of scale.[45]

Whatever the benefits of this approach (and the ward system certainly should not be romanticized, rife as it was with corruption), creating larger districts of experts did serve to further remove decisions about schools from local control and put them into the hands of professional "experts." When Massachusetts consolidated the school boards to various towns and cities, a survey of these changes found that:

> With but few exceptions superintendents had the power to design a course of study, call and conduct teacher meetings, promote pupils, and inspect and direct the work of teachers. In ninety-two of the systems they had full

---

[43] Ethan L. Hutt, "Formalism Over Function: Compulsion, Courts, and the Rise of Educational Formalism in America, 1870–1930," *Teachers College Record* 114, no. 1 (January 2012): 1–2.
[44] David B. Tyack, *The One Best System: A History of American Urban Education* (Cambridge, MA: Harvard University Press, 1974), 143. Tyack notes, "In urging the corporate form of external school governance and internal control by expert bureaucrats, the centralizers were, of course, simply exchanging one form of 'political' decision-making for another. They were arguing for a relatively closed system of politics in which power and initiative flowed from the top down and administrative law or system took the place of decisions by elected officials," 147.
[45] Berry, "School Inflation," 60. See also Lawrence W. Kenny and Amy B. Schmidt, "The Decline in the Number of School Districts in the U.S.: 1950–1980," *Public Choice* 79 (1994): 1–18.

control over the selection of textbooks. ... A study of the duties of school superintendents in 1923 indicated that the managers were continuing to win power to initiate board actions on such crucial decisions as hiring staff, determining new education policies, firing staff, and determining the scope of the curriculum and selecting textbooks.[46]

Other cities passed similar measures consolidating school districts and widening the scope of power put into fewer hands. In 1905, the Philadelphia legislature "reduced the central board by half to twenty-one members, appointed by judges and chosen from the city at larger rather than the ward."[47] In 1917, the Chicago legislature passed legislation "cutting the board from twenty-one to eleven [and] providing for appointment of the board by the mayor."[48]

Concordant with this consolidation was a belief in centralizing decision-making power in a top-down system of management by "experts." These progressives were enthralled "by the emerging power of scientific and business techniques, they were convinced, would make schooling more efficient and effective."

> In this form, which draws heavily on the factory model, expertise and hence power reside at the top rather than on the front lines, work is prescribed from above, and teachers are motivated by external incentives set by their superiors rather than by internal motivations to do quality work.[49]

Decisions would not be made by local teachers and administrators in a parochial way—each school making different decisions based on local context and local demand; rather, educational experts would make decisions (on everything from textbook and curricular decisions to how staff would be hired, fired, and evaluated), decisions that would apply to all schools within the district. To correct the problem of "variability of performance and amateur political control," these progressive reformers saw that

---

[46] Tyack, *The One Best System*, 145.
[47] Tyack, *The One Best System*, 156–57.
[48] Tyack, *The One Best System*, 171.
[49] Jal Mehta, *The Allure of Order: High Hopes, Dashed Expectations, and the Troubled Quest to Remake American Schooling* (New York: Oxford University Press, 2013), 39.

"technocratic rationalization was the antidote."[50] In the common school era, Horace Mann once urged that boards of education should have the power to

> collect such information, on the great subject of Education, as now lies scattered, buried and dormant; and after digesting, and as far as possible, systematizing and perfecting it, to send it forth again to the extremist borders of the State; so that all improvements which are local, may be enlarged into universal; that what is now transitory and evanescent, may be established in permanency; and that correct views, on this all-important subject, may be multiplied by the number of minds capable of understanding them.[51]

By consolidating, strengthening, and centralizing the power of political authorities and school districts to make educational decisions for schools in its purview, the progressive reformers arguably fulfilled much of Mann's vision. "The overall effect was to transform the small, informal, community-controlled schools of the 19th century into centralized, professionally run school bureaucracies. The American public school system as we know it today was born during this brief, tumultuous [progressive] period."[52]

While the common school movement saw the ascendancy of the tax-funded public school (and the fall of the various models of private schooling available in the Republic's early years), the progressive period consolidated and centralized control of those public schools. Both of these movements arguably took power away from families to control the education of their children. This is the educational situation to which the libertarian intellectuals were reacting. Schooling was now almost entirely a state affair; the state regulated whether and at what ages children must attend school, dictated the parameters of what public and private schools could and could not do, and administered its own tax-supported schools.

---

[50] Mehta, *The Allure of Order*, 41.
[51] Horace Mann, *Lectures and Annual Reports on Education* (Cambridge, MA: M.T. Mann, 1867), 39–40.
[52] Berry, "School Inflation," 60.

2

Albert Jay Nock: Pessimism About Education by State or Market

Albert Jay Nock is often cited as an intellectual precursor to the libertarian movement in the United States. Indeed, Nock considered himself an anarchist and an individualist, edited *The Freeman*, a decidedly libertarian magazine, and inspired such libertarians as Frank Chodorov, Murray Rothbard, and Ayn Rand.

Nock also had strong conservative tendencies, particularly in his cultural criticism and educational philosophy. In this chapter, I will argue that while Nock had a strong laissez-faire attitude on economic and political issues, his social conservatism led him to distrust private enterprise as much as government as unable to create and administer (worthwhile) educational institutions. Particularly, while Nock believed private enterprise to be more efficient, less corrupt, and more conducive to people's liberty than government bureaucracies, Nock believed that private industry would likely cater too much to consumer preferences, rather than offer the kind of education consumers *should* have. Nock, then, was pessimistic that truly educative institutions could be sustained either by government or private industry.

Nock as Individualist Libertarian

Albert Jay Nock (1870–1945) was an essayist, news magazine editor, and public intellectual. A member of what is now often called the "Old Right," a loosely knit group of intellectuals in the 1930s and 1940s who stood against the encroaching statism they saw in Roosevelt's New Deal—Nock is often regarded as an ideological precursor to the current libertarian movement.[1] In Murray Rothbard's words, "Albert Nock more than any other person supplied 20th-century libertarianism with a positive, systematic theory."[2]

Nock considered himself an anarchist and an individualist. He was both highly skeptical of the state and embracing of laissez-faire approaches to social problems. In his 1935 book *Our Enemy the State*, Nock wrote:

> There are two methods, or means, and only two, whereby man's needs and desires can be satisfied. One is the production and exchange of wealth; this is the economic means. The other is the uncompensated appropriation of wealth produced by others; this is the political means.[3]

Whereas private individuals gained wealth by positive-sum market exchanges, the state gained their wealth by zero-sum confiscation from those it claimed as its subjects. Unlike his progressive colleagues, Nock did not see the state—even a democratic one—as likely to work in the people's best interest. Nock's libertarian skepticism of the state's power to coerce led him to suspect that those who had hold of state power would abuse that power at every turn. As "the State originated in conquest and confiscation," so would the state remain a device for "maintaining the stratification of society permanently into two classes—an owning and an exploiting class, relatively small, and a propertyless dependent class."[4]

---

[1] Brian Doherty, *Radicals for Capitalism: A Freewheeling History of the Modern American Libertarian Movement*, 1st ed. (New York: PublicAffairs, 2007), chap. 1.
[2] Murray Rothbard, *The Betrayal of the American Right*, 1st ed. (Auburn, AL: Ludwig von Mises Institute, 2007), 31, epub edition. See also Justin Raimondo, *Reclaiming the American Right: The Lost Legacy of the Conservative Movement*, 2nd ed. (Wilmington, DE: Intercollegiate Studies Institute, 2008).
[3] Albert Jay Nock, *Our Enemy the State* (New York: William Morrow, 1935), 15.
[4] Albert Jay Nock, "Anarchist's Progress," in *On Doing the Right Thing and Other Essays* (New York: Harper & Brothers, 1928), 150.

2 Albert Jay Nock: Pessimism About Education by State or Market

Influenced heavily by philosopher Herbert Spencer, Nock preferred that social institutions be left to private enterprise. In contrast to the state's powers of "unconfiscated appropriation," private enterprise operated on the principle of voluntary exchange, where transactions only took place when parties agree to mutually beneficial terms. Largely because of what Nock saw as the one-sided nature of government action (government confiscates with no need to provide value to consumers in return), government bureaucracies are "notoriously and flagrantly slow, costly, inefficient, improvident, unadaptive, unintelligent, and that it tends directly to become corrupt." Private industry, on the other hand, tends to be more responsive to people's wants and needs, more enterprising and innovative, and leaves people free to pursue their own ends as they see fit.[5]

Nock lamented the gradual usurpation by the state of roles that used to be the domain of private enterprise. In Western Europe (where Nock did a fair amount of travel) as in the United States, Nock noted that the state:

> now undertakes to tell the individuals wat he may buy and sell; it limits his freedom of movement; it tells him what sort of quarters he may occupy; what he may manufacture; what he may eat; what the discipline of his family shall be. It "manages" his currency, "manages" the worth of his labor, his sales-prices and buying-prices, his credit, his banking facilities, and so on with an almost limitless particularity; and it keeps an enormous, highly articulated bureaucracy standing over him, to see that its orders are carried out.[6]

To Nock, such paternalistic exercises by the state only serve to increase the people's material and psychological dependence on the state. Restricting human action by legislation restricts people's responsibility over themselves, "and thus retards and cripples the education which can be a product of nothing but the free exercise of moral judgment." In this way, state action deprives individuals of the ability to rely on themselves and their own judgment, leading them into a "mere routine of mechanical assent."

---

[5]Albert Jay Nock, "Life, Liberty, and …," in *The Disadvantages of Being Educated and Other Essays* (Tampa, FL: Hallberg, 1996), 33–34; Herbert Spencer, *The Man Versus the State* (Caldwell, ID: Caxton, 1940).
[6]Nock, "Life, Liberty, and …," 32.

Paradoxically, by taking away people's responsibility for themselves and giving that responsibility to the state, Nock believed that the paternalistic legislation made people less self-reliant and perpetuated further growth of the state.[7]

It is here where Nock's social thought parallels that of nineteen-century English philosopher Herbert Spencer, a strong influence on Nock.[8] Throughout Spencer's career, he premised his own laissez-faire belief in small government on the idea of a moral Law of Equal Freedom, wherein each would pursue their own happiness using only means that left others equally free to do likewise. Government limits on human behavior—even when motivated by a desire to preserve the equal freedom of all—was undesirable in large part because it would leave people dependent on law and government coercion in their pursuit of happiness, getting in the way of individuals exercising and improving their self-reliance and self-discipline. "And hence the belief that endeavours to elude this discipline [by government intervention to constrain private action], will not only fail, but will bring worse evils than those to be escaped."[9]

For Nock, as for Spencer:

> The practical reason for freedom, then, is that freedom seems to be the only condition under which any kind of substantial moral fibre can be developed. Everything else has been tried, world without end. Going dead against reason and experience, we have tried law, compulsion and authoritarianism of various kinds, and the result is nothing to be proud of.[10]

Compulsion and paternalistic legislation only succeeds in making the people more dependent on an inefficient, coercive, and often corrupt state. On the other hand, private enterprise allows individuals to retain the liberty to pursue their own ends as they see fit, engage in mutually beneficial

---

[7] Albert Jay Nock, "On Doing the Right Thing," in *On Doing the Right Thing and Other Essays* (New York: Harper & Brothers, 1928), 173.
[8] Robert M. Crunden, *The Mind and Art of Albert Jay Nock* (Chicago: Henry Regnery, 1964), 63–67.
[9] Herbert Spencer, "From Freedom to Bondage," in *The Man Versus the State* (Indianapolis: Liberty Fund, 2008), 248, http://oll.libertyfund.org/title/330. See also Herbert Spencer, *Social Statics* (Indianapolis: Liberty Fund, 1850), http://oll.libertyfund.org/title/273.
[10] Nock, "On Doing the Right Thing," 173.

exchange with others, and retain the kind of personal responsibility that allows individuals to exercise their freedom responsibly.

There is a tension in Nock's thought, though, coming from his much less laissez-faire attitude toward cultural and aesthetic standards. Where Nock's libertarian sentiments were on the side of private enterprise as a way for people to exercise freedom and engage in voluntary exchange, Nock's culturally conservative sentiments, though, distrusted private enterprise in several areas (like literature, art, and, as we'll see, education) to deliver goods and services of culturally superior quality. This meant that, in absence of external pressures guiding their choices, consumers would prefer the average to the culturally superior, and profit-seeking producers would be all too happy to give consumers what they want rather than what would be best for them. As we will see, this trepidation played a large part in Nock's pessimism that private enterprise could ever create and sustain truly educational institutions.

Nock as Cultural Conservative

As a social critic, one of Nock's chief concerns was the preservation of culture—what Nock often called "the humane life"—among people. By *culture*, Nock meant "knowledge of the best that has been thought and said in the world."[11] Those who acquire habits of culture are those who learn "never to be satisfied with a conventional account of anything, no matter what, but always instinctively to cut through it and get as close as you can to the reality of things."[12] Acquaintance with the best that has been thought and said equips individuals to exercise truly independent thought and aids society by preserving the cultural knowledge and dispositions that allow society to remain civilized.

While Nock never believed it possible that the majority of people could acquire the kind of culture he had in mind, Nock believed (in the vein of his peer, Jose Ortega y Gasset)[13] that those who have the mental ability should

---
[11] Albert Jay Nock, *Memoirs of a Superfluous Man* (New York: Harper, 1943), 47.
[12] Albert Jay Nock, "The Value of Useless Knowledge," in *The Disadvantages of Being Educated and Other Essays* (Tampa, FL: Hallberg, 1996), 85.
[13] Jose Ortega y Gasset, *The Revolt of the Masses* (New York: W. W. Norton, 1993).

acquire a cultured mind. The difficulty was that acquiring a cultured mind was a very difficult endeavor: "This exercise will keep you busy for many years. In preparation for it, you must spend a great deal of time in learning a great many things, and then you must spend more or less time in forgetting them."[14] Because acquiring a cultured mind requires such sustained effort, Nock believed that, left to their own natural inclination, people would choose the easier, sensual pleasures to the hard-earned intellectual ones. People, Nock wrote, would pursue their taste for the bathos "until, perverted by custom or example, he is brought, or rather compelled, to relish the sublime."[15]

The United States, in Nock's opinion, had no real institutions that could provide this perversion, or social pressure of a kind strong enough to counteract people's natural taste for the bathos and encourage them toward cultural acquisition: no powerful church, royal court, or permanent leisure class to inspire in the people a zeal for cultural improvement. Add to this a democratic and populist ethos in the United States with its aversion to tradition and class distinctions. "In other civilizations the natural taste for the bathos has been, by common consent, severely modified through processes of perversion but in ours it has been glorified, by common consent, into unapproachable dominance."[16]

As hostile as Nock was to the state and as favorable as he was to private industry, Nock was skeptical that private industry could or would provide the "processes of perversion" necessary to induce people to strive for cultural enrichment. As cultural acquisition requires significant effort where acquiring the bathos doesn't, all but the most unusual consumer would choose the path of least resistance and easiest gratification.

Nor were producers likely to undertake the "processes of perversion." Producers produce what they anticipate consumers will want, not what producers think consumers *should* want. Where Nock, in his more libertarian political writings, often wrote that private industry was more

---

[14] Nock, "The Value of Useless Knowledge," 85.

[15] Albert Jay Nock, *On Doing the Right Thing and Other Essays* (New York: Harper & Brothers, 1928), 77; Matthew Arnold, *Culture and Anarchy: An Essay in Political and Social Criticism* (London: Smith Elder, 1869), 112.

[16] Albert Jay Nock, "A Cultural Forecast," in *On Doing the Right Thing and Other Essays* (New York: Harper & Brothers, 1928), 79–80.

effective, efficient, intelligent, and dynamic than government bureaucracies, he also believed that in certain cultural pursuits, people were best served by consuming culturally superior goods where markets might cater more to consumers' base preferences. Where Nock the liberal wrote of people's right to transact as they judged fit, Nock the conservative feared free markets in areas where cultural discernment would cater to the lowest common denominator, a:

> horde of commercial enterprisers busily encouraging the popular taste for the bathos to believe that it was good taste, just as good as anybody's, that its standards were all right, and that all it had to do was to keep on its natural way in order to come out as well as need be, and to realize as complete satisfaction as the human spirit demands.[17]

Another possibility, equally distressing to Nock's conservative temperament, was that people might pay "a kind of acknowledgement to the superiority of culture," by "assum[ing] the appearance of culture and counterfeit its superficial qualities."[18] Whether reading a truncated popularization of a work of classic literature or seeing a poorly executed but inexpensive performance of a great opera, some consumers may want to enjoy certain benefits of culture (such as appearing cultured to oneself or others) without enduring the labor and experiencing the transformative effects that come from truly working toward cultural betterment. Nock laments that producers have been all too eager to capitalize on this consumer tendency. Rather than attempting to nudge potentially interested consumers toward enjoying the benefits of culture, businesses would appeal to consumers' desire to buy what has the appearance of culture (popularization of great books, inferior performances of great musical works) without the substance:

> Commercial enterprise has seized upon this disposition and made as much of it as it can, thereby administering to the natural taste for the bathos the subtlest flattery of all. Thus in literature, education, music, art, in every department of spiritual activity, we have a developed and impressive

---
[17] Nock, "A Cultural Forecast," 85.
[18] Nock, "A Cultural Forecast," 87.

system of passive exercise in culture, a system proposing to produce a sound natural development while the mind of the patient remains completely and comfortably inert upon its native plane of thought and imagination.[19]

Philosophers and economists with market libertarian leanings have long argued that consumer sovereignty was a virtue of markets.[20] Economist Ludwig von Mises, for instance, put the idea of consumer sovereignty at the very center of his defense of market capitalism. When Mises wrote that "what counts in the frame of the market economy is not academic judgment of value, but the valuation actually manifested by people in buying or not buying," Mises saw this consumer sovereignty as an argument for market capitalism.[21]

Yet, for Nock's cultural conservative concerns, this customer sovereignty risked giving in to consumers' preference for the bathos, even if consumers (and society) might be better served by "processes of perversion" exerted on consumers to consume culturally superior goods. Mises (and other economists writing in the tradition of the marginalist revolution, with its value subjectivism)[22] was content to leave aside normative questions of whether what people choose in market transactions is what they *should* choose.[23] Nock, though, wrote as a social critic, and often *did* focus on such questions.

---

[19] Nock, "A Cultural Forecast," 87–88.
[20] Joseph Persky, "Retrospectives: Consumer Sovereignty," *The Journal of Economic Perspectives* 7, no. 1 (1993): 183–91; Israel Kirzner, "Mises and His Understanding of the Capitalist System," *Cato Journal* 19, no. 2 (1999): 215–32.
[21] Ludwig von Mises, *The Anti-Capitalist Mentality* (Auburn, AL: Ludwig von Mises Institute, 2008), 13, epub ed.
[22] James M. Buchanan, *Cost and Choice: An Inquiry in Economic Theory* (Chicago: Markham, 1969), chaps. 1 and 2.
[23] "Now, nobody ever contended that under unhampered capitalism those fare best who, from the point of view of eternal standards of value, ought to be preferred. What capitalistic democracy of the market brings about is not rewarding people according to their "true" merits, inherent worth and moral eminence." Mises, *The Anti-Capitalist Mentality*, 12.

Why Neither Government Nor Private Enterprise Can Truly Educate the Remnant

Nock was no egalitarian; he certainly did not think that everyone should (let alone *could*) experience the benefits of cultural refinement. Yet Nock did appear to lament the fact that few people (of high mental ability) chose to pursue the "the profound transformations of character that can only be effected by the self-imposed discipline of culture."[24] Similarly, Nock did not think that everyone was truly educable. Most of the population, Nock suggested, was trainable in that they could learn basic skills and be trained into a profession. A minority of people, by contrast, were educable. Education, as different from training, requires:

> not only a disciplined mind, but an experienced mind; a mind that instinctively views any contemporary phenomenon from the vantage-point of an immensely long perspective attained through this profound and weighty experience of the human spirit's operations.[25]

Training, Nock wrote, was the preparation for basic life tasks (learning things like the mechanics of literacy or the ability to perform basic math), and the learning of (probably a low-level) profession. Education was more than this: not only learning the mechanics of literacy but also learning how to think about, and adequately appraise the quality of, what one reads; not just learning a profession, but learning the capacity for abstract thinking and cultural appreciation. By way of example, Nock suggested that education "produces something in the way of Emerson; while training, properly applied … produces something in the way of Edison."[26]

---

[24] Nock, "A Cultural Forecast," 89. In many of Nock's essays, he writes in very deterministic language, and throughout "A Cultural Forecast," Nock suggests that he does *not* lament this trend—that "it is a situation to be remarked, not a condition to be complained of" (79). I believe that his argument and language often betray him on this point. Nock very clearly talks of cultural attainment as a desideratum, as it enriches spiritual life—something Nock regards clearly as desirable. Also, Nock uses normative quite a bit in this and similar essays, for instance, calling preference for the bathos a preference for "inferior goods" (77).

[25] Albert Jay Nock, *The Theory of Education in the United States* (Auburn, AL: Ludwig von Mises Institute, 2008), 52.

[26] Nock, *Memoirs of a Man*, 270; Nock, "Towards a New Quality Product"; Nock, *The Theory of Education in the United States*; McElroy, "Albert Jay Nock on Education."

Nock's recognition that individuals varied in their capacity to receive education/training, and that schools should differentiate instructional expectations based on student capacity, was not at all outside the educational mainstream. Such well-respected educational theorists as the psychologist Edward Thorndike supported different educational "tracks" for students with differing educational abilities. Thorndike, for instance, celebrated that educators have been "devising varieties of schools to make education profitable in the case for those whom existing types of training do little or no good." Reviewing then-recent trends in educational tracking—sorting students into ability groups to determine whether they would receive vocational training or academic instruction, Edward Cubberley approvingly noted that "our city schools will soon be forced to give up the exceedingly democratic idea that all are equa ... and to begin a specialization of educational effort along many new lines in an attempt better to adapt the school to the needs of these many classes in the city life." Far from attempting to teach all students to the same academic level, educational trends in Nock's time more often sorted students by (perceived or anticipated) ability, educating each group quite differently in a way Nock might have partially approved of.[27]

While Nock wrote much on the practice of education, he wrote very little in regard to the proper method of training. What he did write, in fact, gave the impression that, as far as schools exist to train rather than educate, "I could not see but that it [the school system] was doing an extremely good job."[28] Nock's biggest criticism of then-current schools was that, while they may do a fair job in their training function, they did so only at the expense of neglecting the educative function.

But for the minority, those capable of absorbing and benefitting from *education*, state-run institutions were not serving them well. Nor, to Nock, were state-run schools likely to serve them well, as "persons of intelligence

---

[27] E. L. Thorndike, *Human Nature and the Social Order* (New York: Macmillan, 1940), 310; Elwood P. Cubberley, *Changing Conceptions of Education* (Cambridge, MA: Houghton Mifflin, 1909), 56–57. For more on the widespread trends toward academic tracking in public schools, see Diane Ravitch, *The Death and Life of the Great American School System: How Testing and Choice Are Undermining Education* (New York: Basic Books, 2010), chaps. 4 and 7.

[28] Nock, *Memoirs of a Superfluous Man*, 279. Similarly, Nock wrote that, as far as schools' training function goes, "I would make hardly any actual changes, and those I would make are only such as should enable our system to go on doing practically what it is doing now, but to do it better." Nock, *The Theory of Education in the United States*, 110–11.

2 Albert Jay Nock: Pessimism About Education by State or Market 33

and wisdom were no asset to the State."[29] Nock believed that the state was more likely to desire well-trained and submissive citizens than educated ones capable of independent thought, capable of questioning the validity of the state.

Of course, as little value as educated individuals are to the state, they are equally of little value to a society devoted largely to what Nock, citing arguments by Edmund Burke, calls "economism," or, the acquiring of material wealth at the neglect of cultural and spiritual depth.[30] Those who would pursue true education of the kind envisioned by Nock would find themselves, as educated Nock considered himself, superfluous to economism-valuing society.

Also, just like cultural acquisition, Nock recognized that acquiring true education was hard work. There may be some willing to endure such hard work, motivated by an intrinsic thirst for real education (as opposed to being motivated by extrinsic incentives like upward mobility or social recognition). Nock referred to this small group as "the Remnant"—a group that, while likely small in number, had the ability and motivation to counteract the human tendency to settle for easy attainments and cultural inferiority, and continually seek out cultural betterment. Even if existing educational institutions focused on training the trainable at the expense of educating the educable, the Remnant would likely turn out educated by their own initiative.

Nock recognized that there likely exist a good many (even if only a large portion of a minority) who were educable yet lacked the intrinsic motivation of the Remnant. This, in the same way that Nock supposed there were many people who were capable of, but lacked any internal motivation to achieve, cultural betterment. Yet unless pushed to do so by some external force (the church, admiration for a cultured leisure class, etc.), these able-minded but not intrinsically motivated people might forgo such cultural strivings.

Just as Nock argued that markets in cultural wares may lack the "processes of perversion" to induce people toward cultural betterment, he made a similar case Nock's regarding private enterprise in education. At

---

[29] Nock, *Memoirs of a Superfluous Man*, 275.
[30] Nock, *Memoirs of a Superfluous Man*, 111.

best, Nock was pessimistic about private industry's ability to provide the truly educative institutions he believes necessary for educable minds.

First, Nock frequently expressed pessimism that educable people (excepting the intrinsically motivated Remnant, perhaps) would seek truly educational experiences. Particularly in a society that prized material acquisition over cultural and spiritual pleasures, educated persons would find themselves in a situation where they have attained many of the skills—appreciation for and ability to think deeply about politics, philosophy, the arts, etc.—that would not be of any value to a society dedicated to the philosophy of economism. Moreover, Nock supposed that education would equip the educated with the ability to evaluate social arrangements and entertain alternative, superior, ones; this, Nock supposed, would leave the educated not only in a world where their educated minds would leave them out of step with the current social order but also with the reflective skills that would surely leave them dissatisfied.

Nock contrasts this with the effects of training on the minds of the trainable. In Nock's essay "On the Disadvantages of Being Educated," he writes that training

> tends to satisfy him with very moderate and simple returns. A good income, a home and a family, the usual run of comforts and conveniences, diversions addressed only to the competitive or sporting spirit or else to raw sensation - training only makes directly for getting these, but also for an inert and comfortable contentment with them.[31]

Nock suggested that individuals who were capable of being educated but may not have the intrinsic motivation of the Remnant would more likely choose the path that would equip them for the economism-focused world. Thus, in the same way as Nock argued that, if left to their own devices, consumers would likely forego cultural attainments for easier amusements, Nock predicted that educable individuals would likely prefer the safer road of training to the more difficult road of education.

Also, just as Nock saw the risk that consumers would settle for the appearance (without reaping the substance of) of cultural attainment, one finds a similar concern in Nock's educational writing. Nock often

---

[31] Nock, *The Disadvantages of Being Educated*, 19.

2 Albert Jay Nock: Pessimism About Education by State or Market 35

criticized then-current educational institutions for operating on faulty egalitarian premises that all students were educable. Nock suggested that this led to a gradual watering-down of the curriculum; since the majority were not capable of absorbing true education, schools began teaching only what the trainable could learn and merely calling it education.

Yet Nock was careful to point out that this was not done to people as much as by people's behest—not done from any ill motive on the part of the state, but by the good motives of parents.

> An educational system was set up in our country, and lavishly endowed in response to the noble sentiment of parents for the advancement of their children. It was to be equalitarian, as the average man understands equality; that is to say, everybody should be regarded as able to take in its benefits. It should be democratic, as the average man understands democracy; that is to say, no one has any natural right to anything that everybody could not get.[32]

Parents, Nock wrote, want their children to be educated to at least the same level of other children, and no one wants to believe (or maybe admit) that their children are among those not capable of education. While Nock believed that the majority of children, in the end, were not capable of education, parents, as parents, never wanted to believe that their children were only capable of training. Over time, this meant that "we set at once on the business of hauling, recasting, readjusting, and tinkering the mechanisms of our system" in order to find the level of instruction that would fit with our egalitarian desire that all children appear successful in education.

Yet if parents' aspirations to see their children successful in school led to a gradual easing of curricular difficulty, surely a similar thing would be likely if education were administered by private industry rather than the state. If parents, as political actors, pushed for or allowed changes in curricula over time in order to improve their children's likelihood of academic success, parents as consumers would be just as likely to shop for schools with similarly diluted curricula. In fact, as one of the virtues of the market is its propensity to satisfy consumer demand (without regard for normative

---

[32] Nock, *The Theory of Education in the United States*, 53–54.

questions of what consumers *should* demand), it could be argued that curricular dilution (if desired, even subconsciously, by consumers) would be more likely to happen if schools were run by profit-seeking business than by the state.

Consumers were as unlikely to choose the type of truly educational institutions that Nock envisioned as producers were likely to offer it. Nock wrote that if his ideal educational institution—an undergraduate college "cover[ing] (1) the whole range of Greek and Roman literature, (2) mathematics up as far as the differential calculus, [and] (3) … informal logic"—were established in the private sector, "probably not a single student would enter it for the first six or seven years, and if it had a baker's dozen at the end of ten years." As this college was unlikely to be profitable or even popular, he conceived that it "should have its experimental status established in such economic security that it need not care twopence whether any students ever came to it or not."[33]

Similarly, toward the very end of Nock's *Theory of Education in the United States,* Nock wrote that "private enterprise in this country, it is true, might establish a set of institutions for the educable only, consecrated to the unswerving services of the Great Tradition." Yet these institutions would likely prove unsuccessful and, as such, would not be sustainable if it had to rely on turning a profit for its existence. It would either fail to attract more than a handful of customers (probably, members of the intrinsically motivated but numerically insignificant Remnant), or experience market pressure to compromise its strenuous curriculum for one more congenial to the less educable (or less intrinsically motivated) masses. It is worth quoting Nock here at some length:

> For obvious reasons this set of institutions would stand a long time with its doors locked, waiting for eligible persons to seek it out. Then when it began to exist as a going concern, it would be existing against all of the force of wind and tide, under every temptation to eviscerate itself by concession and compromise. Then when it began to exist as a going concern, it would be existing against all of the force of wind and tide, under every temptation to eviscerate itself by concession and compromise. If it is kept to its intention, it would of course triumph gloriously in the long-run; but the run would be

---

[33] Nock, "Towards a New Quality Product," 118–19.

so long, and the chances of its fidelity so doubtful, that private enterprise, however enlightened and public spirited, could hardly be expected not to hesitate.[34]

Matthew Arnold, whose writings very much influenced Nock's educational and cultural criticism,[35] had similar concerns about private enterprise's ability to provide the kind of culturally robust education that was best for consumers, rather than simply cater to consumer demands. (Recall that Nock quoted Arnold to bolster his argument that most consumers, in the absence of extrinsic "upward" pressures on them, would prefer to indulge their taste for the bathos than strive toward the sublime.)

> The mass of mankind know good butter from bad, and tainted meat from fresh, and the principle of supply and demand, perhaps, may be relied on to give us sound meat and butter. But the mass of mankind do not so well know what distinguishes good teaching and training from bad; they do not here know what they ought to demand, and therefore, the demand cannot be relied on to give us the right supply. Even if they knew what they ought to demand, they have not sufficient means of testing whether or not this is really supplied to them. Securities, therefore, are needed.[36]

Libertarian economists like Ludwig von Mises defended market capitalism in part with the idea that markets cater to consumer demand, rather than what politicians or intellectuals believe consumers should have. Under capitalist markets, "the real bosses are the consumers … . They, by their buying and by their abstention from buying, decide who should own the capital and run the plants. They determine what should be produced and in what quantity and quality."[37]

Yet, for Nock as for Arnold, this type of consumer sovereignty might be an obstacle toward the maintenance of truly educative institutions; people may know what they want, but they may not know what will be best for them. Businesses, in turn, will cater to the former rather than the latter.

---

[34] Nock, *The Theory of Education in the United States*, 152–53.
[35] Crunden, *The Mind and Art of Albert Jay Nock*, 61–63.
[36] Matthew Arnold, *A French Eton, or, Middle Class Education and the State* (London: Macmillan, 1864), 44.
[37] Ludwig von Mises, *Bureaucracy* (Indianapolis: Liberty Fund, 2007), 24, epub ed.

For both Arnold and Nock, this meant that for educational institutions to remain truly educative, they needed to be immune from market forces. For Arnold, this meant that the state should provide educational institutions under the guidance of enlightened and knowledged supervisors, free from the forces of the market. Nock, a bit more ambiguous, certainly did not believe that the state could (or would be willing to) provide education to those capable of it—maybe training, but not education. In order for truly educational institutions to be established and maintained, Nock's requirement was that they be established "in such economic security that it need not care twopence whether any students ever came to it or not."[38]

Nock, the Economic Libertarian and Educational Conservative

In his history of conservatism, historian George H. Nash referred to Albert Jay Nock as "the common ancestor" of libertarians like Frank Chodorov and conservatives like Russell Kirk. Nock was a libertarian in his insistence on laissez-faire in economic affairs and his antipathy toward state interference in individuals' private affairs but was conservative in his emphasis on the importance for society of preserving certain cultural values, at least in those capable of safeguarding them. As Nash wrote, "While libertarians asserted the right of the individual to be free, the right to be oneself, the traditionalists [conservatives] were concerned with what an individual *ought* to be."[39]

And on the subject of education, Nock's conservative sympathies largely won the day. While Nock was very libertarian in his insistence that individuals be free from state interference to pursue their interests as they judge them to be, in the end, Nock feared both that consumers would demand educational opportunities of dubious quality and that producers, in their desire to make profits, would cater to these tastes.

Nock's protégé Frank Chodorov adapted Nock's social philosophy almost entirely, from Nock's anarchist views toward the state to his belief

---

[38] Nock, "Towards a New Quality Product," 118–19.
[39] George H. Nash, *The Conservative Intellectual Movement in America Since 1945* (New York: Basic Books, 1979), 82.

2 Albert Jay Nock: Pessimism About Education by State or Market

that only a special minority were truly educable, rather than trainable.[40] Yet Chodorov was very resolute in his belief that education be provided by a market of competing schools rather than almost exclusively by the state's public schools. Then again, Chodorov's writings (on education and beyond) exhibited more reticence to question whether consumer preferences were as they should be, or at least to suggest that anyone but the consumer be able to decide what is in the consumer's interest.[41]

Unlike Chodorov and subsequent libertarians (like Murray Rothbard) who were influenced by Nock's thought, Albert Jay Nock's culturally conservative concerns dampened his libertarian enthusiasm for private enterprise, at least as far as education was concerned. Where markets were to be valued for their efficiency in supplying people with wanted goods and service, while leaving people free to pursue their own ends, Nock exhibited little to no enthusiasm for the viability of private enterprise providing educational institutions. As far as training schools went, Nock seemed content to leave that function to the state. As for the prospects of private enterprise providing truly educational institutions, Nock distrusted that consumers, with their taste for the bathos, and producers, with their willingness to cater to those tastes, could do the job.

---

[40] Charles Gerald Nitsche, *Albert Jay Nock and Frank Chodorov: Case Studies in Recent American Individualist and Anti-Statist Thought* (College Park: University of Maryland, 1981); Gregory T. Eow, "Fighting a New Deal: Intellectual Origins of the Reagan Revolution, 1932–1952," PhD diss., Rice University, 2007, 212–18.
[41] Frank Chodorov, "A Really Free School System," *The Freeman*, July 1954.

3

Frank Chodorov: Consumer Sovereignty, Markets in Education, and "A School on Every Corner"

Frank Chodorov first met Albert Jay Nock in 1936:

> In New York, in the fall of 1936, I happened in one night club at the Players Club. As I sat at a table with a couple of men, I noticed a dignified, elderly gentleman playing pool. He was very deliberate—painfully so to his opponent—in the selection of hi shots, and quite accurate too. At the end of the game he came over to our table, on request, and I was introduced to Albert Jay Nock.

Up to this point, the forty-nine-year-old Chodorov had had several jobs, from traveling salesman to managing a clothing factory (where Chodorov's already-libertarian outlook led to a showdown with a worker's union, which Chodorov called "my fortuitous licking of the union").[1] By this point, though, Chodorov had already become deeply read in the liberal free market, economists like Turgot, Bastiat, and—an economist who also

---

[1] Brian Doherty, *Radicals for Capitalism: A Freewheeling History of the Modern American Libertarian Movement*, 1st ed. (New York: PublicAffairs, 2007), 102; Frank Chodorov, *Out of Step* (Auburn, AL: Ludwig von Mises Institute, 2007), 60.

© The Author(s) 2019
K. Currie-Knight, *Education in the Marketplace*,
Palgrave Studies in Classical Liberalism,
https://doi.org/10.1007/978-3-030-11778-8_3

deeply influenced Albert Jay Nock—Henry George.[2] Owing to a mutual affinity for Georgist and libertarian ideas, Chodorov was almost certainly quite familiar with Nock's writings prior to their meeting at the billiard table.

It was a friendship that would continue until Nock's death in 1945. In the year after their first meeting, Frank Chodorov would take a job as the director of the Henry George School of Social Sciences (where adults could enroll in courses on the political economy of economist Henry George) and established a school paper called *The Freeman*, named for a defunct journal Nock had edited in the 1920s. There, Chodorov and other contributors "took delight in attacking the New Deal and Mr. Roosevelt, mainly on economic grounds."[3] When Chodorov began criticizing American entry into World War II, pressure from the Henry George School's board of directors forced the paper to close, and Chodorov to lose his job as director, after several years. From 1944 to 1951, Chodorov produced and distributed his own small news magazine, *analysis* (sic.), and in 1954, he would be asked to edit *The Freeman*—a resurrected iteration of the magazine Nock edited decades earlier.[4] In other words, Frank Chodorov became a public intellectual and champion of libertarian ideas learned from "liberal" intellectuals and, of course, Nock.

Chodorov's thought exhibits marked similarities to Nock's. First, Chodorov roughly held the same lowly view of government as Nock expressed in his *Our Enemy the State*. While Nock and Chodorov both considered themselves anarchists (of the individualist variety), neither had much of a problem with government protecting "negative liberties" like life, liberty, and property. To Chodorov, government "was manufactured by men out of whole cloth, and for a specific purpose, the maintaining of social order. It had no other function and no competence for anything else."[5] Where Chodorov (and Nock before him) took issue with government is when it overstepped the protection of life, liberty, and property,

---

[2] Chodorov, *Out of Step*, chap. 4; Albert Jay Nock, *Henry George: An Essay* (New York: W. Morrow, 1939).
[3] Chodorov, *Out of Step*, 79.
[4] Aaron Steeman, "Frank Chodorov: Champion of Liberty," *The Freeman*, 1996, www.thefreemanonline.org/features/frank-chodorov-champion-of-liberty.
[5] Chodorov, *Out of Step*, 62–63.

and engaged either in administering "social services" or in redistributions of wealth. These latter (illegitimate) functions of the state, Chodorov believed, were increasing more rapidly thanks to the recent (1919) passage of the Constitution's Sixteenth Amendment, giving Congress the ability to levy taxes on incomes. For Chodorov, not only did this newly granted Congressional power violate the sanctity of individuals' right to their property (as Congress could now confiscate the fruits of one's labor), but it "also gave the American State the means to become the nation's biggest consumer, employer, banker, manufacturer, and owner of capital."[6] Unless jealously guarded, state actors would continue expanding into new areas, at the expense of both individual liberty and the free market.

Chodorov was concerned not only that the state's encroachment into "social services" was dangerous to individual liberty, ensuring individuals developed dependencies on the state, but also that the state would prove incompetent in many of these functions. Like Nock, Chodorov believed that private enterprise, particularly in a competitive market, provided goods and services better, faster, and more efficiently than governments could. In a market, those offering goods and services have to compete for business with others offering similar goods and services. One's income, then, is proportional to how much profit one can make, a combination of producing goods and services that individuals are willing to pay for and finding a way to do it in a cost-effective way. Government services, on the other hand,

> are enterprises which have nothing at all to do with the market place, are not subject to competitive conditions, do not exist because Society has chosen them to exist, and would not exist but for the power of political management to impose them on Society. Society [as opposed to a group of voluntary consumers] is compelled to keep them going.[7]

While Chodorov considered himself a radical individualist rather than a conservative (as detractors often accused), he exhibited many of the same (to our eyes) socially conservative views as did Albert Jay Nock. First,

---

[6] Frank Chodorov, *The Rise and Fall of Society* (Auburn, AL: Ludwig von Mises Institute, 2007), 24.
[7] Chodorov, *The Rise and Fall of Society*, 96.

and apropos of other individualists at the time,[8] Chodorov often lionized the era of America's founding, finding its emphasis on the importance of property rights, individual liberty, and limited government preferable to what Chodorov saw as an increasing egalitarian ethos. Chodorov celebrated what he called "the peddler class" of previous generations, "the middle class man who prided himself on his own initiative, self-reliance, independence, and above all, his integrity," who "never asked favors and certainly did not expect society to take care of him."[9] His admiration for virtues of the peddler-class caused him to look with disdain at "The New Psychology," which emphasized extrinsic influences on individual behavior—economic or structural reasons for poverty and social maladjustment, for instance—deemphasizing individual responsibility.[10] This "New Psychology," thought Chodorov, was largely responsible for keeping people dependent on government "social services" rather than on individual initiative.

Chodorov also held "socially conservative" views similar to Nock's regarding education. Chodorov believed that only a minority of people were capable of actual academic education as opposed to vocational and menial training.[11] And like Nock, Chodorov was concerned that the public education system was more devoted to training than to education, attributing this fact to the "democratic impulse" of the people:

> With education a governmental enterprise, and with every parent a voter, the voice of the people had to be heard. And the voice insisted on the educability of their offspring, no matter what the school authorities thought about it.... Not only that, but attendance at school has been made compulsory until the

---

[8] Rose Wilder Lane, *The Discovery of Freedom* (New York: The John Day Company, 1943); John T. Flynn, *The Decline of the American Republic* (Auburn, AL: Ludwig von Mises Institute, 2007).
[9] Chodorov, *Out of Step*, 3.
[10] Chodorov, *Out of Step*, chap. 2.
[11] Like Nock, also, Chodorov did not voice this belief in a way that demeaned those who might not be capable of academic education. "They may be quick-witted, far more so than are the educable, and capable of mastering the practical affairs of life, but find the disciplines incomprehensible or boring," 31. Possibly, because Chodorov had worked in the business world (where Nock did not), Chodorov was quick to point out that "in respect to functional ability the noneducable are usually better endowed than the educable, and their contribution to material progress is certainly greater." Frank Chodorov, "Education and Freedom: My Friend's Education," in *Fugitive Essays: Selected Writings of Frank Chodorov*, ed. Charles H. Hamilton (Indianapolis: Liberty Fund, 1980), 119.

sixteenth, and in some states, until the eighteenth, birthday, regardless of any interest in learning, and the current trend is to subsidize the "rubbish" through college. Everyone has to be educated.[12]

In all of these ways, Chodorov's thought strongly resembles that of Albert Jay Nock.[13]

Despite these philosophical similarities, however, Chodorov departed from Nock's pessimism regarding whether private industry could properly provide educational services. While Nock had no love for government-run public education, he was skeptical that private producers would offer, or consumers would demand, education of truly good quality. In contrast, Chodorov consistently championed the idea that private industry could and should offer educational services and that competitive educational markets would and should loosen the quasi-monopoly in education government had set up for itself.

Chodorov defended this pro-market stance in several ways. First, Chodorov was a stern advocate of natural rights—the natural rights of life, liberty, and property, primarily—and argued that, as the child is the offspring of the parents, responsibility for taking care of the child, and the right to direct the child's education, lies with the parent rather than "society" or, worse, the state. Proclaimed Chodorov:

> We must put it [power to direct children's educations] back where it belongs, in the hands of parents. Theirs is the responsibility for the breeding of children, and theirs is the responsibility for the upbringing. The first error of public schooling is the shifting of this responsibility, the transformation of the children of men into wards of the state.[14]

Additionally, Chodorov defended private educational markets on grounds of intellectual diversity and freedom of thought. He argued that

---

[12] Chodorov, *Out of Step*, 29–30.
[13] Chodorov's thought bore so much resemblance toward Nock's that historian Christopher Eow somewhat uncharitably concluded that "much of Chodorov's oeuvre reads like Nock-light." Gregory T. Eow, "Fighting a New Deal: Intellectual Origins of the Reagan Revolution, 1932–1952," PhD diss., Rice University, 2007, 217.
[14] Frank Chodorov, "Why Free Schools Are Not Free," in *Fugitive Essays: Selected Writings of Frank Chodorov*, ed. Charles H. Hamilton (Indianapolis: Liberty Fund, 1980), 125–26.

state-controlled education led not only to uniformity of thought but also to a uniformity of thought molded by, in the interest of, the state. Because he saw the state as "not an impersonal or impartial deity," but rather a "committee of persons, replete with desires, prejudices, values," Chodorov argued that state control of education meant that "the kind of education the state dispenses will be that which those in control think desirable."[15]

For Chodorov, education—the transmission of knowledge from elders to students—"can never be free from the prejudices and preconditions of elders"; from decisions about what to teach and exclude, how to present what is taught, and what teaching methods to use in presentation, the act of teaching was the transmission of not only neutral facts, but also, to some degree, the teacher's and school's values.[16] The question, then, was whether the state or the parents should determine what is taught.

In addition to Chodorov's odium toward the idea that children belonged to the state before the parents, Chodorov suggested that allowing the state to control children's education would lead to a conformity incompatible with a free society. Continuing a theme echoed by previous liberal thinkers—including Frederic Bastiat and John Stuart Mill—argued that a free society should be one where individuals have been educated for individuality rather than conformity, an idea inconsistent with government control of curriculum and teaching methods.[17]

Chodorov similarly argued that as people had different points of view and values, state control of education meant that conflicts over what should be taught and how were inevitable. Chodorov was writing in an era rife with legal and political battles regarding religion's proper role in public education in a diverse society. In 1925, when Chodorov was forty-two, the Supreme Court famously decided, in *Pierce v. Society of Sisters*, that an Oregon state law demanding that all children attend *public* schools (largely in order to outlaw Catholic schools) was unconstitutional.[18] Chodorov's 1948 essay "Why Free Schools Are Not Free" was written largely in response to then-recent events in Dixon, New Mexico,

---

[15] Chodorov, "Why Free Schools Are Not Free," 125.
[16] Chodorov, "Why Free Schools Are Not Free," 132.
[17] Frank Chodorov, "A Really Free School System," *The Freeman*, July 1954, 24.
[18] *Pierce v. Society of Sisters* (1925); David B. Tyack, "The Perils of Pluralism: The Background of the Pierce Case," *The American Historical Review* 74, no. 1 (October 1, 1968): 74–98.

3 Frank Chodorov: Consumer Sovereignty, Markets in Education …

where the (majority Catholic) school district closed its public schools and mandated that citizens instead attend the local Catholic school in order, presumably, to be taught values in line with the Catholic Church. These events formed the 1950 case of *Zellers v. Hoff*; the Supreme Court of New Mexico decided that the school board had violated the separation of church and state recently acknowledged by the U.S. Supreme Court in the previous year's *Everson v. Board of Education*. (*Everson* controversially established that even government funding of student transportation to and from parochial schools unconstitutionally violated the separation of church and state.[19])

With *Zellers* in mind, Chodorov wrote of the dangers inherent in a state quasi-monopoly on education amid a society with diverse values and a social system that purports to respect freedom of thought. When people of different religions, political persuasions, and moral outlooks are compelled to financially support (and attend, under penalty of paying both tax and private school tuition) public schools, each seeks to see their own values (religious, political, or moral) reflected in the curriculum. "By right of ownership every citizen feels that his values should be included in the curriculum, but by the same right others press their values and in the end somebody must be cheated."[20] And, per the article's title—and probably with the recently decided *Everson* in mind—Chodorov argued that private schools are only free to the extent that they are independently funded and operated. Private schools whose quality must be regulated by the state, or who receive funding in any way by government, may be more free and autonomous than public schools, but their existence (to greater or lesser degrees) was dependent on the state and its demands or conditions: "In the full sense of the word, a free school is one that has no truck with the state, via its taxing powers. The more subsidized it is, the less free it is."[21]

A believer in the efficacy of free markets and opponent of state provision of "social services," Chodorov advocated a "separation of the school from

---

[19] *Zellers v. Huff*, 236 P. 2d 949 (NM Supreme Court 1951); *Everson v. Board of Education*, 330 U.S. 1 (1947).
[20] Chodorov, "Why Free Schools Are Not Free," 123.
[21] Chodorov, "Why Free Schools Are Not Free," 125.

the state."[22] By this, he meant that schools should operate completely privately, competing for business in a market. The state, in turn, should neither subsidize nor regulate schools.

As an anarchist, Chodorov's ideal was a *completely* private school system, where schools were private entities, parents paid schools with private funds, and government neither regulated nor subsidized education in any way. Schools would compete for business, and parents would choose how to provide education for their children with the resources they had (or could get from private charities if need be). This, though, was an ideal that Chodorov recognized was highly improbable, given how dependent American society had become on the public school system. Chodorov recognized that "in the transition from all-public to all-private schools many children may have to go without any education at all," surely an undesirable outcome.[23] This, because a sudden transition from an all- (really, most-) public and all-private system of education would mean that a "market" where only a few private schools existed (catering to the rare family that decided to pay both taxes to public schools and tuition to a private school) would need to transition to a system with enough private schools to cater to all students. (While Chodorov didn't mention it, others—like John Stuart Mill and Milton Friedman—have argued that, without some government funding of education, the poor would often have to go without for lack of resources.)

Short of this ideal, Chodorov championed the more pragmatic idea of having governments allow parents who choose private schools for their children to deduct the tuition fees from their taxes.[24] In that way, Chodorov was satisfied that while public schools would exist for those who need them (presumably funded both by those whose children attended the schools and by citizens who paid taxes but had no children currently in school), we could bring the benefits of a market into education without having to abolish the public education system outright.

---

[22] Chodorov, "Why Free Schools Are Not Free," 125.
[23] Chodorov, "A Really Free School System," 23.
[24] Ibid.; Frank Chodorov, "Private Schools: The Solution to America's Educational Problems," in *Fugitive Essays: Selected Writings of Frank Chodorov*, ed. Charles H. Hamilton (Indianapolis: Liberty Fund, 1980), 130.

3 Frank Chodorov: Consumer Sovereignty, Markets in Education ...

Allowing parents to deduct the cost of private school tuition from their taxes would bring several market elements to bear on the public education system. First, it would mean that public schools could no longer take their funding for granted,[25] but would have to provide educational services "customers" *want* to pay for over alternatives. Second, it (partially)[26] avoids the problem that results from compelling individuals to pay toward schools whose teaching (or methods) may be at odds with one's personal beliefs.

Perhaps the most important benefit to Chodorov of this semi-separation of school and state was that it allowed families to choose what kind of education to give to their children. Should families disapprove of the manner of education available in their public schools, they could pay for private tuition (at least partly) with the tax money they would have paid into the public school system. Not only would this mean that parents could choose schools for their children that accord with their personal convictions, but it would also break the ideological heterodoxy that Chodorov saw in the government's quasi-monopoly on schooling for the young. In other words, this partial-privatization of schools would lead to a kind of competitive pluralism where different schools with different approaches compete for consumers' business. Were the school system to be privatized in this way, as Chodorov approvingly saw it:

> Every pedagogue with an educational theory, and with gumption enough to try it out, would open up shop and put his merchandise on display. There would be a school "on every corner" competing for trade. It would become customary for young mothers to query experimental matrons as to the relative merits of the various masters of their system, even as they do now with respect to doctors, hat shops, and grocers.[27]

---

[25] While Chodorov doesn't specify this, his suggestion assumes that those who do not have children in school will still be compelled to pay taxes toward schools. Since this is so, at least some of the public schools' revenue would be from those who are forced to pay. Additionally, this would likely mean that public school "tuition" (the taxes an individual pays per child they have in public school) will be "subsidized" by those compelled to pay toward the public school while not using the school's services.

[26] "Partially," because those who have no children in school would still be compelled to pay into the public school system.

[27] Chodorov, "A Really Free School System," 23.

In another essay, Chodorov similarly writes approvingly of the pluralism he believed would come from this kind of separation of school and state. Were the state simply allowed to administer public schools (that students need not attend and parents need not support), and not regulate or control private competitors:

> Every pedagogue who takes pride in his profession would be tempted to start on his own, to ply his skill free from institutional restrictions. Every school of thought would offer its wares to the public. Every pedagogical theory would have a chance of proving itself. Every denomination would expand its parochial activities. There would be, so to speak, a private school on every city block.[28]

Like John Stuart Mill, Chodorov argued that "heterodoxy is a necessary condition of a free society." While one could argue that society would function more smoothly if all believed similarly (or held "correct" beliefs), a free society must be one where people are free to choose from competing ideas. "The freedom of selection is necessary to my sense of personality; it is important to society, because only from the juxtaposition of ideas can we hope to approach the idea of truth."[29] By allowing private schools to enter an (at least relatively) unregulated educational market, and parents to remove their funding and their children from public schools with relative ease, Chodorov hoped that a climate would emerge where families could choose between several schools competing with different instructional methodologies, curricula, or even ideological emphases.

Chodorov believed that private enterprise, competing for consumers in the marketplace, would provide the kind of educational climate most concordant with a free society. Government could not dictate or monopolize how citizens must be educated, families would be allowed to choose the

---

[28] Chodorov, "Private Schools: The Solution to America's Educational Problems," 131. Chodorov didn't seem to entertain the possibility—maybe the probability—that his scheme would lead to government regulation of private schools. If families may make tax deductions if they can show evidence that they are paying private school tuition, surely governments will regulate what counts as a valid private school, if only to avoid fraudulent deductions.

[29] Frank Chodorov, "How to Curb the Commies," in *Fugitive Essays: Selected Writings of Frank Chodorov*, ed. Charles H. Hamilton (Indianapolis: Liberty Fund, 1980), 95.

manner in which their children would be educated, and schools would survive and flourish only to the degree that they could satisfy consumers.

Since Chodorov's thought is strikingly similar to Nock's in so many areas, Chodorov's championing of educational markets is a marked exception. Nock was ambivalent at best about the possibility of private enterprises' ability to offer education. Following Matthew Arnold, Nock believed that in areas like education, consumers were not likely to be the best judges of what was best for them. People would prefer the cheap and easy to meritorious but arduous, training that would lead to a comfortable living and little else than education that would lead to a rich and happy life. While Nock did not trust governments to provide good education (as opposed to watered-down training), he exhibited none of Chodorov's enthusiasm for educational markets.

Perhaps this divergence between Nock and Chodorov over the desirability of education markets is best explained by noting Chodorov's respect for the economic ideas of consumer sovereignty and value subjectivism. Both ideas were prevalent in defenses of markets by laissez-faire economists at the time at which Chodorov was writing, particularly the "Austrian school" of economists, who Chodorov was quite familiar with.

As we have seen, Chodorov's vision of educational markets relied heavily on the idea that families should be able to choose educational models for their children that best suit the family's preferences. The more government reserved for itself the right to be people's primary educator (and regulator of all private alternatives), the less schools either would or could be responsive to families' individual preferences.

Chodorov's Appreciation for Consumer Sovereignty

At the time Chodorov was writing (and since), a central part of laissez-faire economists' defenses of markets was (and continues to be) the idea of consumer sovereignty: the power markets give consumers to effectively determine what goods and services are produced. While the term *consumer sovereignty* was coined in 1946 by Austrian economist William H. Hutt,[30] Hutt suggested that the idea of consumer sovereignty—expressed in such phrases as "the customer is always right"—has been a part of laissez-faire economics and the market system long before the term was coined.[31] Hutt invoked the idea of consumer sovereignty in order to argue that, by giving consumers the power to patronize companies that effectively served their interests and refuse companies who didn't, competitive markets were often a better tool for advancing people's well-being (by way of satisfying people's needs and wants) than government services (or regulation of markets to discourage or limit competition).[32] Even the most democratic of governments satisfy in meeting the needs of certain groups (the majority, namely). Competitive markets (and for Hutt, this only worked when markets were sufficiently competitive, which often meant government should avoid regulating entry into the market when possible) meant that each consumer could decide to use the resources they had to obtain products and services that best met their individual needs. Competition for business between firms, in other words, meant that diverse consumers (whether in the majority or minority by way of preference, whether rich or poor) would be able to choose between firms trying to satisfy consumers' preferences. In other words, competitive markets would likely allow more (diverse) preferences to be satisfied than would even the most democratic governments.

While Chodorov does not mention Hutt in his writings, he was very familiar with another author whose pro-market ideas relied crucially on respect for consumer sovereignty: Ludwig von Mises.[33] In books like

---

[30] Joseph Persky, "Retrospectives: Consumer Sovereignty," *The Journal of Economic Perspectives* 7, no. 1 (1993): 183–91.

[31] W. H. Hutt, "The Concept of Consumers' Sovereignty," *The Economic Journal* 50, no. 197 (March 1940): 66–67, note 2.

[32] W. H. Hutt, *Economists and the Public: A Study of Competition and Opinion* (New Brunswick, NJ: Transaction Publishers, 1990), chap. 26.

[33] Chodorov had at one point attended (at least) one lecture that Ludwig von Mises had given, likely at New York University. Frank Chodorov, "Why Teach Freedom?," in *Fugitive Essays: Selected Writings of Frank Chodorov*, ed. Charles H. Hamilton (Indianapolis: Liberty Fund, 1980), 115. Additionally, Mises contributed an article to *The Freeman* while Chodorov was editor, and was also affiliated with the Intercollegiate Society of Individualists, an educational organization headed by Frank Chodorov. Jörg Guido Hülsmann, *Mises: The Last Knight of Liberalism* (Auburn, AL: Ludwig von Mises Institute, 2007), 913, 1029.

Socialism, and later, *Human Action*, Mises discussed the problem of economic calculation in socialist economies, whereby socialist governments could not calculate what to produce based on consumer needs and wants in an effective way. Mises suggested that producers in capitalist markets avoid this problem by using the price system to facilitate calculate what goods and services should be offered at what quantities. Producers anticipate demand by looking at what prices consumers are paying for what (including the prices producers-as-consumers were paying for labor, materials, etc.). While individual firms might miscalculate what consumers will demand (or calculate correctly but fail in satisfying that demand adequately), industries as a whole did quite a good job figuring out what to produce by looking at relative prices as measures of consumer demand, compared with socialist governments, who frequently wrestled with vast shortages and surpluses.[34]

Elsewhere, Mises made clearer the centrality of consumer sovereignty to his defense of markets:

> Neither the capitalists nor the entrepreneurs nor the farmers determine what has to be produced. The consumers do that. The producers do not produce for their own consumption but for the market. They are intent on selling their products. If the consumers do not buy the goods offered to them, the businessman cannot recover the outlays made. He loses his money. If he fails to adjust his procedure to the wishes of the consumers, he will very soon be removed from his eminent position at the helm.[35]

To Mises and Hutt, goods and services were best provided by free markets than because, unlike government services run by planners, competitive markets put customers at the helm. Not only does the price system make it (relatively) easy to anticipate customer demand (and provide incentives to find improved ways to satisfy it), but also, as long as the market is competitive (at least, easy for new firms to enter at low cost, and at most, containing several firms offering competing products), consumers are also sovereign in the sense that they may choose between several competing

---

[34] Ludwig von Mises, *Socialism: An Economic and Sociological Analysis* (New Haven: Yale University Press, 1951); Ludwig von Mises, *Human Action: A Treatise on Economics* (Indianapolis: Liberty Fund, 2010), chaps. 11–13.
[35] Ludwig von Mises, *Bureaucracy* (Indianapolis: Liberty Fund, 2007), 2, ebook pdf edition.

firms, choosing whose product/service is closer to what they are looking for.

This type of consumer sovereignty is at the heart of Chodorov's educational vision—a variety of schools competing for business, allowing families to choose that education approximating the approach they believe is best. Of course, Nock *recognized* that consumers would be sovereign in educational markets (and markets in any cultural goods or services). Nock was simply pessimistic about consumers' ability to demand what they ought to demand. For Nock, unlike for Chodorov, the educational freedom allowed by consumer sovereignty in markets opened the distressing possibility that owing to their natural preference for "the bathos," people would demand educational opportunities of dubious quality.

Chodorov, though, expressed none of this tendency to second-guess consumers' choices in educational (or other) markets. As Chodorov was well-versed in the works of laissez-faire economists, including the Austrian school, he not only agreed that consumer sovereignty was a virtue of market- over government-provision of goods and services; he also accepted the idea that economic value is subjective, an idea commonly held by economists of the marginalist tradition like Carl Menger and Ludwig von Mises. Chodorov summarized the subjective theory of value in the following way:

> The laissez-faire economist as economist, does not question or evaluate men's desires; he has no opinion on the "ought" or "should" of their aspirations. Whether they prefer culture to gadgets, or put a higher value on ostentation than on spiritual matters, is not his concern; the free market, he insists, is mechanistic and amoral.[36]

This subjective theory of value at the heart of Ludwig von Mises's economic ideas. Value, Mises wrote, is not an objectively determined quality—whether through calculating the number of labor hours used to bring x to market, comparison to philosophers' standards of what should be valued, or any other way. Rather, value was a subjective quality that reflects the valuer's appraisal of x at the moment of choice. While one

---

[36] Frank Chodorov, "What Individualism Is Not," in *Fugitive Essays: Selected Writings of Frank Chodorov*, ed. Charles H. Hamilton (Indianapolis: Liberty Fund, 1980), 110.

3 Frank Chodorov: Consumer Sovereignty, Markets in Education ...   55

could certainly make normative judgments about others' valuations or try to encourage them to adopt different valuations, these, too, were subjective values, rather than evaluations based on objective appraisal. For Mises, there simply was "no such things as absolute values, independent of the subjective preferences of erring men. Judgments of value are the outcome of human arbitrariness."[37]

The same went for Hutt. Central to his vision of consumer sovereignty was that competitive markets succeed in allowing consumers to satisfy their preferences. And while some—like Nock, in the case of education—might have protested that consumer preference might mistakenly prefer the inferior to the superior, Hutt did not see a nonarbitrary way to argue that there were objectively correct values or preferences to measure actual consumer preferences against.

> Rejecting all systems of absolute ethics and aesthetics, judgment as to the goodness or badness of the result of any valuation process can only be personal; so that we have no more satisfactory criteria of the goodness of society's preferences in the objective of the goodness of society's preferences in the objective expression than we have of the goodness of individual taste.[38]

Partly, Mises, Hutt, and other economists put such importance on the idea that value was ultimately subjective because economics was to be a science; while it could determine the proper means for advancing particular social ends, Mises et al. were careful not to opine on the desirability or merit of particular ends.[39] Partly, though, defending the subjective theory of value was based on a conviction that no one was likely better situated to determine what consumers should have than consumers themselves. For instance, Mises admitted that consumer valuations

---

[37] Mises, *Bureaucracy*, 31.
[38] Hutt, *Economists and the Public*, 292.
[39] It is worth noting, though, that both Mises and Hutt (and certainly Chodorov) *did* actively advocate for pro-market economic policies. To do this, they had to go beyond the goal of making pronouncements on what means would best achieve particular ends (without opining on what ends were worth pursuing). See W. H. Hutt, *Politically Impossible ...?* (London: Institute of Economic Affairs, 1971); Ludwig Von Mises, *Liberalism: The Classical Tradition* (Indianapolis: Liberty Fund, 2008).

reflect all the shortcomings and weaknesses of their authors. However, the only alternative to the determination of market prices by the choices of all consumers is the determination of values by the judgment of some small groups of men, no less liable to error and frustration than the majority, notwithstanding the fact that they are called "authority."[40]

Hutt, also, was sensitive to the idea that, even if we *could* say that consumers may be misinformed about what they should prefer (and he entertained this possibility more explicitly than Mises or Chodorov), the alternative was to accept the untenable idea that external (usually government) authorities could ascertain what people should prefer, or should not be allowed to prefer, better than the consumers themselves. If consumers choose wrongly, the best (albeit imperfect) remedy may be for the chooser to live with and for them and others to learn from the mistake, getting wiser over time about what to choose or avoid in the future. At very least, thought Hutt, "we have no reasons for believing that the controllers of modern States have more practical wisdom than the social classes whom they might wish to help."[41]

Chodorov's Argument for Consumer Sovereignty in Education

The appreciation of the consumer sovereignty that comes with competitive markets as well as the recognition that consumers' valuations are essentially subjective qualities are both evident in Chodorov's enthusiasm for markets in education. So, too, was his recognition that not trusting families to make decisions over what kind of education is best for their children leaves only one option: allowing the state to determine what kind of education children should have. Like Hutt, Chodorov saw no reason to assume that families were more likely to choose badly than the state, "a committee of persons, replete with [their own] desires, prejudices, values."[42]

---

[40] Mises, *Bureaucracy*, 31.
[41] Hutt, *Economists and the Public*, 288.
[42] Chodorov, "Why Free Schools Are Not Free," 125.

In fact, Chodorov argued, trusting families to choose wisely for their children was preferable to trusting governments because parents had more vested interest in ensuring their children received quality education. Chodorov envisioned that parents who were not well informed regarding educational choices might "query experimental matrons as to the relative merits of the various masters of their system, even as they do now with respect to doctors, hat shops, and grocers." The very responsibility of having to choose educational opportunities for their own children "would tend to make parents even more conscious of their responsibility, and thus strengthen the family tie."[43] Even if some parents will choose wrongly or irresponsibly, Chodorov believed that, on the whole, there was no reason to think governments would choose better.

Chodorov exhibited an enthusiasm for educational markets that his friend Albert Jay Nock never possessed. Ideally, there would be a complete separation between school and state, but failing that, a system where private school tuition could be deduced from one's taxes, and few to no regulatory parameters as to what schools can't and can't try. For Chodorov, competition within markets would decide which educational ventures were successful and unsuccessful.

At the heart of Chodorov's thought was a respect for the idea of consumer sovereignty—that the best educational system is one where various producers attempt to serve consumer demands, where consumers could each search for schools that would best meet their individual preferences. For Chodorov, unlike Nock, what mattered was that consumers could choose educational models based on their preferences, not evaluating the merit of what educations consumers would likely choose. Influenced by the subjective theory of value (and arguments about consumer sovereignty) being voiced by laissez-faire economists like Ludwig von Mises, Chodorov argued that there was little reason to think that governments were apt to better appraise (let alone provide) what consumers *should* demand educationally better than consumers themselves.

---

[43] Chodorov, "A Really Free School System," 23.

4

Ayn Rand: Isabel Paterson, Private Education for a Free Society, and Education for Galt's Gulch

In 1957, when Frank Chodorov was writing articles for news magazines like *The Freeman*, Ayn Rand published what would quickly become her most successful and influential novel, *Atlas Shrugged*. Born Alisa Rosenbaum, Ayn Rand immigrated to New York from Soviet Russia in 1926 at the age of twenty-one. In the years that followed, she found work as a screenwriter and a playwright. By the time Rand published *Atlas Shrugged*, she had written three other novels, all with strong anti-socialistic (and pro-individualist) themes: *We the Living* (1936) *Anthem* (1938), and the influential *The Fountainhead* (1943). Committed to the ideas of small government, free markets, and individualism, Rand became politically active in the 1940s, working as a volunteer on the 1940 presidential campaign of Wendell Willkie and becoming acquaintances with such free-market notables as economist Ludwig von Mises and economics writer Henry Hazlitt.

Rand's philosophy, which she would come to call Objectivism, centered largely around intellectual and economic individualism. Individuals should use their individual reason (rather than faith or passive obedience to authority) as their guide to action, and a just economic system

© The Author(s) 2019
K. Currie-Knight, *Education in the Marketplace*,
Palgrave Studies in Classical Liberalism,
https://doi.org/10.1007/978-3-030-11778-8_4

(of free markets) was largely justified because it rewarded or penalized people based on their own actions.

While Rand wrote little on education (a passage in *Atlas Shrugged* followed by a handful of nonfiction essays), Rand's thoughts on education emphasized the intellectual individualism at the heart of her philosophy of Objectivism. Much like another libertarian writer, Isabel Paterson, who appears to have influenced Rand's thought, Rand believed that the intellectual individualism (and dynamism) that capitalism depended on was put in danger by the public school system.

Rand's Critiques of Public Education

Like her other novels (particularly *The Fountainhead*), *Atlas Shrugged* had strong philosophic overtones. *Atlas* depicted the United States in a dystopian condition where successful entrepreneurs and inventors see their wealth increasingly expropriated, and their economic behavior regulated, by a malicious federal government. The main character, a dynamic railroad vice-president named Dagney Taggart, notices that these entrepreneurs and inventors are vanishing with increasing frequency. Toward the novel's end, Taggart discovers that these figures have been voluntarily escaping to a secret community referred to as Galt's Gulch. There, productive individuals are left free to create and thrive without government management and to interact in unregulated capitalist markets.

While the novel devotes little space to discussion of Rand's educational views, the subject does come up late in the book, when Dagny Taggart discovers Galt's Gulch (unintentionally via a plane crash that lands there). While there, she notices two young boys who, she thought, exhibited the kind of self-confidence she seldom saw in children:

> The two boys had the open, joyous, friendly confidence of kittens who did not expect to get hurt, they had an innocently natural, non-boastful sense of their own value and as innocent a trust in any stranger's ability to recognize it, they had the eager curiosity that would venture anywhere with the certainty that life held nothing unworthy of or closed to discovery, and they looked as if, should they encounter malevolence, they would reject it

contemptuously, not as dangerous, but as stupid, they would not accept in bruised resignation the laws of existence.[1]

Taggart discovered that these children belonged to a woman in Galt's Gulch who owned a bakeshop. When Taggart inquired about what led the woman to defect to Galt's Gulch, the woman suggested that, in large part, she

> came here in order to bring up my sons as human beings. I would not surrender them to the educational systems devised to stunt a child's brain, to convince him that reason is impotent, that existence is an irrational chaos with which he is unable to deal, and thus reduce him to a state of chronic terror. You marvel at the difference between my children and those outside, Miss Taggart? Yet, the cause is so simple. The cause is that here, in Galt's Gulch, there is no person who would not consider it monstrous ever to confront a child with the slightest suggestion of the irrational.[2]

Rand did not describe the kind of education these two boys receive, but the implication is that these are self-confident, mindful, and rational boys—the kind who fit in well in a utopian gulch of entrepreneurs and creators—because their parents did not "surrender them to the" American (and presumably public) educational system.

Thirteen years later, Rand wrote an essay called "The Comprachinos," which in many ways elaborates on the themes of the above passage.[3] In the essay, Rand critiqued (her interpretation of) of then-current trends in American public education, trends she believed educated toward conformity and collectivism rather than creativity and individualism.

The term *comprachinos* was coined by novelist Victor Hugo in his novel *The Man Who Laughs* and roughly means "child buyers." As Hugo depicts them, comprachinos captured children and physically disfigured them so that they could be sold to royal courts as court jesters or clowns. In using the term as the title of her essay, Rand suggested that (particularly progressive) educators and school administrators were similar to comprachinos.

---

[1] Ayn Rand, *Atlas Shrugged*, 50th anniversary epub ed. (New York: Signet, 2007), 813.
[2] Rand, *Atlas Shrugged*, 814.
[3] Ayn Rand, "The Comprachinos," in *The New Left: The Anti-Industrial Revolution* (New York: Signet, 1975), 187–239.

Today, it [the public education system] leaves traces in his mind, not on his face. In both cases, the child is not aware of the mutilation he has suffered. But today's comprachinos do not use narcotic powders; they take a child before he is fully aware of reality and never let him develop that awareness.[4]

Rand believed that the public schools, influenced by progressive educators like John Dewey, put undue emphasis on the importance of "'self-expression' (in the form of anything he might feel like doing) and conformity to the group."[5] Instead, children should learn to think for themselves (which included reasoned evaluation more than emotive self-expression).

As a consequence of the emphasis Rand believed schools put on the ideas of social adjustment and group conformity, students' ability to think for themselves (and trust in their ability to think for themselves) becomes stunted. Students do not develop a healthy sense of ambition or self-esteem. "Reality, to him, is no longer an exciting challenge, but a dark, unknowable threat, which evokes a feeling he did not have when he started; a feeling not of ignorance, but of failure, not of helplessness, but of impotence—a sense of his own malfunctioning mind."[6]

Rand argues that "the indoctrination of children with the mob spirit—under the category of 'social adjustment'" is deliberate on the part of the state, whose goal is to "destroy a child's individuality and turn him into a stale little conformist" who will accept the state's collectivist ideology.[7]

In *Atlas Shrugged* and elsewhere, Rand envisions and argues for a society based on entrepreneurship, economic productivity, and laissez-faire market competition between competing firms. Such a society, Rand argued, requires creative, ambitious, and thinking individuals to serve

---

[4] Rand, "The Comprachinos," 189.
[5] Rand, "The Comprachinos," 190. One could justly see the accusation that schools put undue influence both on self-expression and on group conformity as contradictory. Rand, who's philosophy emphasized both reason and individualism, argued elsewhere that individuals who correctly use reason will necessarily reject group conformity and embrace intellectual individualism (both because reason is an individual faculty and because one who can reason will reach their own conclusions, negating any need to defer to the authority of the group). Conversely, to not teach children how to reason will leave them ill-equipped for independent thought and individual action.
[6] Rand, "The Comprachinos," 202.
[7] Rand, "The Comprachinos," 210.

both as entrepreneurs and as workers.[8] Public schools, as Rand depicted them, did not allow students to sufficiently develop these traits, traits that Rand thought crucial to the maintenance of a market society. This philosophy—of what traits individuals need for a market society to flourish, and how public education thwarts them—shares much in common with an early influence on Rand, Isabel Paterson.

Rand's Philosophy of Education and Isabel Paterson's Influence

According to Rand biographer Ann Heller, Ayn Rand first met journalist Isabel Paterson at a literary cocktail party in 1936 at the New York Literary Tribune, where Paterson worked as a celebrated book reviewer and (like Rand) an outspoken critic of President Franklin Roosevelt. Over the next few years, Rand and Paterson would become very close, discussing issues of politics, philosophy, and history long into the night, the Russian-born Rand learning much about American politics and history from (Canadian-born) Paterson.[9] Paterson clearly had an influence on Rand. As Rand wrote to Paterson years later, "I learned from you the historical and economic aspects of Capitalism [sic.], which I knew before only in a general way, in the way of general principles."[10]

In 1943, the same year Rand published *The Fountainhead*, Isabel Paterson published her own libertarian tract, *The God of the Machine*, which Albert Jay Nock called one of the "only intelligible books on the philosophy of individualism that have been written in America this century."[11] In the

---

[8] While Rand often emphasized the importance of creators and entrepreneurs to a market society, she also believed that creativity and the ability to think critically were essential characteristics of a good worker/employee. In John Galt's famed speech toward the end of *Atlas Shrugged*—an exposition of Rand's own philosophy—Rand writes, "That all work is creative if done by a thinking mind, and no work is creative if done by a blank who repeats in uncritical stupor a routine that he has learned from others." Rand, *Atlas Shrugged*, 1057.
[9] Anne Conover Heller, *Ayn Rand and the World She Made* (New York: Anchor, 2010), 171–73, epub ed.
[10] Ayn Rand, *Letters of Ayn Rand* (New York: Dutton, 1995), 215, italics in original.
[11] Albert Jay Nock, *Letters from Albert Jay Nock*, ed. Frank W. Garrison (Caldwell, ID: Caxton Printers, 1949), 181. Rand reviewed *The God of the Machine* for her own news magazine, *The Objectivist Newsletter*, in 1963, a review later used as an introduction to a reprint of the book in 1983. Stephen

book, Paterson argued that society is best thought of as a machine with moving parts—individuals—who provide the energy for the machine. Human energy is expended to produce goods and services for consumption, whether the creator's own or that of other consumers. Government did have a strictly minimal role to play in protecting individuals and enforcing contracts—both things that enhance individuals' ability to use their energy productively. Beyond these functions, though, Paterson saw government as parasitic, diverting energy from the production of goods and services to paying for the maintenance of government regulation and bureaucracy (which often served to needlessly limit how humans could harness their energies). "In the social organization, man is the dynamo in his productive capacity. Government is an end appliance, and a dead end in respect to the energy it uses."[12]

In order for individuals to make appropriate use of their energies, though, individuals must act on their own initiative, be free to think and act for themselves in a manner where they are responsible for the (positive or negative) consequences of their actions. People need freedom to associate through voluntary transactions in the marketplace, where they are responsible for deciding with whom and under what terms to interact with others. To Paterson, political agencies, by either dictating what people must do or prohibiting people from doing what government officials think is unwise, are "directly prohibitory and must tend to stop men thinking," blunting individuals' ability to act freely.[13]

One political agency highly responsible for blunting humans' capacity for independent thought and action was the American public school. In a chapter called "Our Japanized Education System," Paterson argues that educational trends (which Paterson doesn't name, but are almost certainly a reference to progressive education) have increasingly neglected to teach independence of thought and action, instead infusing children with a collective and socialistic ethos.

Cox, "Merely Metaphorical? Ayn Rand, Isabel Paterson, and the Language of Theory," *Journal of Ayn Rand Studies* 8: 237.
[12] Isabel Paterson, *The God of the Machine* (Baltimore, MD: Laissez Faire Books, 2012), 97.
[13] Paterson, *The God of the Machine*, 159.

When called upon to think, they cannot, because they have been trained to accept the class, the group, or the "social trend," as the sole authority. As far as it can be done, they have been reduced to "ganglions," neural processes in a collective "body," instead of persons.[14]

In this way, "the natural outlet of energy in human beings, which in childhood is properly directed toward the development of intelligence and character, is choked down and subverted."[15]

Much of what Paterson had to say in *God of the Machine* is detectable in Rand's own work, from the emphasis on independently thinking individuals as the backbone of society to Rand's use of energy circuits and motors as symbols of human achievement.[16] For both Paterson and Rand, society is best organized when individuals have the maximum amount of space (consistent with a like space for others) to act on their initiative and creativity. Likewise, both authors shared a concern that American public schools were teaching an overly collective ethos that did not adequately stress individualism and the use of reason to guide one's individual behavior.

Paterson went a bit further than Rand, however, in directly attributing much of this educational problem to the fact that American schools were largely public—political agencies of the kind Paterson thought blunted people's abilities of independent thought. First, as with previous libertarian thinkers, Paterson thought that it was inevitable that

> every politically controlled education system will inculcate the doctrine of state supremacy sooner or later whether as the divine right of kings, or the "will of the people" in "democracy." Once the doctrine has been accepted, it becomes an almost superhuman task to break the stranglehold of the political power over the life of the citizen. It has had his body, property, and mind in its clutches from infancy. An octopus would sooner release its prey.[17]

---

[14] Paterson, *The God of the Machine*, 246.
[15] Paterson, *The God of the Machine*, 247.
[16] Heller, *Ayn Rand and the World She Made*, 173.
[17] Paterson, *The God of the Machine*, 249.

For Paterson, "a tax-supported, compulsory educational system is the complete model of the totalitarian state."[18] It kills the individuality (and individualistic spirit) necessary for a free society, unwisely violates property rights, and expands the government beyond its proper minimal presence in people's lives. Instead, Paterson defended a completely private system of education, where

> anyone who wished could open a school, to which persons could send their children on payment of the necessary fees, which would naturally vary a good deal. Primary education could be given at home, as it generally was in the United States up to fifty years ago.[19]

Like Chodorov, Paterson realized that, under a completely private system, some would go without schooling. Like Nock, though, Paterson differentiated between schooling and education. It is certainly possible, argued Paterson, that a private system would leave some poor children unschooled and illiterate. Paterson argued, though, that while political control of schools would ensure that all children went to school, it did so only at the expense of reducing education to the teaching of that which can be forced onto students by the state. One might teach students the mechanics of how to read under state compulsion, Paterson argued, but not how to appreciate literature. One could learn facts about various subjects under state compulsion, but, argued Paterson, the habits of mind necessary for perpetuating free society—like creativity, critical thinking, and self-reliance—could only be learned outside the sphere of state compulsion. "The free mind has persisted in the United States, in spite of the steady intrusion of the political power into the primary field of freedom in education."[20]

It may be worth noting that Rand's (and Paterson's) interpretation of the then-current state(s) of American schools can justly be challenged as

---

[18] Paterson, *The God of the Machine*, 249–50.

[19] Paterson, *The God of the Machine*, 250. "As it generally was in the United States up to fifty years ago" is a strong overstatement. By 1893 (fifty years before *God of the Machine* was published), twenty-seven U.S. states and territories had compulsory education laws. By 1900, the number had climbed to thirty-three. Michael B. Katz, "A History of Compulsory Education Laws," *Phi Delta Kappan Fastback Series*, no. 75 (1976).

[20] Paterson, *The God of the Machine*, 251.

overexaggerated or uninformed. In the 1930s John Dewey, whose philosophy of education Rand describes as being averse to reason and individuality, actively wrote in effort to correct similar misimpressions that existed in his own day.[21] In 1938, Boyd Bode—himself an enthusiastic supporter of progressive education—wrote a book criticizing the progressive education that Paterson and Rand accused of being too collectivistic for being too *libertarian* in spirit.[22]

Paterson's and Rand's painting of progressive education as an overly collectivistic educational doctrine may have owed to many progressive educators' aversion to laissez-faire individualism and capitalism. For instance, several of the most widely read progressive educators did push to use schools as a vehicle for social change toward collectivism. In 1932, progressive educator George Counts released an anthologized collection of speeches given at meetings of the Progressive Education Association. The title speech—"Dare the Schools Build a New Social Order?"—suggested that "if Progressive Education is to be genuinely progressive, it must … become less frightened than it is today at the bogies of 'imposition' and 'indoctrination.'" Teachers, he suggested, should help create a new social order by educating youth to reject competition and laissez-faire capitalism and to accept that a "fairly larger measure of deliberate control [social planning by governments] is desirable and even essential to social survival."[23] Writing in Rand's own time, progressive educator Theodore Brameld similarly admonished progressive educators to use the schools as a tool for social

---

[21] Dewey did not argue against the importance of reason, but argued that reasoning ability is but one (important) aspect of a child's development with which schools should be concerned. While Dewey was averse to the kind of laissez-faire individualism Rand later endorsed, his philosophy of education was quite concerned with ensuring that children develop as, and are instructed as, individuals. John Dewey, *Experience and Education* (New York: Macmillan, 1938); John Dewey, "How Much Freedom in New Schools?" (Greenwich, CT: Information Age, 2006).

[22] Boyd Henry Bode, *Progressive Education at the Crossroads* (New York: Newson, 1938). Bode was not alone here. Several critics of progressive education argued that its highly individualistic methods were at odds with, and would undermine, its goals of increasing social cohesiveness. See William C. Bagley, *Education and Emergent Man* (New York: T. Nelson & Sons, 1934); Isaac Leon Kandel, *American Education in the Twentieth Century* (Cambridge: Harvard University Press, 1957).

[23] George Counts, *Dare the Schools Build a New Social Order? and Other Essays* (New York: Arno Press, 1969), 9, 18.

reconstruction away from capitalism and toward social democracy with strong central planning.[24]

Whether an accurate reflection of the then-current educational climate or not, Paterson's critique of public schools as bodies unable to educate the kind of independent minds necessary for a free society (one with a limited government) bears much resemblance to, and very probably influenced, Rand's own educational views. In *Atlas Shrugged*, the two boys educated in Galt's Gulch are depicted as just the kind of "free minds"—confident, independent, rational—that Paterson argued cannot be educated via government-run public schools. Rand's later essay, "The Comprachinos," could easily be read as an attempt to elaborate on the (collectivizing) psychological effects on students that Paterson had argued were inherent in America's "Japanized" public education system.

Natural Rights Contra State Education

Apart from Rand's belief that America's public education system was unduly collectivist in spirit, Rand's moral and political philosophy left no room for public education (or other "public service" functions of government). Morally, Rand advocated a philosophy of rational egoism. Each person should pursue their own happiness according to their own (rational) judgment, holding their own lives as his or her ultimate value. Toward that end, Rand argued that

> there is only one fundamental right (all others are its consequences or corollaries): a man's right to his own life. Life is a process of self-sustaining and self-generated action; the right to life means the right to engage in self-sustaining and self-generated action—which means: the freedom to take all the actions required by the nature of a rational being for the support, the furtherance, the fulfillment and the enjoyment of his own life. (Such is the meaning of the right to life, liberty and the pursuit of happiness.)[25]

---

[24]Theodore Brameld, *Education for the Emerging Age: Newer Ends and Stronger Means* (New York: Harper & Row, 1965); Theodore Brameld, *Patterns of Educational Philosophy* (New York: Holt, Reinhart, and Winston, 1971).
[25]Ayn Rand, "Man's Rights," in *The Virtue of Selfishness* (New York: Signet, 1964), 97.

Since Rand believed that humans morally ought to pursue their own happiness, she believed that humans had a right to live their lives as their reason dictates; as with many libertarians, the right to life and self-ownership extends to a right individuals have over property acquired via their own labor or voluntary trade with others. This right to self-ownership (and by extension, property) guarantees humans "freedom from physical compulsion, coercion or interference by other men."[26] Government's role is to enforce this right by protecting against, and redressing, the use of force between people and enforcing private contracts between people. Otherwise, people should be left free to pursue their own happiness.[27]

Given this, public education would be problematic for two reasons. First, as long as schooling is compulsory, it could be argued that the child, and maybe the parents, are compelled to either attend or send their children to a school against their will.[28] Second, public education—like other "social services"—demands that some pay for others' services. (Compulsory) tax-supported public schooling would force some students and parents into attending or financially supporting schools they do not wish to submit to. To Rand, this was unacceptable: "No man can have a right to impose an unchosen obligation, an unrewarded duty or an involuntary servitude on another man."[29]

Thus, commenting on the Democratic Party's 1960 platform (which included support for such things as the "right of every family to a decent home" and "the right to a good education"),[30] Rand noted that social services (homes, education, etc.) must be provided for some by others, with a third party (rather than the consumers) paying the cost. "If some men are entitled by right to the products and work of others, it means that

---

[26] Rand, "Man's Rights." As an aside, it has been noted that Rand's jump from her moral argument (what humans *should* pursue) to what rights humans *do* have is philosophically problematic. Patrick M. O'Neil, "Ayn Rand and the Is-Ought Problem," *Journal of Libertarian Studies* 7, no. 1: 81–99.

[27] Ayn Rand, "The Nature of Government," in *The Virtue of Selfishness*, 111–19 (New York: Signet, 1964).

[28] Of course, a child may equally be coerced should her parents send her to a private school, as the school is of the parents, not the child's, choosing. Rand seemingly did not write on the issue of whether, given Rand's view of rights, coercion of children by parents is justified. As we will see, Murray Rothbard did write about this problem.

[29] Rand, "Man's Rights," 101.

[30] "Democratic Party Platform of 1960," *The American Presidency Project*, 1960, www.presidency.ucsb.edu/ws/index.php?pid=29602.

those others are deprived of rights and condemned to slave labor."[31] Thus, individuals could not claim social services—whether housing, education, or other—as rights at all.

Rand, like Paterson, believed that goods and services should be provided by people interacting voluntarily, whether it be through capitalist markets or other voluntary means. (Rand supported charity toward others, as long as one gave because one believed the recipients deserving in some way, rather than from a sense of moral or societal obligation; schools funded by charity would likely at least some support with Rand.)[32] "In a capitalist society, all human relationships are voluntary. Men are free to cooperate or not, to deal with one another or not, as their own individual judgments, convictions, and interests, dictate."[33]

This vision of a laissez-faire society certainly finds voice in *Atlas Shrugged*'s Utopian society of Galt's Gulch, where inhabitants provide goods and services for each other within unregulated markets and transactions are purely voluntary. While Rand's characters discuss how education looks in Galt's Gulch only briefly and vaguely, there is no mention of any formal (let alone tax-supported!) school existing there. The boys, we ascertain, are taught by their mother, who is not a teacher by trade, but an owner of the town's bake shop. In Rand's seemingly ideal world—at least as portrayed in *Atlas Shrugged*—education is a matter of private initiative, and no public schooling exists.

---

[31] Rand, "Man's Rights," 101.
[32] In an essay on the morality of accepting scholarships (both private and public), Rand draws a distinction between the morality of accepting a private scholarship funded by private donations and accepting government scholarships based on a perceived right to them. While Rand writes that her philosophy of Objectivism doesn't prohibit giving or accepting charity, she writes tepidly, stopping short of condoning charity. "The fact that a man has no claim on others (i.e., that it is not their moral duty to help him and that he cannot demand their help as his right) does not preclude or prohibit good will among men and does not make it immoral to offer or to accept voluntary, non-sacrificial assistance." Ayn Rand, "The Question of Scholarships," in *The Voice of Reason: Essays in Objectivist Thought*, ed. Leonard Peikoff (New York: New American Library, 1988), 40.
[33] Ayn Rand, "What Is Capitalism?" in *Capitalism: The Unknown Ideal* (New York: Signet, 1986), 20.

Rand's Surprising Support for Tax Credits in Education

In 1973, however, Rand endorsed the use of educational tax credits in order to open up what she saw as a governmental monopoly on schooling to market forces. Public education bureaucracies, Rand argued, were becoming larger and larger while education was declining in quality.[34] Rand noted, as have other market libertarians, that while governments do not hold an outright monopoly on education—private schools are permitted to exist—government maintains a de facto monopoly on schooling largely owing to their ability to use tax money to compel support for public schools and avoid charging tuition. Thus, parents who wish to send their children to a private school must pay that tuition as well as taxes to support the public school they do not wish their children to attend. Rand found this objectionable not just because it made for unfair competition between private and public schools. As with Chodorov, Rand also worried that public schools' reception of tax money meant that parents would often be forced to contribute tax money to schools they do not ideologically support. (Rand, though an atheist, used the example of religious parents subject to the "double burden of a forced necessity to pay for the support of secular schools" in addition to tuition to a religious school.[35]) Rand argued that this unfair competition between public and private schools was further aggravated because departments of education had the ability to regulate private schools, creating a scenario where "one contestant is forced to obey the rules arbitrarily set by the other."[36]

Like Chodorov's vision of a tax-credit policy for education, Rand's vision was that "an individual citizen would be given tax credits for the money he spends on education, whether his own education, his children's, or any person he wants to put through a bona fide school of his own choice (including primary, secondary, and higher education)." Rand further sug-

---

[34] Rand cites no actual evidence of this decline, stating that "the scope, the depth, and the evidence for this failure are observable all around us." Rand does briefly mentions a proliferation in student drug use and violence as well as a decline in functional literacy, without citing sources to back these claims. Ayn Rand, "Tax Credits for Education," in *The Voice of Reason: Essays in Objectivist Thought*, ed. Leonard Peikoff (New York: New American Library, 1988), 248.
[35] Rand, "Tax Credits for Education," 252.
[36] Rand, "Tax Credits for Education," 251.

gested that there be a limit on how much any individual could spend on their own or another's education, equivalent to the likely cost for the same education at a public school.[37]

Rand's vision for an education policy involving tax credits seemingly allowed a moderate scope for government involvement in education. First, and by Rand's own admission, "the public school would remain in existence and be financed out of general tax revenues."[38] Second, Rand placed a ceiling on how much money any individual could spend on education, presumably allowing for government to set this ceiling and use its police power to enforce this ceiling (curtailing individuals' freedom of contract to some degree). Lastly, Rand would allow individuals to receive tax credit only for educational expenses toward a "bona fide school," and while it could be argued that private accreditation agencies could demarcate legitimate from illegitimate schools, it is more likely that government agencies, like departments of education, would become the accrediting bodies.

For Rand, though, a tax-credit policy for education was necessary if only to upend the government monopoly.

> It would give private schools a chance to survive (which they do not have at present). It would bring their tuition fees within the reach of the majority of people (today, only the well-to-do can afford them). It would break up the government's stranglehold, decentralize education, and open it up to competition—as well as to a free marketplace of ideas.[39]

Rand let her readers know that, for her, advocating tax credits in education was something of a compromise position:

> I want to stress that I am not an advocate of public (i.e., government-operated) schools, that I am not an advocate of the income tax, and that I am not an advocate of the government's "right" to expropriate a citizen's money or control his spending through tax incentives. None of these phenomena would exist in a free economy. But we are living in a disastrously mixed economy, which cannot be freed overnight. And in today's context, the

---

[37] Rand, "Tax Credits for Education," 249.
[38] Rand, "Tax Credits for Education," 250.
[39] Rand, "Tax Credits for Education," 250.

above proposal would be a step in the right direction, a measure to avert an immediate catastrophe.[40]

That Rand was willing to support a tax-credit policy in education as a necessary "step in the right direction" is made problematic by Rand's career-long insistence that one never compromise one's philosophic principles, particularly regarding the immorality of government interventions in the economy. Most explicitly, in a 1962 essay titled "Doesn't Life Require Compromise?" (to which Rand answers an emphatic "No!"), Rand writes that

> there can be no compromise between freedom and government controls; to accept "just a few controls" is to surrender the principle of inalienable individual rights and to substitute it for the principle of the government's unlimited, arbitrary power, thus delivering oneself into gradual enslavement.[41]

Why, then, was Rand so willing to support educational tax credits—a position she recognizes as a compromise—by 1973? Without much-written evidence to go on, we can only speculate. It is, of course, possible that Rand did not see the support of tax credits in education as a problematic compromise. This is unlikely. In her 1962 article, Rand argues that compromise of one's own moral principles is never just (while one could be justified in conceding a personal want for something one believes to be of greater value).[42] It seems clear, though, from the above passages that Rand regarded the doctrine of inalienable individual rights (presumably the rights to life and property) as very basic moral principles and the idea of advocating any government interventions into the marketplace as

---

[40] Rand, "Tax Credits for Education," 249.
[41] Ayn Rand, "Doesn't Life Require Compromise?," in *The Virtue of Selfishness* (New York: Signet, 1964), 68.
[42] Rand differentiates between an acceptable concession and morally unacceptable compromise with some examples: one may justly accompany one's spouse to a concert of music one doesn't personally like, but one may not justly "surrender … to his or her irrational demands for social conformity, for pretended religious observances or for generosity toward boorish in-laws. Working for an employer who does not share one's ideas is not a 'compromise;' pretending to accept his ideas is." Thus, one can justly modify one's actions and behaviors in order to obtain or secure something one values, but acting out of accord with, or misrepresenting, one's own moral values in order to obtain a desired end constitutes unjust compromise. Rand, "Doesn't Life Require Compromise?" 69.

an impermissible and potentially disastrous breach of these inalienable rights. (Rand, of course, was no anarchist, so she did permit that government could tax, justified on the grounds that the tax was necessary for government to secure our rights to life and property. Since Rand did not believe in a general right to education, Rand would not have viewed collecting tax to support educational institutions in that same light.)

Rand's support for tax credits in education could have had to do with the political climate in which she was writing in the early 1970s, when the issue of tax credits for education was in the air. The Republican Party used educational tax credits as a minor campaign issue before the 1972 election. In their 1972 platform, the Republican Party publicly announced its support for educational tax credits as a "means which are consistent with the Constitution can be devised for channeling public financial aid to support the education of all children in schools of their parents' choice, nonpublic as well as public."[43] While Rand hadn't aligned herself with the Republican Party since campaigning for Wendell Wilkie in 1940, there is evidence that, by 1972, Rand came to support the Republicans, even if a bit reluctantly. When asked her thoughts on the recently formed Libertarian Party and its presidential candidate John Hospers, for instance, Rand warned against support for Hospers. Even though the Libertarian Party's politics were arguably closer to Rand's own than Republican politics, she expressed concern that John Hospers's candidacy would take potential votes away from Republican candidate Richard Nixon and help Democratic candidate George McGovern win the election. Said Rand, "If Hospers takes ten votes away from Nixon (which I doubt he'll do), it would be a moral crime."[44] Rand's support for tax credits, then, may have at least partly been influenced by the Republican Party's support for the idea in the run-up to the 1972 presidential election, but the evidence for that conclusion is admittedly circumstantial.

---

[43] "Republican Party Platform of 1972," *The American Presidency Project*, 1972, www.presidency.ucsb.edu/ws/?pid=25842.

[44] Ayn Rand, *Ayn Rand Answers: The Best of Her Q & A*, ed. Robert Mayhew (New York: New American Library, 2005), 72. Nixon subsequently won the 1972 election on the above platform, and while his and the Republicans' stance on tax credits for education was likely a very small part of the victory, Richard Nixon continued to champion the cause of educational tax credits throughout his presidency, keeping the issue of tax credits for education at least somewhat in the national spotlight. Jim Carl, *Freedom of Choice: Vouchers in American Education* (Santa Barbara, CA: Praeger, 2011), 83.

Whatever the reason, Ayn Rand ended up, like Frank Chodorov, supporting educational tax credits. For Chodorov, this was an admitted compromise (as he feared that, given the political realities of the time, leaving education entirely to the free market would leave some families unable to pay tuition toward schooling, at least until market competition brought prices down). For Rand, though, the seeming compromise is a bit more troubling, largely because of her career-long aversion to the idea of compromising political principles for the sake of expediency or pragmatism. Ayn Rand's political philosophy of strict adherence to natural rights (of person and property) simply left no room for government interference in education (whether government regulation of private education, or government administration of education via public, tax-supported schools, both allowed under Rand's envisioned tax-credit plan).

Rand's chief concern regarding state control of education (similar to that of her mentor, Isabel Paterson) was a concern that it would not respect or nurture individuality, but would indoctrinate collectivism and allegiance to the state. Rand's philosophy of individualism, free markets, and strictly limited government depended on strong, independently thinking, and rational individuals, and Rand believed that then-current public education—with its progressive emphasis on social adjustment—was ill-suited to produce the kinds of individuals necessary to perpetuate a free society. As we will see, Rand's (and Paterson's) concern that government education will produce conformity rather than individuality, uncritical support for the state rather than independent thought, was a concern shared by Rand's sometimes political ally, Murray Rothbard.

5

Murray Rothbard: Separating Education and the State Beyond Left and Right

Murray Rothbard had a tense and sporadic relationship with Ayn Rand. By the early 1950s, both were visible advocates of libertarian ideas—Rand with her novel *The Fountainhead*, and Rothbard for his articles in such magazines as *The Freeman* and *National Review*. Since at least 1954, they frequently got together (often in Rand's apartment) to discuss libertarian ideas, though Rothbard was often uneasy with what he saw as Rand's dogmatism.[1]

The 1957 publication of Rand's *Atlas Shrugged* renewed Rothbard's enthusiasm for Rand and her ideas. Shortly after the book's publication, Rothbard wrote Rand an enthusiastic personal letter, praising the novel as having "carved out a completely integrated rational ethic, rational epistemology, rational psychology, and rational politics."[2] Rothbard's rekindled enthusiasm for Rand's philosophy lasted only another year or so, however.

---

[1] Justin Raimondo, *An Enemy of the State: The Life of Murray N. Rothbard* (Amherst, NY: Prometheus Books, 2000), 1015–72.
[2] Ludwig von Mises and Murray N. Rothbard, "Mises and Rothbard Letters of Ayn Rand," *Journal of Libertarian Studies* 21, no. 4 (Winter 2007): 13. Shortly after, Rothbard published a rebuttal to a particularly scathing review of *Atlas Shrugged* in the magazine *Commonweal*. Murray Rothbard, "Atlas Shrugged," *Commonweal*, December 20, 1957.

Still uneasy with the perceived dogmatism of Rand and her followers, Rothbard ceased associating with Rand in 1958.[3]

Unlike Ayn Rand (but like Frank Chodorov), Rothbard came to libertarian ideas largely by reading economists of the Austrian school like Carl Menger and, specifically, Ludwig von Mises (whose New York University lectures Rothbard would attend while pursuing his doctorate at Columbia). Mises and the Austrian economists emphasized the subjective nature of value and, by extension, the necessity of market-determined price systems to convey knowledge about the availability and (economic participants' subjective appraisals of) desirability of goods and services. Further, the Austrians were quick to emphasize that since value was a subjective function of individuals, and market-determined price systems were a way to convey knowledge about actors' preferences, government intervention in the economy (through such things as price controls, subsidies, or regulations) distort the effectiveness of prices to convey accurate information about the "value" of goods and services.

Unlike Rand—or Austrian economists like Mises, for that matter—Rothbard took free market libertarianism (and Austrian economics) to an arguably extreme conclusion: all social functions, including those traditionally handled by the state, would be best handled by private market transactions. As Rothbard put it, "My conversion to anarchism was a simple exercise in logic".[4]

Rothbard's libertarian anarchism led to increased tension with his conservative colleagues. Referring to his time writing for *National Review*, Rothbard writes that in "this formidable but profoundly statist grouping, interest in individual liberty was minimal or negative."[5] After leaving *National Review* in 1961, Rothbard began to see his radical libertarianism as aligning historically more with the political left than the right. Rothbard began thinking that a libertarian belief in human liberty had more often been an ideal espoused historically by the political *left*; "in the eighteenth and nineteenth centuries, laissez-faire liberals, radicals, and revolutionar-

---

[3] Raimondo, *An Enemy of the State*, 1172–97.
[4] Murray Rothbard, *The Betrayal of the American Right* (Auburn, AL: Ludwig von Mises Institute, 2007), 74.
[5] Rothbard, *The Betrayal of the American Right*, 161.

ies constituted the 'extreme left' while our ancient foes, the conservatives … constituted the right-wing enemy."

Therefore, starting in the mid-1960s, Rothbard began attempts to forge an alliance between his market anarchism and the burgeoning New Left movement. With Rothbard, this anti-authoritarian outgrowth of the American left wing was concerned with protesting the United States' increasingly aggressive foreign policy and increasingly bureaucratic government. In 1965, Rothbard founded an academic journal called *Left and Right*, offering a forum for New Leftist and "Old Right" (pro-market advocates a la Frank Chodorov) intellectuals to discuss issues of common interest. There and elsewhere, Rothbard attempted to forge an alliance between his own pro-market libertarianism and the libertarianism of the New Left by highlighting the similarities between them. Rothbard's educational writings (and those discussing the rights of children in a libertarian society) fit firmly within that project.

Murray Rothbard and Children's Liberation

Nock, Chodorov, and Rand were all silent on the issue of what rights children should have in a libertarian society—very likely assuming that libertarian arguments against coercion did not apply, or applied in very limited fashion, to the coercive relationship between parents and children. Implicit in the thought of all three is the idea that freedom of choice in education (and other matters) applies to parents, whose custodial rights permitted them to make choices for the child that the child must obey.

For Rothbard, the question of children's rights was worth addressing for a few reasons. First, Rothbard—particularly in his later career—was something of a system-builder, who aimed to construct a comprehensive vision of what an anarchist libertarian society might ultimately look like, from how markets could provide private law and security to specifics about how law in a libertarian society might look. As such, Rothbard gave some attention to the question of children's rights, whether or how far libertarian freedoms against coercion applied to children against parents.

Also, to Rothbard's credit, he recognized that the question of children's rights had the potential to vex libertarian theory. As Rothbard wrote,

"Libertarians are well trained to handle the problems of adults; each adult is clearly possessed with the right of self-ownership. So far so good. But what of the newborn babe" whose survival and well-being largely depends on parents taking some sort of ownership of the child—in a manner to which libertarians would likely object if directed toward an adult?[6]

Lastly, Rothbard—who by the time he wrote on the subject of children's rights in the 1970s considered himself a man of the left—was writing at a time where several New Left authors were arguing for a more expansive view of children's rights, some arguing the cause of "children's liberation."[7] In 1960, A. S. Neill wrote a book arguing for a "radical approach to child rearing" based on his experience founding and directing an alternative school called Summerhill, where students were not forced to learn what they didn't want to learn and took full political participation in the government of the school.[8] Social critic Paul Goodman advocated for such children's rights as freedom of sexual expression, freedom to work, and freedom to direct their own education (whether they chose to attend a conventional school or seek alternative forms of education).[9] With "Kid Lib," Rothbard's most comprehensive essay on children's rights, Rothbard sought to give his own libertarian solution to the issue of children's rights, an issue Rothbard believed "seemed to be waiting in the wings."[10]

As a natural law theorist who believed that each person has a natural right to own their own person and the fruits of their labor, Rothbard argued that the answer to the question of what rights children have against the state and parents will "invariably to be found in focusing on the rights of property. Where do the property rights lie?"[11] Rothbard suggested that children, like the parents, have a natural right to their own persons and that, as such, they have the right to exit arrangements that they did not

---

[6] Murray Rothbard, "Kid Lib," in *Egalitarianism as a Revolt Against Nature*, 2nd ed. (Auburn, AL: Ludwig von Mises Institute, 2000), 115.

[7] Philip E. Veerman, *The Rights of the Child and the Changing Image of Childhood* (Boston: Martinus Nijhoff, 1992), chap. 9.

[8] Alexander Sutherland Neill, *Summerhill: A Radical Approach to Child Rearing* (New York: Hart, 1960).

[9] Paul Goodman, *Growing Up Absurd: Problems of Youth in the Organized System* (New York: Random House, 1960).

[10] Rothbard's essay originally appeared in the October 1972 issue of left-libertarian magazine *Outlook*. Rothbard, "Kid Lib," 115.

[11] Rothbard, "Kid Lib," 115.

choose. However, Rothbard argued, the parents have a natural right to their own property; unless the child chooses to exit the parents' care, the child, like a house guest, tacitly agrees to live by the rules parents impose. To Rothbard, the child "then becomes a self-owner whenever he chooses to exercise his right to run-away freedom."[12] The child, like any self-owner in a libertarian society, must find her own way; though she may ask for support from others if need be, no support—from the parents or society—is guaranteed to her by right.

Rothbard's solution, then, sought to strike a balance between the libertarian intuition that coercion is unjustifiable (that he shared with many advocates of children's liberation) and the more general intuition that children should not have absolute freedom while under their parents' care (that he shared with critics of attempts at children's liberation).[13]

One could argue, though, that Rothbard's solution is inelegant and problematic in several ways. First, one might point out the very high exit costs associated with children deciding to leave home, such that even a miserable or abused children might choose to remain with their parents simply because the cost of exit is too high. Second, while Rothbard suggests that parents may not "forcibly prevent [a child] from running away,"[14] Rothbard's definition of "forcibly" includes only direct acts of physical force. This still gives parents significant latitude to manipulate the child in order to prevent running away—choosing indoctrinating education, disallowing the child to search for foster parents or save up enough money to leave home. (Most problematically, perhaps, since Rothbard believes that parents should not be legally compelled to provide for their children,[15]

---

[12]Rothbard, "Kid Lib," 117. Rothbard did place a limit, however, on what parents may do with a child in their care. Parents' power over the child "cannot be absolute, cannot involve the right of the parent to mutilate, maim, or murder the child, for this would be criminal aggression against the body of the child, who, being an independent human entity, cannot come under the absolute jurisdiction of anyone." Rothbard—an anarchist—left the enforcement of this provision to private actors, who were free to step in, defend, or even remove the child if they believe the child is mistreated. "The role of the parent, then, is to be, not an absolute owner, but a trustee-owner or guardian, with the right to regulate the child but not to aggress against his person," 118, 119.

[13]Rothbard reiterates this view in his chapter on "Children and Rights" in his book *The Ethics of Liberty*. Murray Rothbard, *The Ethics of Liberty* (New York: New York University Press, 2003), chap. 14.

[14]Rothbard, "Kid Lib," 118.

[15]"Can we say that the law—that outside enforcement agencies—has the right to step in and force the parents to raise their children properly? The answer must be no. For the libertarian, the answer must

parents could voluntarily withhold nourishment from their children; while not an act of physical force, this could achieve the effect of weakening the child to the point where they physically cannot run away.)

While Rothbard's libertarian solution to the issue of children's rights might seem inelegant, it bears similarity to the solution envisioned by John Holt, who some consider "one of the most important exponents of the Children's Liberation Movement" of the 1970s.[16] In 1974 (the same year "Kid Lib" was published as part of a larger collection of Rothbard's essays), Holt wrote *Escape from Childhood*, a book proposing ten rights children should have. As with Rothbard, Holt argued that the child as self-owner should have the right to leave home (living on her own or with others who agree to take her in), work, and own property. Like Rothbard, Holt also believed that whoever the child chooses to live under and receive care from should be permitted to make rules about the living arrangement. In a very Rothbardian passage, Holt writes:

> In a voluntary community, there is no contradiction at all between freedom and rules. If you come of your own free will, and truly have the option to stay or go, then the community has a right to say to you, "If you want to stay here there are the things you have to do, and if you don't want to do them you can leave."[17]

Like Rothbard, Holt's conception of children's rights is grounded in the idea that exit rights are important to ensure that relationships remain voluntary between parties. Yet Holt had a very different idea of what the necessary conditions for having exit rights were. One of Holt's ten proposed rights for children was the right to receive a guaranteed minimum income from the state if the child requested it. For Holt, this was largely in order to strengthen children's (and others') exit rights: "The right to leave home, to travel, to seek other guardians, to live where they choose, and alone if they choose, cannot be an active or meaningful right for

---

be no. For the libertarian, the law can only be negative, can only prohibit aggressive and criminal acts by one person upon another. It cannot compel positive acts, regardless of how praiseworthy or even necessary such actions may be. And so a parent may be a moral monster for not caring for his child properly, but the law cannot compel him to do otherwise." Rothbard, "Kid Lib," 152–53.
[16] Veerman, *The Rights of the Child and the Changing Image of Childhood*, 133.
[17] John C. Holt, *Escape from Childhood* (New York, NY: E. P. Dutton, 1974), 215.

most young people unless they can get the money they need to live."[18] Despite similarities in how they handle the question of children's rights, Rothbard's insistence that children have the freedom to exit current living arrangements is purely formal: as long as the child may not be forcibly prevented from leaving, the child's choice to stay must be regarded as voluntary (regardless of whether the child stays purely because the cost of leaving is prohibitively high). For Holt, children's exit rights exist in name only unless the child's freedom to exit is financially realistic, a standard that a guaranteed minimum income would seek to address.

Despite differences like these, those who wrote in the 1960s and 1970s advocating for an expansion of children's rights—Rothbard included, with his advocacy of children's right to exit from existing filial relations—had at least one thing in common: a strong aversion toward compulsory schooling for children. In *Escape from Childhood*, John Holt proposed that children should always have the right to control their own education—"to decide what they want to learn, and when, where, how, how much, how fast, and with what help they want to learn it."[19] Holt argued that compulsory education grossly abridges this freedom based, as the idea of compulsory schooling is, on "the highly authoritarian notion that someone should and could decide what all young people were to learn and, beyond that, could do whatever might seem necessary (which now includes dosing them with drugs) to compel them to learn it."[20]

Similarly, in a 1964 book, *Compulsory Mis-Education*, Paul Goodman wrote that compulsory schooling for youth was largely a tool for killing creativity and spontaneity, replacing it with conformity and deference to authority. Instead of allowing students to pursue diverse modes of education—from attending less authoritarian "free schools," choosing to apprentice in a trade, to attending more traditional schools if the child chooses—"100% of all children are supposed to remain for at least 12 years in one kind of box."[21] For Goodman, compulsory education mistakenly treated learning as something that could be engineered by experts rather than an organic process that could not be forced and might look

---

[18]Holt, *Escape from Childhood*, 221.
[19]Holt, *Escape from Childhood*, 153.
[20]Holt, *Escape from Childhood*, 241.
[21]Goodman, *Compulsory Mis-Education*, 48.

different for each learner. "Thus," concluded Goodman, "if we are going to experiment with real universal education that educates, we have to get rid of compulsory schooling altogether."[22]

While Rothbard may have been more measured in his vision of children's rights than Holt or Goodman (in the sense that Rothbard "limits" children's rights only to very formal exit rights from parental authority), he shared his colleagues' mistrust of compulsory education as a tool of the elites for engineering conformity out of diversity and individuality.

Against Compulsory State Education and Other State Bureaucracies

Murray Rothbard's book-length argument against compulsory state-administered education, *Education: Free and Compulsory*, originally appeared in 1971 as two essays appearing in issues of libertarian magazine *The Individualist*. There, Rothbard makes a largely historical case that the evolution of American public education was tied almost entirely to elites' desires to impose homogeneity and conformity on the population. By 1971—and certainly into the 1970s—arguments depicting commonly revered institutions (like public schools) as instruments of control and manipulation were finding increasingly sympathetic audiences, especially among the young on the political left.

In the United States, the 1960s was a decade marked by disillusionment with the increasing skepticism of centralized governmental power. In 1956, sociologist C. Wright Mills warned that social power was centralizing in the hands of leaders in business, military, and government he called the "power elite."[23] World War II had given rise to what was being called a Cold War, and an ever-expanding U.S. military led exiting President Eisenhower to warn against a coming "military industrial complex."[24] By 1965, the United States had entered into the Vietnam War, and by 1968,

---

[22] Goodman, *Compulsory Mis-Education*, 48.
[23] C. Wright Mills, *The Power Elite* (Oxford, UK: Oxford University Press, 1956).
[24] Dwight Eisenhower, "Transcript of President Dwight D. Eisenhower's Farewell Address (1961)," www.ourdocuments.gov, January 17, 1961, www.ourdocuments.gov/doc.php?flash=true&doc=90&page=transcript.

the majority of polled Americans believed the United States should not have sent troops to Vietnam.[25]

Many Americans, particularly the young, were coming to distrust a growing and increasingly distant national government. Leftist political activist Sidney Lens expressed the concern well in his 1964 book *The Futile Crusade*:

> But since we are only in a "half war," a Cold War, we stand midpoint between the values of individualism and those of the garrison state, continuing to manifest characteristics of the former, but yielding to the demands of the latter. In this Cold War, the central government inevitably gains more power over its citizens. Countervailing checks and balances by the people are reduced and "participative" democracy is subtly transformed into "manipulative" democracy.[26]

Lens was giving voice to a rising anti-authoritarian sentiment where more and more areas of government and society were seen as repressive and distant from the concerns of the masses. In this vein, historian Gabriel Kolko argued that the progressive era in American politics and its resulting welfare state was less a benevolent act of government to regulate business in the interests of the masses and more a collusion of business and government to insulate business monopolies.[27] Philosopher Herbert Marcuse pointed out the dehumanizing effects of centralized power (in business and government) implicit in "advanced industrial society."[28] Psychiatrist and activist Thomas Szasz was questioning the practice of compulsory psychiatry (institutionalizing or treating the "mentally ill" against their will) as a tool of impermissible social control.[29]

---

[25] Frank Newport and Joseph Carroll, "Iraq Versus Vietnam: A Comparison of Public Opinion," www.gallup.com, August 24, 2005, www.gallup.com/poll/18097/Iraq-Versus-Vietnam-Comparison-Public-Opinion.aspx.

[26] Sidney Lens, *The Futile Crusade* (Chicago: Quadrangle Press, 1964), 143–44.

[27] Gabriel Kolko, *The Triumph of Conservatism: A Re-Interpretation of American History, 1900–1916* (New York: Free Press of Glencoe, 1963).

[28] Herbert Marcuse, *One-Dimensional Man: Studies in the Ideology of Advanced Industrial Society* (Boston: Beacon Press, 1964).

[29] Thomas Szasz, *Law, Liberty, and Psychiatry: An Inquiry into the Social Uses of Mental Health Practices* (New York: Macmillan, 1963).

Likewise, the 1960s and 1970s produced similar scholarship directing skepticism at America's public school system, calling for an end to repressive and coercive compulsory education. By the time Rothbard's book appeared, Paul Goodman had been arguing that "compulsory (mis)education" was designed to strip students of individuality and prepare them for an impersonal world of bureaucratic monotony.[30] In his 1971 book *Deschooling Society*, Ivan Illich argued against the idea that compulsory schooling did anything but injure and repress the poor who it was (in theory) designed to help.[31] In 1972, historian Joel Spring argued that the evolution of public schools—with their regimentation and increasingly centralized administrative structure—paralleled the rise of the corporate structure of both business and American government.[32] Outside of the intelligentsia, folk singer Bill Paxton encapsulated this growing anti-authoritarian sentiment toward public schools in his song "What Did You Learn in School Today?"

> What did you learn in school today, dear little boy of mine?
> What did you learn in school today, dear little boy of mine?
> I learned our government must be strong.
> It's always right and never wrong.
> Our leaders are the finest men.
> That's why we elect 'em again and again.
> That's what I learned in school today.
> That's what I learned in school.[33]

It was into this anti-authoritarian climate that Rothbard's *Education: Free and Compulsory* appeared. It made both a philosophical and historical argument that government-operated schools had the intent and effect to teach conformity and obedience and to stamp out individuality and independence of thought.

---

[30] Goodman, *Growing Up Absurd: Problems of Youth in the Organized System*; Goodman, *Compulsory Mis-Education*.
[31] Ivan Illich, *Deschooling Society* (New York: Harper & Row, 1971).
[32] Joel Spring, *Education and the Rise of the Corporate State* (Boston: Beacon Press, 1972).
[33] Bill Paxton, "What Did You Learn in School Today?," *Ramblin' Boy* (Elektra Records, 1964).

Rothbard's historical examination of public schooling's history in Europe and the United States aimed to show that the institution of public schools has always been accompanied by the rationale of imposing a uniform ideology on the governed. Searching the history of Europe, where several countries made education compulsory before the United States did, Rothbard found that the rationale in each case was toward producing citizens who would accept, and be obedient to, the state and its favored doctrines. Rothbard began with mention of the (generally Lutheran and Calvinistic) religious motivations behind much of early European compulsory education:

> In [1560s] Geneva, [John] Calvin established a number of public schools, at which attendance was compulsory. What was the spirit that animated Calvin's establishment of the State school system? The spirit was the inculcation of the message of Calvinism, and obedience to the theocratic despotism which he had established.[34]

Similarly, Rothbard noted that in France, compulsory primary schooling was written into the revolutionary Constitution as part of the French Revolution, its rationale largely being to ensure that the "the French language be the sole language of the 'republic, one and indivisible.'"[35] Later in the nineteenth century, defeat in the Franco-Prussian war renewed French vigor for compulsory public schooling, "so that every French child would be inoculated in republicanism and immune to the lures of monarchical restoration" and receive "training in citizenship."[36]

Rothbard paid particular attention to compulsory state schooling in Prussia, making much of the inspiration American educational reformers like Horace Mann took in its centralized and standardized methods. Prussian officials, in their ardor to create a strong military state that could head a unified Germany, mandated compulsory attendance at state schools as early as 1717, teaching students of their duties toward the Prussian state. "This despotic Prussian system," wrote Rothbard, "formed an inspiring

---
[34] Murray Rothbard, *Education: Free and Compulsory* (Auburn, AL: Ludwig von Mises Institute, 1999), 22–23.
[35] Rothbard, *Education: Free and Compulsory*, 28.
[36] Rothbard, *Education: Free and Compulsory*, 30.

model for the leading professional educationists in the United States, who ruled the public school systems here and were largely responsible for its extension."[37]

Rothbard wrote of the various conflicts over attempts to establish compulsory education and state schools in the colonies, and later, American states. Of attempts in the American (particularly New England) colonies, Rothbard focused on the religious motivations behind attempts to make denominational education compulsory, and particularly, conflicts between religious factions (where religious majority groups would enact laws outlawing attempts by minority groups to erect their own schools).[38]

Rothbard was similarly convinced that later attempts by American states to erect public schools and compulsory education laws were motivated by both a condescending paternalism and a desire for collective homogeneity. For example, Rothbard depicted Benjamin Rush's (unsuccessful) appeal for public schooling in Pennsylvania as motivated by a vision of general education to "establish a uniform, homogeneous, and egalitarian nation."[39] Mid-nineteenth-century educationists like Horace Mann, Henry Barnard, and Archibald Murphy

> saw themselves as using an expanded network of free public schools to shape and render uniform all American citizens, to unify the nation, to assimilate the foreigner, to stamp all citizens as Americans, and to impose cohesion and stability on the often unruly and diverse aspirations of the disparate individuals who make up this country.[40]

Philosophically, *Education: Free and Compulsory* made several arguments as to why education should not be handled by the state. First, Rothbard argued that state-administered education is incompatible with humanity's natural diversity. As he argued in his historical recount, govern-

---

[37] Rothbard, *Education: Free and Compulsory*, 26. Rothbard also argues that compulsory education, in nations such as England, Ireland, and Canada, has been at least partly motivated by a desire to "dragoon ... national minorities into the public schools run by their masters." Rothbard, *For a New Liberty*, 46.

[38] Rothbard, *Education: Free and Compulsory*, 40.

[39] Rothbard, *Education: Free and Compulsory*, 44.

[40] Murray Rothbard, "Historical Origins," in *The Twelve Year Sentence: Radical Views on Compulsory Schooling*, ed. William F. Rickenbacker (San Francisco: Fox & Wilkes, 1974), 17.

ments' primary rationale for administering public education has been to homogenize diversity, making homogeneous populations more cohesive and, hence, manageable (to govern). Some students have a high aptitude for academics, while others might be suited for apprenticeships in a particular trade (whom Rothbard unfortunately termed "subnormal children"). "To force these [subnormal] children to be exposed to schooling, as the State does almost everywhere, is a criminal offense to their natures."[41]

Like Rand and Paterson, Rothbard also feared that public schooling would unavoidably tend toward teaching collectivistic, rather than individualistic, doctrines. In Rothbard's historical depiction, state-administered schooling was largely a self-serving act of the state, not only to render citizens homogeneous, but also to render them loyal to the state. (Here, Rothbard's connection of mid-nineteenth-century American reformers to "the most notoriously despotic State in Europe—Prussia" set the stage for Rothbard's ideological case that states educate largely to command obedience.[42]) As the American system of government is democratic (a system of government Rothbard criticized as incompatible with individual liberty because it subordinated that liberty to majority rule),[43] Rothbard argued that the American public school curricula would teach the collectivistic doctrines of democracy inimical to individual liberty. In a passage that could have easily come from the pen of Ayn Rand, Rothbard wrote:

> All emphasis is on the "group," and the group votes, runs its affairs by majority rule, etc. As a result, the children are taught to look for truth in the opinion of the majority, rather than in their own independent inquiry, or in the intelligence of the best in the field.[44]

Rothbard argued that state-run schools are incompatible with liberty, first, because they violate natural rights by taking the property of some to educate others. Beyond that, state education violates liberty by violating

---

[41] Rothbard, *Education: Free and Compulsory*, 9.
[42] Rothbard, *Education: Free and Compulsory*, 24.
[43] Murray Rothbard, *Power and Market: Government and the Economy* (Auburn, AL: Ludwig von Mises Institute, 2004), 233–45, epub edition.
[44] Rothbard, *Education: Free and Compulsory*, 55.

the freedom of conscience of both parents and children: the parents, to educate their children as they see fit, and the children, to exit social arrangements they find to be intolerable. Public schools "dragoon the entire youth population into vast prisons in the guise of 'education,' not giving parents (who might choose another school) or children (who might choose different living arrangements in part to pursue a different educational path) a way to choose differently."[45]

Lastly, to Rothbard, the fact that public schools are controlled by governments means that they will not be as responsive to "customers" as if the schools were private. Historically, the story Rothbard told about U.S. education is one of gradual centralization of decision-making authority from families to communities to states (and state education reformers, particularly). Similar to historian Michael Katz's presentation, Rothbard saw the history of American education as a tale of education reforms wherein reformers and decision makers became increasingly detached from those being forced to utilize the public schools and what they wanted.[46] "The fact that teachers are under Civil Service is one of the most damning indictments against the American compulsory system of today," because, Rothbard argued, it means that teachers (and schools) are not at all accountable to those they serve—not by democratic processes nor by market pressures.[47]

To emphasize his arguments regarding the dangers of a state-run education system, and the justice of a private education system, Rothbard used an analogy, the one which we saw in the present book's introduction. He asked readers to imagine a "proposal for the government, federal or state, to use the taxpayers' money to set up a nationwide chain of public magazines or newspapers, and then to compel all people, or all children, to read them." This proposal, as with the American school system, would not directly outlaw private news, but (a) demand that those who consume private news not only pay for that private news, but also pay taxes that will support the public news they choose not to consume, and (b)

---

[45] Rothbard, *For a New Liberty*, 124–25.
[46] Michael B. Katz, "From Voluntarism to Bureaucracy in American Education," *Sociology of Education* 44, no. 3 (July 1, 1971): 297–332.
[47] Rothbard, *Education: Free and Compulsory*, 49.

heavily regulate private news, ensuring that its content is governmentally approved.

> A compulsory public press would rightly be considered an invasion of the basic freedom of the press; is not scholastic freedom at least as important as press freedom? Aren't both vital media for public information and education, for free inquiry and search for the truth? In fact, the suppression of free schooling should be regarded with even greater horror than the suppression of a free press, since here the tender and unformed minds of children are more directly involved.[48]

To Rothbard, one particular danger of leaving any institution whose primary function is to pass on information and knowledge to quasi-monopolistic government control is that government may use their power to control what information is dispensed and how. As with the example of news media, one can imagine governments controlling the flow of information for self-serving purposes, disseminating information in a way biased toward the interests of those in government power.[49]

Yet, as much as the analogy was invoked to point out the dangers of government control of schools, the analogy could also be used to demonstrate the virtues of private control of schools. Because of the freedom of press guaranteed by the U.S. Constitution's First Amendment, the United States has always enjoyed a private press, relatively free of government constraints. As such, private news sources compete for readership, leaving consumers free to decide what news sources they trust, and producers to compete for consumers' trust. Thus, should one news source become untrustworthy (by consumer opinion), consumers have a choice to use another news source. Not only does this give customers the ability to choose their sources for news (rather than being compelled or pushed toward a government source), but it also takes the power to control what

---

[48] Rothbard, *For a New Liberty*, 133.
[49] Whether Rothbard had Walter Lippman's arguments in mind, Lippman provided arguments that government officials (more knowledgeable about intricate issues of public policy) should manipulate the media's flow of information in order to "manufacture consent" of the general population toward their preferred policy outcomes. Walter Lippmann, *Public Opinion* (New York: Harcourt Brace, 1922).

news gets covered away from government.[50] (A Nockian critic, however, might suggest that just as private control of news means that news agencies gear their output toward viewership and ratings at the expense of rigorous news coverage, private educational outlets might gear curriculum toward what is attractive to consumers at the possible expense of true rigor.)

The same virtues Rothbard sees in a free press could arguably be applied to education.

> The advantages of unlimited development of private schools is that there will tend to be developed on the free market a different type of school for each type of demand. Schools will tend to be developed especially for bright children, for average children, and for dull ones, for those with broad aptitudes, and for those for whom it would be best to specialize, etc. But if the State decrees that there may be no schools which do not, for example, teach arithmetic, it would mean that those children who may be bright in other subjects but have little or no aptitude for arithmetic will have to be subjected to needless suffering. The State's imposition of uniform standards does grave violation to the diversity of human tastes and abilities.[51]

Murray Rothbard Delicate Relationship to the New Left

In the latter stages of her career, Ayn Rand sought to distance herself from the New Left, arguing that the movement advocated a nihilism and disrespect for reason that left the movement severely at odds with her own philosophy.[52] Murray Rothbard, on the other hand, actively sought to forge an alliance between his own free market libertarianism and the New Left's anti-authoritarian brand of libertarianism. From 1965 to 1967, Rothbard

---

[50] One could argue that in a private market of news sources (or schools), monopolistic control by a private actor is still possible. Elsewhere, Rothbard argues that in a free and unregulated market, monopolies cannot exist because the possibility of entry by new rivals always exists. As long as new producers are free to enter the market (and government regulations do not make entrance artificially costly), even in instances where one producer currently controls an entire market, the threat of competition will always limit that one producer's power in that market. Rothbard, *Power and Market*, chap. 10.
[51] Rothbard, *Education: Free and Compulsory*, 9.
[52] Ayn Rand, *The New Left: The Anti-Industrial Revolution* (New York: Plume, 1975).

created and edited an academic journal called *Left and Right*, with contributions from scholars of differing perspectives. The journal's mission, in part, was to highlight contributors' "conviction that the present-day categories of 'left' and 'right' have become misleading and obsolete, and that the doctrine of liberty contains elements corresponding with both contemporary left and right."[53] Rothbard similarly co-edited a collection of historical essays (with then–New Leftist Ronald Radosh) critiquing government bureaucracy from both libertarian and New Leftist directions. The collection involved libertarian scholars like Rothbard and Leonard Liggio, and New Leftist scholars like William Appleman Williams and Martin J. Sklar.[54]

In his writings on education, Rothbard often emphasized the similarity between his own critique of public schooling and those coming from New Leftist figures. In an early issue of *Left and Right*, Rothbard suggested that:

> In their concrete struggles against centralized oppression, the young militants of the New Left are moving, largely unwittingly but more consciously in the work of some of its advanced thinkers, toward a vision of the future that is the fullest possible extension of the ideals of freedom, independence, and participatory democracy: a free market in a free society.[55]

Elsewhere, Rothbard wrote that "it is remarkable that the old libertarian right [referring to figures like Albert Jay Nock and Frank Chodorov] and the New Left, from very different perspectives and using very different rhetoric, came to a similar perception of the despotic nature of mass schooling."[56]

If we see Rothbard as an extension of the "old libertarian right," Rothbard is correct on both counts: his critique of mass schooling bears remarkable similarity to critiques from New Leftists. Yet no matter how similar, these critiques ultimately come from very different perspectives that over-

---

[53] No Author, "The General Line," *Left and Right* 1, no. 1 (1965): 5.
[54] Murray Rothbard and Ronald Radosh, eds., *A New History of Leviathan: Essays on the Rise of the American Corporate State* (New York: E. P. Dutton, 1972). Rothbard's contribution, "Herbert Hoover and the Myth of Laissez-Faire," argued that, far from a laissez-faire president, Herbert Hoover's interventionist policies gave rise to the corporatist structure of the New Deal.
[55] Murray Rothbard, "Liberty and the New Left," *Left and Right* 1, no. 2 (1965): 67.
[56] Rothbard, *For a New Liberty*, 126.

lap, but are parts of very different (ultimately incompatible?) political philosophies.

Rothbard and the New Leftist scholars both wrote of a tension between individuals living freely and interacting voluntarily, and bureaucratic institutions imposing a self-serving conformity from above. They each advocated visions of a less centralized and coercive, and more voluntary and pluralistic, society. For both Rothbard and New Leftists, this meant that public schooling, with its education for uniformity and standardization, must be done away with.

This, however, may be where the similarities end. For, while Rothbard shared recognition with many New Leftists that public mass education was a tool of the governing elites to shape the citizenry, they differed in their explanations of who the governing elite were and what kind of shaping public schools were doing. For Rothbard, the governing elite were pro-government reformers, inspired by the Prussian model of education, who intended to create a patriotic citizenry who would unquestioningly obey state authority. Many New Leftists emphasized the degree to which capitalists—wealthy business owners—were part of the elite and used public schools to shape individuals into workers who would be comfortable in a lowly role of wage laborer. In their 1977 historical and sociological analysis of public schooling in the United States, Gintis and Bowles concluded, "The U.S. educational system works to justify economic inequality, whose … consciousness are dictated in substantial measure by the requirements of profitable employment in the capitalist economy."[57] Ivan Illich and Paul Goodman also stressed public schooling's role in molding individuals into little more than corporate workers and acquisitive consumers.

While Rothbard and members of the New Left took similarly strong stances against coercion, New Left writers tended to employ a broader definition of coercion that not only included Rothbard's "invasive use of physical violence or the threat thereof against someone else's person or (just) property",[58] but also included any form of manipulation by the powerful—government bureaucrats, corporate executives, advertisers—the vulnerable. Thus, Paul Goodman's libertarian vision

---

[57] Samuel Bowles and Herbert Gintis, *Schooling in Capitalist America: Educational Reform and the Contradictions of Economic Life* (New York: Basic Books, 1977), 151.
[58] Rothbard, *The Ethics of Liberty*, 219.

sought to do away with not only brute coercion by the state but also "all the organs of publicity, entertainment, and education so to form the personality that a man performs by his subjective personal choice just what is objectively advantageous for the coercive corporation, of which further he feels himself to be a part."[59] For Rothbard, coercion was the use of brute force or the threat of such use. Goodman's broader definition included the subtle manipulation of advertisements inducing consumers to want a new product, or corporate workplace rules restricting individual self-expression on the job. These, to Goodman and many New Leftists, were as problematic instances of coercion as laws mandating compulsory school attendance or standardized curricula.

This may explain why many New Leftists argued against not only compulsory and state-provided schooling but also any forms of bureaucratically organized schooling. For many in the New Left, even privately administered schools had the potential to be coercive in Goodman's broader sense of the word, as private schools may still attempt to form children's personalities in manipulative ways. For Rothbard, private schools are not potentially coercive as long as individuals (families or children) have the ability to exit contracts made with them.

Differentiating the New Left's version of a coercion-less society form Rothbard's anarcho-capitalism, historian Peter Marshall wrote:

> Anarcho-capitalists are against the State simply because they are capitalists first and foremost. Their critique for the State ultimately rests on a liberal interpretation of liberty as the inviolable rights to and of private property. They are not concerned with the social consequences of capitalism for the weak, powerless and ignorant. Their claim that all would benefit from a free exchange in the market is by no means certain; any unfettered market system would most likely sponsor a reversion to an unequal society.[60]

Possibly for these reasons, Rothbard's hoped-for alliance with the New Left was ultimately unsuccessful. Ronald Radosh—who both contributed to Rothbard's *Left and Right* journal and co-edited *A New History of*

---

[59] Paul Goodman, "A Touchstone for the Libertarian Program," in *American Radical Thought: The Libertarian Tradition* (Lexington, MA: D. C. Heath, 1970), 310.

[60] Peter Marshall, *Demanding the Impossible: A History of Anarchism* (Oakland, CA: PM Press, 2010), 564.

Leviathan with Rothbard—makes no mention of Rothbard in his autobiography.[61] While Carl Oglesby, former president of the New Left group Students for a Democratic Society, credits frequent contact with Murray Rothbard with motivating his own libertarian outlook,[62] Oglesby was ousted from SDS in 1966, ostensibly for not holding sufficiently "progressive" views.

As far as the influence of Rothbard's educational views on New Leftist thinkers, no mention of Rothbard or his educational writings appears in the work of Paul Goodman or Ivan Illich. Historian of education Joel Spring worked closely for a time with Rothbard and the (market) libertarian movement, but later wrote of his gradual disillusionment with (market) libertarians "as conservative donors tightened their nets and discarded the radical cultural elements that had been caught."[63] Reassessing his book *Irony of Early School Reform* over thirty years later, historian Michael Katz feared that his New Leftist arguments against a bureaucratic state-run school system had unwittingly played into pro-market arguments to privatize education that "forced me, along with others, to reconsider our position on the State."[64]

To make matters seemingly worse, while New Leftists may have taken issue with Rothbard's defense of markets and capitalism, the conservative right took issue with Rothbard's libertarianism. In 1969, Frank Meyer, a libertarian-leaning conservative whose educational views resembled those of Albert Jay Nock,[65] categorized Rothbard as a "dropout from the Right" who espouses an "untrammeled libertarianism that tends … directly to

---

[61] Ronald Radosh, *Commies: A Journey Through the Old Left, the New Left and the Leftover Left* (San Francisco: Encounter Books, 2001). Interestingly, Radosh's autobiography chronicles his gradual ideological shift from the New Left to neoconservatism.

[62] Carl Oglesby, *Ravens in the Storm: A Personal History of the 1960s Anti-War Movement* (New York: Scribner, 2010), 120.

[63] Joel Spring, *Political Agendas for Education: From the Christian Coalition to the Green Party* (Mahwah, NJ: Lawrence Erlbaum, 2002), 42. Here, Spring is largely referring to the libertarian CATO institute and its donors, who also parted ways with Rothbard in 1980 owing to ideological differences between Rothbard and CATO president Ed Crane.

[64] Katz, *The Irony of Early School Reform*, xxvii.

[65] Meyer was concerned that the current public education system does not educate in the ability to properly think or inculcate virtuous behavior into students, and is premised on an egalitarian leveling that reduces the overall quality of education. Frank S. Meyer, "In Defense of Freedom," in *In Defense of Freedom and Related Essays* (Indianapolis: Liberty Fund, 1996), 140–46.

anarchy and nihilism."[66] It was Rothbard's often-uncompromising libertarian positions (and refusal to ally with conservatives who didn't share his libertarian values) that led conservative William Buckley to write in his eulogy that "Murray Rothbard had defective judgment."[67]

Rothbard's attempt to craft a libertarian philosophy that advocated market capitalism while also aligning with the New Left led him, first and foremost, to emphasize the dangers of state control of education for a free society. It also led him into an area where few market libertarians had gone before: the question of what rights children have in a free society. While Rothbard hoped to forge an ideological alliance with the New Left, his advocacy of a free market (in education and elsewhere) failed to convince most New Leftists, concerned as they were with the potential of markets to produce equally freedom-inhibiting bureaucratization as governments could. Rothbard's anarchism similarly alienated many conservatives, some of whom believed that government had at least some role to play in education (whether regulating schools to ensure quality standards or redistributing educational funding to ensure that all children could receive some education). This latter group of conservatives (joined by some liberals) found a voice in Milton Friedman and his arguments for educational vouchers.

---

[66] Frank S. Meyer, "Libertarianism or Libertinism?" in *In Defense of Freedom and Related Essays* (Indianapolis: Liberty Fund, 1996), 183.
[67] William Buckley, "Murray Rothbard, RIP," *The National Review*, February 6, 1995.

6

Milton (and Rose) Friedman: Education Vouchers and State Financing of Private Education

In a 1995 interview for libertarian *Reason Magazine*, Milton Friedman described his virtually nonexistent professional relationship with Murray Rothbard. "I had some contact with Murray early on, but very little contact with him overall." Friedman explained that "partly [this was] because whenever he's had the chance he's been nasty to me and my work. I don't mind that but I didn't have to mix with him. And so there is no ideological reason why I kept separate from him, really a personal reason." Friedman also recalled discomfort with the work of Ayn Rand, who, to Friedman, "was an utterly intolerant and dogmatic person who did a great deal of good. But I could never feel comfortable with her."[1]

In both cases, Friedman's antipathy toward Rothbard and Rand (which seems to have been mutual) was borne of a sense that Rothbard and Rand were too unwavering in their ideologies and moralistic in their approaches to defending liberty. Conversely, both Rand and Rothbard saw Friedman as not principled and moralistic enough.

---

[1] Brian Doherty, "Best of Both Worlds," *Reason Magazine*, June 1996, 4, http://reason.com/archives/1995/06/01/best-of-both-worlds.

Tensions between Rand and Friedman and Rothbard and Friedman almost certainly started with a pamphlet Friedman co-wrote with fellow economist George Stigler arguing against rent-control laws. Rand or Rothbard likely would have argued against these controls on moral grounds, that rent controls were morally impermissible infringements on liberty in the free market. However, Friedman and Stigler's argument focused on consequences of such laws, how such laws would inadvertently lead to outcomes (like housing shortages) that hurt those the laws intended to help. Upon reading their pamphlet, Rand wrote a letter to the president of the pamphlet's publisher demanding, in vain, that the pamphlet be recalled and that Rand be allowed to vet future publications.[2] Despite Friedman's status as a respected popularizer of libertarian ideas, including educational vouchers, none of Rand's subsequent essays defending market capitalism or a tax-credit system of public support for private education mention the name or work of Milton Friedman.

Rothbard also voiced skepticism and sometimes outright hostility to the work of Milton Friedman, and for similar reasons. In a 1971 article called "Milton Friedman Unraveled," Rothbard, referencing Friedman's then-role as an economic advisor to President Richard Nixon, declared that "Milton Friedman is the Establishment's Court Libertarian, and it is high time that libertarians awaken to this fact of life." (One focus of Rothbard's criticism in this article was Friedman's preference for vouchers, rather than a *completely* free market in education.) In 1973, Rothbard took issue with Friedman—who he called an "alleged 'libertarian' economist"—in his support of a proposed tax on imported oil by rhetorically asking what cause "has led to Friedman's abandonment of free trade and free market principles this time?"[3]

As the tensions between Friedman and both Rand and Rothbard illustrates, Milton Friedman's brand of libertarianism was more tempered than was Rand's or Rothbard's less compromising approaches.[4] As one histo-

---

[2] Brian Doherty, *Radicals for Capitalism: A Freewheeling History of the Modern American Libertarian Movement*, 1st ed. (New York: Public Affairs, 2007), 191; Gregory T. Eow, "Fighting a New Deal: Intellectual Origins of the Reagan Revolution, 1932–1952," PhD dissertation, Rice University, 2007, 151–55.
[3] Murray N. Rothbard, "Society Without a State," *The Libertarian Forum*, January 1975, 3.
[4] As a quick terminological note, it is quite common to see Friedman referred to as a conservative, likely because of his work as advisor to Republican presidents (Nixon, Reagan) and presidential

rian notes, "Friedman displays an affinity with a more moderate form of neoliberal thought" than many more libertarian colleagues.[5] This moderation led Friedman to advocate several policies where governments would play a larger role than made many libertarians comfortable, from a Federal Reserve actively adjusting interest rates to the tax redistribution necessary for school vouchers.

Friedman's less rigid and government-averse libertarianism might partly be a function of Friedman having started his career as a man of the "New Deal" left. Growing up in a working-class family in New York City, Friedman's first several jobs after obtaining his MA in economics were for the federal government, in the National Resources Committee and the U.S. Treasury (where he worked on wartime tax policy). Biographer William Ruger writes, "Friedman's work at this time displayed no sign of the monetarist and libertarian future."[6]

Friedman's thought went in a more libertarian direction while studying for his Ph.D. in economics at the University of Chicago under "classical liberal" professors like Henry Simons, Frank Knight, and Jacob Viner.[7] As pro-market as these professors were, though, their own thought exhibited the same kind of moderation that Friedman's would later exhibit. As historian Angus Burgin writes of Simons, Knight, and Viner, "Although they shared with their colleagues … an inclination to defend markets against excessively or ill-conceived interventions, they believed that government had an essential role to play in the modern economy."[8]

---

candidates (Goldwater). Like many other pro-market thinkers, Friedman preferred to classify himself as a liberal (in the old sense of the word), but later in his life, referred to himself as a libertarian. In a 1995 interview, Friedman suggested that "I have a party membership as a Republican, not because they have any principles, but because that's the way I am the most useful and have most influence. My philosophy is clearly libertarian" (Doherty, "Best of Both Worlds," 4).

[5] David Stedman Jones, *Masters of the Universe: Hayek, Friedman, and the Birth of Neoliberal Politics* (Princeton, NJ: Princeton University Press, 2012), 98.

[6] William Ruger, *Milton Friedman* (New York: Continuum, 2011), 21.

[7] In the preface of his seminal 1963 book *Capitalism and Freedom*, Friedman acknowledged the intellectual influence of Knight and Simons (as well as other pro-market colleagues like F. A. Hayek and George Stigler). Friedman wrote: "I have learned so much from them and what I have learned has become so much a part of this book that I would not know how to select points to footnote." Milton Friedman, *Capitalism and Freedom*, 40th anniversary edition (Chicago: University of Chicago Press, 2002), 15.

[8] Angus Burgin, *The Great Persuasion: Reinventing Free Markets Since the Depression* (Cambridge: Harvard University Press, 2012), 43.

In particular, Henry Simons had a noticeable effect on Friedman's intellectual development in a libertarian direction. Particularly formative was Simons's widely read essay, "A Positive Programme for Laissez Faire." There, Simons articulates a philosophy similar to that which Friedman would later exhibit: a passionate belief that, while markets tend to produce the best results when left free of government interferences such as price controls, government has a vital role in fostering competition (by breaking up private monopolies) and, in Simons's words, ensuring "the drastic reduction of inequality through [progressive] taxation."[9] Like his University of Chicago brethren, Simons championed free markets less on moralistic grounds (as Rothbard and Rand often did) and more on consequentialist economic grounds; markets were to be judged by the results they produced, and government interventions were necessary to the point where they aided markets in producing socially beneficial results. In a similar way, Friedman developed views that were more willing to grant governments some role in ensuring that all citizens had educational opportunities. Where Chodorov and Rand allowed *some* role to government here, that role was the minimal one of allowing tax credit for monies spent on educational services. For Rothbard, government had absolutely no role to play in education. For Friedman, per his more pragmatic Chicago School approach, government had a more active role of distributing funding to families in the form of educational vouchers they could use to purchase educational services.

Milton Friedman and the Role of Government in Education

In 1955, Milton Friedman wrote an essay applying his economic and political thought to the field of education, arguing that the existing sys-

---

[9] Henry Simons, "A Positive Program for Laissez Faire," in *Economic Policy for a Free Society* (Chicago: University of Chicago Press, 1948), 65. Rothbard also saw Simons's influence on Friedman's thought, but in a decidedly negative light: "And while Friedman has modified and softened Simons's hard-nosed stance, he is still, in essence, Simons redivivus; he only appears to be a free-marketeer because the remainder of the profession has shifted radically leftward and stateward in the meanwhile." Murray N. Rothbard, "Milton Friedman Unraveled," *Journal of Libertarian Studies* 16, no. 4 (n.d.): 38.

tem of public schooling should be replaced by a voucher system, allowing families to purchase private (or public) schooling at public expense. Originally appearing in a collection of academic essays in economics, "The Role of Government in Education" reached a much broader audience when it became a chapter (with minor changes) in Friedman's 1962 book *Capitalism and Freedom*.[10]

Up until the late 1940s, Friedman's economic work focused on economic issues, geared toward specialists, like monetary policy. In 1947 Friedman began attending meetings of the Mont Pelerin Society, an international consortium of academics devoted to defending classical liberal ideas of a free society in academia and to the wider public. Around this time, Friedman began supplementing his technical writings in economic theory with writings both defending classical liberal principles and applying these principles to concrete policy areas. As Friedman reflected later, "The Role of Government in Education" was less about any concrete interest Friedman had in education policy than a desire to apply his existing libertarian ideas of personal and economic freedom to the area of education. "My interest was in the philosophy of a free society. Education was the area that I happened to write on early."[11]

Friedman's original proposal for education vouchers was as follows:

> Governments could require a minimum level of schooling financed by giving parents vouchers redeemable for a specified maximum sum per child per year if spent on "approved" educational services. Parents would then be free to spend this sum and any additional sum they themselves provided on purchasing educational services from an "approved" institution of their own choice. The educational services could be rendered by private enterprises operated for profit, or by non-profit institutions.[12]

---

[10] Milton Friedman, "The Role of Government in Education," in *Economics and the Public Interest*, ed. Robert A. Solo (New Brunswick, NJ: Rutgers University Press, 1955), 123–44; Friedman, *Capitalism and Freedom*, chap. 6.
[11] Milton Friedman, "School Choice: A Personal Retrospective," in *The Indispensable Milton Friedman*, ed. Larry Ebenstein (Washington, DC: Regnery, 2012), 125.
[12] Friedman, *Capitalism and Freedom*, 92.

Why was this approach more desirable than the existing educational system, where the large majority of students went to public schools paid for and administered by governments? Like other market libertarians, Friedman embraced the "nineteenth-century liberal emphasis in the fundamental importance of the individual" and argued that a competitive order was necessary to ensure that individuals had the maximum freedom to direct their lives free from the dictates and exploitation of others. Friedman's brand of competitive order would "seek to use competition among producers to protect the consumer from exploitation, competition among employers to protect workers and owners of property, and competition among consumers to protect the enterprises themselves."[13] Similarly, in the first chapter of *Capitalism and Freedom*, Friedman argued that economic and political freedom are strongly interrelated, emphasizing that "by removing the organization of economic activity from the control of political authority, the market eliminates this source of coercive power."[14]

A primary rationale for government administration of schools had been (and continues to be) "that it might otherwise be impossible to provide the common core of values deemed requisite for social stability."[15] While Friedman had some broad sympathy with this argument, he believed that maintaining a state quasi-monopoly on schooling in order to achieve this end conflicts with the preservation of a free society. For Friedman, "drawing a line between providing for the common social values required for a stable society, on the one hand, and indoctrination inhibiting freedom of thought and belief, on the other" was necessary for the preservation of a free society.[16] Avoiding the latter "indoctrination" option meant moving away from a governmental quasi-monopoly on schooling and toward markets that, if necessary, were mildly regulated to ensure that all students received some common education while preserving much space for the diversity and choice necessary for a free society.

Yet, Friedman was unwilling to keep government completely out of education (like Rothbard) or even keeping it to the minimal role of

---

[13] Milton Friedman, "Neoliberalism and Its Prospects," in *The Indispensable Milton Friedman*, ed. Larry Ebenstein (Washington, DC: Regnery, 2012), 22.
[14] Friedman, *Capitalism and Freedom*, 30.
[15] Friedman, *Capitalism and Freedom*, 93.
[16] Friedman, *Capitalism and Freedom*, 93.

allowing individuals to exempt money spent on education from taxation (like Chodorov or Rand). Friedman's plan of governmental redistribution of educational vouchers opened education to the marketplace while allowing the government a role in redistributing educational funding to families.

Friedman justified this role for government in education primarily by appealing to the indirect benefits (what Friedman calls "neighborhood effects" and economists generally know as externalities) that education produces on those who did not directly consume it. For Friedman, maintaining robust markets where individuals can buy and sell goods and services was an important criterion for deciding whether and when government intervention is necessary (thus, Friedman favored governmental intervention to guard against monopolistic practices when those practices interfere with the competitive efficacy of markets). Toward this end, one area where Friedman believed government intervention was justified was when the purchase of goods or services produces significant neighborhood effects where "the action of one individual imposes significant costs on other individuals for which it is not feasible to make him compensate them or yields significant gains to others for which it is not feasible to make them compensate him."[17] For Friedman, instances where it would be excessively costly or impossible to charge every beneficiary of particular goods and services would likely result in those goods and services going underproduced.

Education, and particularly civic education of a kind that prepared individuals to be responsible democratic citizens, was one such service. Friedman worried that

> the education of a child is regarded as benefitting not only the child and his parents, but also other members of society, since some minimum level of education is a prerequisite for a stable and democratic society. Yet, it is not feasible to identify the particular individuals benefited by the education of any particular child, much less the money value of the benefit, and so to charge for the services rendered. In consequence there is justification on

---

[17] Milton Friedman, "Liberalism, Old Style," in *The Indispensable Milton Friedman*, ed. Larry Ebenstein (Washington, DC: Regnery, 2012), 11–24, 20.

liberal grounds for the state requiring some minimum amount of education for children.[18]

The Intellectual Origins of Vouchers

Friedman's original intent in formulating a voucher proposal owed less to concrete concerns over education policy than the more intellectual exercise of applying "the philosophy of freedom" to the area of education. It might be instructive, then, to note that at the time of Friedman's writings, not only had the idea of vouchers already been theoretically formulated (by John Stuart Mill) but policies resembling Friedman's vouchers had already been put into place, from the GI Bill of Rights to various southern states' use of voucher plans to avoid integrating public schools after *Brown v. Board of Education*. Looking at these precedents might help us put Friedman's voucher proposal in historical context.

Whether Friedman was conscious of it or not, he very likely read a similar (if not as developed) "voucher plan" advocated a century before by philosopher and economist John Stuart Mill, who Friedman elsewhere recalled he "must have read in my first or second year of college."[19] Like Friedman, Mill was a "liberal" who justified his libertarian political philosophy on consequentialist grounds: individual liberty is valued not because humans have natural rights, but by the good consequences respect for liberty produces overall. Like Friedman, then, Mill was concerned with the infringements on liberty caused by state education, but recognized that as all children should be educated (to better exercise liberty as adults), government may have a legitimate role in funding and regulating private education and compelling parents to purchase suitable education for their children.

For Mill, "a general State education is a mere contrivance for moulding people to be exactly like one another: and as the mould in which it casts them is that which pleases the predominant power in the government. ... In proportion as it is efficient and successful, it establishes a despotism

---

[18] Friedman, "Liberalism, Old Style," 20.
[19] Milton Friedman, "My Five Favorite Libertarian Books," in *The Indispensable Milton Friedman*, ed. Larry Ebenstein (Washington, DC: Regnery, 2012), 17–111, 107.

over the mind, leading by natural tendency to one over the body."[20] Mill believed that the state could avoid this potential despotism by restricting itself to helping parents provide for their children's education in the private sphere:

> It [the state] might leave to parents to obtain the education where and how they feel pleased and content itself with helping to pay the school fees of the poorest classes of children, and defraying the entire school expense of those who have no one else to pay for them. The objections which are urged with reason against State education, do not apply to the enforcement of education by the State, but to the State's taking upon itself to direct that education: which is a totally different thing.[21]

Like Friedman (at least before he and his wife wrote their 1980 book *Free to Choose*), Mill believed that the state should make education compulsory for school-aged children. Contra Friedman's "neighborhood effects" rationale for compulsory education, though, Mill's rationale rested on parents' obligation to provide for and protect their children, "to provide food for its body, but instruction and training for its mind." In cases where parents shirked this duty, "the State ought to see it fulfilled at the charge, as far as possible, of the parent."[22] (While Friedman justified compulsory education laws by appeal to the positive neighborhood effects education produced on society, he, like Mill, believed that there was a strong liberal case to be made for laws protecting certain rights children have against parental abuse and neglect: "The children are responsible individuals in embryo, and a believer in freedom believes in protecting their ultimate rights."[23] Interestingly, though, Friedman did not use this justification in arguing for compulsory education laws.)

While "The Role of Government in Education" is mostly a theoretical work, Friedman did suggest that there were several existing (imperfect) examples of what his voucher program would look like in practice. In addition to limited programs in Britain and France where governments

---

[20] John Stuart Mill, *On Liberty, and the Subjection of Women*, Henry Holt 1879 edition (Indianapolis: Liberty Fund, 2011), 97.
[21] Mill, *On Liberty*, 97.
[22] Mill, *On Liberty*, 96.
[23] Friedman, *Capitalism and Freedom*, 33.

paid the fees of some students to attend non-state schools, "an excellent example of a program of this sort is [in] the United States educational program for veterans after World War II."[24] Friedman was referring to the 1944 Servicemen's Readjustment Act. Better known as the "GI Bill" (or "GI Bill of Rights"), the law paid the tuition of servicemen whose educations had been interrupted by military service to the college or trade school of their choice, up to a certain amount per month for a period of either one year or the duration of the participant's military service (if more than a year). Under the "GI Bill," as described by a pamphlet explaining the bill to servicemen, "the government will pay to the school you have chosen up to $500 for an ordinary school year to cover tuition, laboratory, library, health, infirmary, and other similar fees and may pay for books, supplies, equipment, and other necessary expenses" as well as up to $75 per month for living expenses.[25] While differing from Friedman's voucher idea in that the federal government would pay the institution directly (rather than distribute a voucher to the participant), the similarities with Friedman's voucher proposal come from the fact that state funding was used to pay for private educational options, allowing the servicemen to shop for (state-approved) educational institutions that suited their needs. (Of course, the government's allowance of educational choice likely owed less to a libertarian faith in markets or skepticism toward public universities, and more to a recognition that, as a robust market in higher education already existed, it would be most expedient to fund servicemen's use of those institutions.)

While Friedman mentions the similarity between his voucher proposal and the Servicemen's Readjustment Act only once in "The Role of Government in Education," he would invoke the similarities between the two with increasing frequency in his later career. After the U.S. Supreme Court struck down two voucher-like tuition-reimbursement programs as violations of the First Amendment's Establishment Clause, Friedman argued that school choice programs like his own were similar to the Servicemen's Readjustment Act, which allowed servicemen to receive education at reli-

---

[24] Friedman, *Capitalism and Freedom*, 89.
[25] Army Times Publishing Company, *The GI Bill of Rights and How It Works* (Washington, DC: Army Times, 1945), 4.

gious institutions and had never been subject to constitutional scrutiny.[26] In the later *Free to Choose*, Milton and Rose Friedman wrote that "the voucher plan embodies exactly the same principles as the GI bills."[27] Other proponents of vouchers, like those of Christopher Jencks, Judith Areen, and David Kirkpatrick, also invoked the idea of the Servicemen's Readjustment Act as a rough blueprint for how vouchers at the K–12 level might operate.[28]

While Friedman did not highlight the fact, vouchers for primary and secondary education were already in effect in several southern states, albeit with a different purpose than Friedman likely had in mind. In 1954, the U.S. Supreme Court decided *Brown v. Board of Education*, which demanded the integration of racially segregated public schools. In an attempt to maintain de facto racial segregation in schools but do so in a seemingly constitutional way, these southern states experimented with offering vouchers to parents who wished to purchase private (and almost certainly segregated) private schooling for their children. A 1960 law in New Orleans, Louisiana, for instance, offered parents a voucher equivalent to one year's per student expenditure for public schooling that could be used for tuition at any nondenominational, nonprofit private school. While the voucher was offered to both white and black students, "all of the schools that accepted tuition grants in New Orleans (and across the state) were racially segregated" up until the program's end (by federal decree) in 1967.[29] By 1960 (five years after Friedman originally proposed education vouchers), six southern states had similar voucher laws in effect.[30]

As we have seen, Friedman did point to a few examples where "features of the proposed [voucher] arrangement [were] present in existing educational systems" (voucher-like systems in areas of France and Britain, the

---

[26] Milton Friedman, "Selling Schools Like Groceries: The Voucher Idea," *New York Times Magazine*, September 1973.
[27] Milton Friedman and Rose Friedman, *Free to Choose: A Personal Statement*, 1st ed. (New York: Harcourt Brace Jovanovich, 1980).
[28] Judith Areen and Christopher Jencks, "Educational Vouchers: A Proposal for Diversity and Choice," *The Teachers College Record* 72, no. 3 (1971): 327–36; David W. Kirkpatrick, *Choice in Schooling: A Case for Tuition Vouchers* (Chicago: Loyola University Press, 1990).
[29] Jim Carl, *Freedom of Choice: Vouchers in American Education* (Santa Barbara, CA: Praeger, 2011), 48.
[30] Carl, *Freedom of Choice*, 33.

GI Bill of Rights). Yet Friedman did not mention the voucher programs already in effect in the several southern states (many of which, like the one in Louisiana, bore marked similarity to his own proposal). Historian Jim Carl suggests that this oversight may have been deliberate, that "Friedman … maintained a careful aloofness from southern voucher programs."[31] This interpretation, while plausible, should be approached with caution. Friedman's original article on vouchers appeared in 1955 and while several states were considering and crafting potential voucher legislation, none had yet enacted such laws. When Friedman's original essay appeared in slightly modified form in the 1962 book *Capitalism and Freedom*, it was not amended to include mention of the several voucher laws that, at that time, existed in several southern states. Yet *Capitalism and Freedom*'s chapter on education was immediately followed by a chapter titled "Capitalism and Discrimination," which contained a section on "Segregation in Schooling." There, Friedman acknowledged that "the preceding chapter" was "written initially without any regard at all to the problem of segregation or integration." Friedman, though, maintained that his voucher proposal "gives the appropriate solution that permits the avoidance of both evils" of forced segregation and forced integration.[32] In this "Segregation in Schooling" section, Friedman *did* mention the voucher laws in Prince Edward County, Virginia and predicted that while "adopted for the purposes of avoiding compulsory integration … the ultimate effects of the law will be very different"[33] if allowed to continue for several years to come. This was for two reasons: First, Friedman argued that over time, parents and families would allow considerations of educational quality to trump considerations of racial segregation in their choice of schools for their children. (This, of course, assumed that parents in these southern states would not view the racial makeup of the student body as an indicator of or influence on the quality of education at particular schools.) Second, using his own city of Chicago as an example, Friedman argued that public schools in many areas were already, in a sense, segregated by government fiat—not in the sense that governments disallowed racial integration in schools, but that governments zoned students to particular

---

[31] Carl, *Freedom of Choice*, 91.
[32] Friedman, *Capitalism and Freedom*, 116.
[33] Friedman, *Capitalism and Freedom*, 117.

schools based on where they lived. This meant that by disallowing freedom of choice between schools, governments of homogeneous districts enforced homogeneity in district schools. "If the Virginia plan were introduced in Chicago," Friedman writes, "the result would be an appreciable decrease in segregation, and a great widening in the opportunities available to the ablest and most ambitious Negro youth."[34] Ultimately, Friedman saw Prince Edward County's voucher plan as a test for his idea: "If the voucher system is not abolished, Virginia will provide an experiment to test the conclusions of the preceding chapter [arguing for vouchers in education]."[35]

Ultimately, Prince Edward County's voucher plan would turn out to be an odd one with which to make his case that vouchers would lead to a more integrated school environment than public schools. The plan was ultimately found unconstitutional by the U.S. Supreme Court in 1964 as a violation of the Fourteenth Amendment's Equal Protection Clause. This plan also included a clause to shut down integrated public schools in that students could choose private schools, but private school regulations were such that "white children there have accredited private schools which they can attend, while colored children, until very recently, have had no available private schools, and even the school they now attend is a temporary expedient."[36] Though the tuition program did not last long enough to prove Friedman's suspicions about vouchers leading to

---

[34] Friedman, *Capitalism and Freedom*, 117.
[35] Friedman, *Capitalism and Freedom*, 117.
[36] *Griffin v. School Board of Prince Edward County*, 37, 377 (U.S. 1964). The Supreme Court ruled that African-Americans' rights to the equal protection under the law was violated because only students in Prince Edward Co. operated without the benefit of tax-funded public schooling. While the voucher program was non-discriminatory—students were able to take advantage of the same voucher regardless of race, and schools for African American students were not prohibited from opening in the county—the voucher program had an undeniably disparate effect of whites and blacks. Whites were able to attend the financially well-endowed Prince Edward Academy, which enrolled "about 93 percent of white students" in 1959. Blacks in Prince Edward County had "far lower average incomes, [and] did not have the economic resources to create authentic private schools by themselves." While white segregationist groups did offer financial help to create black schools, these offers risked "jeopardiz[ing] the desegregation lawsuit, [and] never received serious consideration." Thus, while most whites attended a comprehensive "white only" private school, African-Americans either attended makeshift" training centers staffed by volunteers, or were sent to live with relatives or volunteer foster parents in counties and states where public schooling was available. Christopher Bonastia, *Southern Stalemate: Five Years Without Public Education in Prince Edward County, Virginia* (Chicago: The University of Chicago Press, 2012), 106, 131, chap. 4.

integration right or wrong per se, it seems doubtful that Prince Edward County's voucher plan specifically, per its design, would have led to the results Friedman anticipated.

Even Less Role for the State to Play in Education, and the Influence of E. G. West

While Friedman originally wrote his voucher proposal more as an extension of his economic ideas than to reflect a specific interest in education, he continued advocating for his voucher proposal in the coming decades, particularly in newspaper columns he wrote for magazines and newspapers.[37] In 1980, he and his wife, economist Rose Friedman, revisited Friedman's original voucher idea in their book *Free to Choose* (and the ten-part video series for the Public Broadcasting System of the same name). While their arguments about the desirability of a market approach to education remained roughly the same as Milton's earlier arguments in *Capitalism and Freedom*, *Free to Choose* argued for a voucher system with even less government involvement.

Free to Choose was conceived as a book of "more nuts and bolts [and] less theoretical framework"[38] than the more abstract *Capitalism and Freedom*. Chapter 6 of *Free to Choose* ("What's Wrong with Our Schools?") defends a market approach to education less on appeal to individualistic freedom of thought and more on basic economic arguments about the ability of markets to offer choice to consumers and offer services that respond to consumer demand (compared to government services funded and administered through the political process). As an example, the Friedmans argue that the size of public school districts and schools are determined by political processes rather than by consumer demand, as they would be in a system of private providers.[39] The Friedmans also expressed concern that

---

[37] For instance, see: Milton Friedman, "Public Education," *Newsweek*, March 1967; Milton Friedman, "Selling Schools Like Groceries: The Voucher Idea," *New York Times Magazine*, September 1973, The Friedman Foundation for Educational Choice; Milton Friedman, "The Solution to the Public School Crisis," *San Francisco Chronicle*, March 20, 1979.

[38] Friedman and Friedman, *Free to Choose*, ix.

[39] Friedman and Friedman, *Free to Choose*, 156–58.

a public school system unintentionally creates a tiered system: those with financial means who are dissatisfied with their public schools can either pay private school tuition on top of their taxes or move to a district with a better system. Those whose financial means don't allow these options have as their "only recourse … to try to influence the political authorities who are in charge of the public schools, usually a difficult if not hopelessly impossible task."[40]

The details of the Friedman's voucher system were also quite similar to Friedman's earlier proposal: families would receive a voucher equivalent to the amount of money it would take to educate each child in a current public school that they could use at a private or public school of their choice.[41] Like in Friedman's earlier writings, the authors explained their voucher proposal as "embod[ying] exactly the same principle as the GI bills that provide for educational benefits to military veterans."[42]

The Friedmans' discussion of vouchers in *Free to Choose* is different from *Capitalism and Freedom* in several key respects, each reflecting a seemingly increased skepticism of government involvement in education. In *Free to Choose*, the Friedmans' concerns were particularly in the areas of decreasing the governmental role in school financing and compelling attendance. The Friedmans posited "the voucher plan as a partial solution," but insofar as the proposal did not reduce government's role in these two areas, "we favor going much farther."[43]

Later, Friedman suggested that, on educational matters, "I have become more extreme, not because of any change of philosophy, but because of a change in my knowledge of the factual situation and history." Friedman credits his and his wife's reversal on the necessity of compulsory education laws to reading "work that E.G. West and others" have written.[44]

While Friedman did not elaborate on the identity of the "others" who influenced his thinking, the influence of West's writings on the economics

---

[40] Friedman and Friedman, *Free to Choose*, 157–58.
[41] The Friedmans' voucher proposal allowed public schools to exist but noted that it would "require public schools to finance themselves by charging tuition. … The public schools would then have to compete both with one another and with private schools." Friedman and Friedman, *Free to Choose*, 161.
[42] Friedman and Friedman, *Free to Choose*, 161.
[43] *Friedman and Friedman, Free to Choose*, 161.
[44] Doherty, "Best of Both Worlds," 5.

of education on Friedman deserves exploration. To understand the Friedmans' change of mind in favor of a more muted role for government in distributing vouchers (and mandating compulsory schooling), we will look more closely at the aspects of West's writings that convinced the Friedmans that the majority of people did not need government vouchers or compulsory education laws to induce them to send children to school or receive some sort of decent education.

E. G. West was an English economist who first caught Milton Friedman's attention with an article West wrote shortly after the publication of *Capitalism and Freedom* summarizing the debate among classical economists over the role of the public and private spheres in education.[45] The following year, West took a one-year position as a postdoctoral fellow in the University of Chicago's economics department, where Friedman (and other classical liberal economists) worked. That year, West published *Education and the State*, a book-length theoretical and empirical examination exploring the extent to which government intervention in education is justified, a book that was "inspired, in part, as a challenge to Milton Friedman's voucher proposal."[46]

In *Education and the State*, West took square aim at the "neighborhood effects" argument used by Friedman and many other economists to argue that government had a necessary role in financing (or sometimes administering) education. While West never claimed that government should have no role in financing education, he argued both theoretically and empirically that "neighborhood effect" arguments have often been oversold. If government expenditure on education is necessary, West suggested, it is probably necessary only in cases where people are too poor to purchase decent levels of education on their own.

By way of economic theory, West was most concerned that

> the identification of a "neighbourhood effect" is only a necessary but not a sufficient condition for intervention. There are many serious offsetting considerations, the most important being that the task of measuring the

---

[45] E. G. West, "Private Versus Public Education: A Classical Economic Dispute," *Journal of Political Economy* 72, no. 5 (October 1, 1964): 465–75.

[46] James Tooley, "From Universal to Targeted Vouchers: The Relevance of the Friedmans' Proposals for Developing Countries," in *Liberty and Learning: Milton Friedman's Voucher Ideas at Fifty*, ed. Robert C. Enlow and Lenore T. Ealy (Washington, DC: Cato Institute, 2006), 140.

chain reaction of costs and benefits is often insuperable. The administrative costs of intervention alone may be so high as to exceed the net benefits which such action sought to secure, even if they could be measured.[47]

Thus, even if it could be established that education produced substantial enough "neighborhood effects" to warrant government expenditure in education, it must further be shown that such involvement does not impose social costs that outweigh or equal the benefits of government intervention. This was an argument that Friedman would have been quite receptive to. In Friedman's own argument that government intervention was most necessary when "neighborhood effects" might reduce markets' ability to provide the service at appropriate levels, Friedman was already careful to note that

> neighborhood effects cut both ways. They can be a reason for limiting the activities of government as well as for expanding them. ... It is hard to know when neighborhood effects are sufficiently large to justify particular costs in overcoming them and even harder to distribute the costs in an appropriate fashion.[48]

Also, while Friedman originally concluded that the social gains made by government expenditure in education were sufficient to justify his voucher proposal, he was cognizant that "the gain from these measures must be balanced against the costs, and there can be much honest difference of judgment about how extensive a subsidy is justified."[49]

To West, the most obvious cost of government intervention (to be weighed against the benefit of such intervention) was financial. In order to spend on education, governments must raise revenue from taxes, which takes money out of the economy. One valid cost to consider against the potential benefit of governments' expenditure on education is the loss of money circulated in the economy that now goes to taxes. Questioning the belief that any significant number of people would be unable to afford education without government subsidy, West argues that successive gener-

---

[47] E. G West, *Education and the State: A Study in Political Economy* (Indianapolis: Liberty Fund, 1994), 33.
[48] Friedman, *Capitalism and Freedom*, 44.
[49] Friedman, *Capitalism and Freedom*, 90–91.

ations have relied "upon state education financed by taxes on themselves, taxes which so often fall inconspicuously on many goods and services."[50] At best, "since in the absence of an earmarked system, nobody knows which tax pays for which government service, it cannot be demonstrated that even the poorest of families are not paying substantively for their 'free' education."[51] To West, it was at least an open question whether the financial costs of government expenditure on education were worth any social benefit.

In *Capitalism and Freedom*, Friedman argued that education produced positive neighborhood effects by equipping students with "a minimum degree of literacy and knowledge" and "widespread acceptance of some common values" that contribute to the functioning of "a stable and democratic society."[52] To counter Friedman's (and other economists') arguments on these points, West leveled a theoretical and empirical argument against the idea that expenditures in state education correlate with high literacy rates, low crime rates, or social cohesion. In each case, West argues either that data does not support such correlations or that evidence shows that state support for schooling has an unfavorable effect on the variable in question. For instance, West argues that data from Britain in the 1940s should lead one to conclude not only that "the popular belief ... that state education makes the public less crime prone, is unsupported by the available evidence" but also that "the evidence showed a *prima facie* relationship in the opposite direction."[53] West loosely hypothesized that this might be because compulsory education has caused people, in some way, to "overconsume" formal schooling and prolong the number of years before youth enter the workforce. In a way not terribly dissimilar from the more "left-leaning" Paul Goodman, West rhetorically asked: "Why do we accept indiscriminately arguments about the need to protect young people from the 'uncertain pressures of adult life' as long as possible and

---

[50] West, *Education and the State*, 49.
[51] West, *Education and the State*, 50. In the second edition (1970) of *Education and the State*, West used British income and tax data to show that other than for the poor (those who made less than £911 per year), "most people could be 'richer' if the state did not feel itself obligated to provide social services like education 'free,' 51.
[52] Friedman, *Capitalism and Freedom*, 89.
[53] West, *Education and the State*, 41.

neglect the possibility that pressures of school life may be in some cases the crucial ones?"[54]

West also had several arguments specifically against universal voucher programs (as opposed to those targeted only to the very poor who could not otherwise afford education). Among them were that consumers were likely to be "much more alert when spending their own money directly rather than when they are 'spending' a government voucher only" and that issuing vouchers whose total amount must be spent on education might keep prices artificially high where, in a "vigorous market, costs can be expected to fall from time to time."[55] If vouchers were only given to those who needed them to afford education, such effects to the overall pricing of schooling would be minimal.

Another article of West's, "Political Economy of American Public School Legislation," (appearing in later editions of *Education and the State*) had some effect on Friedman's thinking and was cited several times in *Free to Choose*. If Friedman was concerned that compulsory education laws and robust government funding of education were necessary to keep school attendance high, West used historical data to argue that New York's school attendance was quite high before the New York state government erected "free schools" (common schools that were wholly subsidized by taxation, rather than primarily through tuition). According to West, evidence from annual reports by New York State's school superintendents in 1821, school attendance was around 90%—"already almost universal without being compulsory. Moreover, although it was subsidized, it was not free except to the very poor."[56] If the large majority of students were being educated at tuition-charging schools (academies, charity schools, or tuition-charging "common schools"), why did New York State struggle over the next several decades to enlarge the state's responsibility both for financing and ultimately for administering education? Using public choice economic analysis, West suggests that "it is in the interests of individual suppliers, whatever the setting they find themselves in, to seek out those courses of action which bring either better returns for given efforts or the same returns

---

[54] West, *Education and the State*, 43.
[55] West, *Education and the State*, 283, 284.
[56] E. G. West, "The Political Economy of American Public School Legislation," *Journal of Law and Economics* 10 (1967): 105.

for less effort."[57] In seeking to enlarge the role of the state in financing education and making it compulsory (at a time when the state's own data showed continual reluctance to attend public schools in lieu of private), those already close to the state's public school system had some economic interest in seeing the system they were part of depend less on (possibly inconsistent) tuition from parents and more on guaranteed funding from the state.

In "The Political Economy of American Public School Legislation," West, an economist by training, interprets the historical record through the lens of a "new branch of economics which has come to be known as the economic theory of democracy," which, in the 1970s, would become more popularly known as public choice theory. Rather than analyzing economic actors and political actors as differently motivated (economic actors acting from self-interest, and political actors, from public-spiritedness), public choice economists analyze both public and private actors with the same economic model. As E. G. West puts it, "This theory distinguishes itself by an application of the self-interest axiom ('the profit motive') to the actions of voters, governments, public agencies, and to all aspects of political activity in general."[58]

West used this "economic theory of democracy" to answer a puzzling question: if data shows that the large majority of New Yorkers were receiving sufficient (as measured by indirect data such as literacy rates and reports produced by government officials) education before the state established tax-funded "free schools," why did state agencies and reformers continually succeed in expanding the state role in education? West's thesis was that the legislation was driven less by family demand for state-financed schooling than by government actors acting in their own economic self-interest to obtain a monopoly on the provision of schooling and immunize themselves from competition from private schools.[59]

---

[57] West, "The Political Economy of American Public School Legislation," 116.
[58] West, "The Political Economy of American Public School Legislation," 114.
[59] E. G. West, "The Political Economy of American Public School Legislation," *Journal of Law and Economics* 10 (1967): 101–28. The following year, Michael Katz published a similar, and contentious, history in *The Irony of Early School Reform*, suggesting that the growth of public schooling in several areas of Massachusetts had less to do with public demand and more to do with the paternalism of education reformers acting against public demand. Michael B. Katz, *The Irony of Early School Reform: Educational Innovation in Mid-Nineteenth Century Massachusetts* (New

West suggested that "it is in the interests of individual suppliers, whatever the setting they find themselves in, to seek out those courses of action which bring either better returns for given efforts or the same returns for less effort."[60] West believed that applying this economic theory of democracy to the case of New York State's education system explained why the state "so readily brushed aside considerations of administrative improvement as an alternative to the revolutionary step of complete abolition of the rate bill" tuition system where families chose which public or private school to attend and paid tuition (sometimes, with state assistance).[61] If there were families who couldn't afford to pay tuition, the state could have increased subsidies to those families, but instead, moved to abolish the "rate bill" system and erect a tax-funded system of "free schools," thus eliminating competition with private schools and guaranteeing money to state-funded schools. "While conventional history portrays them as distinguished champions in the cause of children's welfare and benevolent participants in a political struggle, it is suggested here that the facts are equally consistent with the hypothesis of self-interest behavior as described above."[62]

The effect of West's work on Friedman is evident in *Free to Choose*. West's *Education and the State* took on Friedman's earlier idea that government funding of education was necessary to prevent any underinvestment in education within the market owing to neighborhood effects. West also cast doubt on the idea that public education systems, universal vouchers, or even compulsory education laws would be necessary to ensure that parents minded their children's education. By *Free to Choose*, the Friedmans preferred a much smaller role for government in education; what was once a support for universal vouchers was now limited to targeted vouchers for the very poor. What used to be a recognition that compulsory education laws were necessary was now a belief that "compulsory attendance at

---

York: Teachers College Press, 2001). Katz's interpretation was contentious and criticized by historians Diane Ravitch and Maris Vinovskis, among others. Diane Ravitch, *The Revisionists Revised: A Critique of the Radical Attack on Schools* (New York: Basic Books, 1978); Maris A. Vinovskis, *The Origins of Public High Schools: A Reexamination of the Beverly High School Controversy* (Madison: University of Wisconsin Press, 1985).

[60] West, "The Political Economy of American Public School Legislation," 116.
[61] West, "The Political Economy of American Public School Legislation," 113.
[62] West, "The Political Economy of American Public School Legislation," 115.

schools is not necessary to achieve that minimum standard of literacy and knowledge."[63]

Milton Friedman and Public Choice Economics

By the time Friedman read E. G. West's work applying public choice economic analysis to the world of education, Friedman was doubtless already familiar with the writings and arguments of public choice economists, and the influence of this strand of economic thought became more evident on Friedman's thought. Particularly, the focus public choice economists placed on highlighting the self-interest of individual actors in explaining the workings of institutions aided Friedman in his critique of the growth of bureaucracy in public education as well as teachers' unions role in blocking vouchers and other educational reforms.

In the late 1950s, Friedman was almost certainly familiar with the growth in standing of the public choice economic approach. In 1957, economist Anthony Downs had published his book *Economic Theory of Democracy* (a book West cited several times in "Political Economy of American Public School Legislation" as providing a theoretical framework for his analysis).[64] In 1962, economists James Buchanan and Gordon Tullock wrote a book widely considered to be a foundational text of public choice theory, *The Calculus of Consent*.[65] In the late 1960s and early 1970s, one of Friedman's close friends and colleagues in the University of Chicago's Department of Economics, George Stigler, would become, in Friedman's words, "one of the pioneers in what came to be called 'public choice' economics."[66] Stigler, with whom Friedman had co-written the aforementioned *Roofs or Ceilings?*, wrote a well-received paper in 1972 called "The Theory of Economic Regulation," whose "general hypothesis [was that] every industry or occupation that has enough political power to

---

[63] Friedman and Friedman, *Free to Choose*, 162.
[64] Anthony Downs, *An Economic Theory of Democracy* (New York: Harper, 1957).
[65] James M. Buchanan and Gordon Tullock, *The Calculus of Consent* (Ann Arbor: University of Michigan Press, 1962).
[66] Milton Friedman, "George Stigler: A Personal Reminiscence," *Journal of Political Economy* 101, no. 5 (October 1, 1993): 772.

utilize the state will seek to control entry."[67] Like West, Stigler argued that regulation—sold as being in the public interest—was often, on further analysis, attempts by private and public actors to use the state's regulatory power to their own economic benefit.

By the publication of *Free to Choose* in 1980, the Friedmans were explicit about the influence of public choice economists on their own economic thinking. In the book's preface, the Friedmans wrote that one key differentiator between *Capitalism and Freedom* and *Free to Choose* was the latter being:

> influenced by a fresh approach to political science that has come from many economists—Anthony Downs, James Buchanan, Gordon Tullock, George J. Stigler, and Gary Becker, who, along with many others, have been doing exciting work in the economic analysis of politics. *Free to Choose* treats the political system symmetrically with the economic system. Both are regarded as markets in which the outcome is determined by interactions among persons pursuing their own self-interest rather than by the social goals the participants find it advantageous to enunciate.[68]

In addition to West's influence, other aspects of the Friedmans' later writing on education show traces of a public choice economic approach. In *Free to Choose*, the Friedmans bring up what they call Gammon's Law. In 1976, physician Max Gammon published a study he'd undertaken of Britain's expanding National Health Service (NHS). The question Gammon sought to answer was whether the expansion and the bureaucratization, of the NHS correlated with an increase in the organization's efficacy (as measured by factors like bed occupancy). Gammon concluded that the organization's size did not positively correlate with its efficacy rather, the larger the organization, the less efficacious it was.[69] The Friedmans summed up Gammon's law in this way: "The more bureaucratic an organization, the greater the extent to which useless work tends to displace useful work."[70] Friedman applied Gammon's Law not only to what he

---

[67] Friedman, "George Stigler," 5.
[68] Friedman and Friedman, *Free to Choose*, ix–x.
[69] Max Gammon, *Health and Security: Report on the Public Provision for Medical Care in Great Britain* (London: St. Michael's Organization, 1976).
[70] Friedman and Friedman, *Free to Choose*, 114.

saw as an increasing governmental presence in U.S. healthcare,[71] but also to the increasing bureaucratization and centralization of the public education system. The Friedmans argued that data on public schools from 1972 to 1977 showed a trend of rising costs per pupil and a number of professional staff, but an overall decrease in number of students and standardized test scores. "*Input clearly up. … Output clearly down.*"[72]

While public choice economists did not reference Gammon's Law, it is similar to many public choice economists' study of the inefficiency of bureaucracy. Public choice economist Gordon Tullock suggested that as public-sector bureaucracies get larger, top-down communication often becomes more difficult and clumsy. The larger the bureaucracy, the less likely its bureaucrats would act in full accord with the bureau's mission and directives. This would reduce the efficiency of the bureau toward its mission, which would often lead governments to expand the bureaucracy in order to (ironically) enhance its efficiency. "The whole situation is highly paradoxical. The inefficiency of the overexpanded bureaucracy leads to still further expansion and still further inefficiency."[73]

Other public choice economists explained the correlation between growing bureaucracy and shrinking inefficiency by appealing more to the self-interest of the bureaucrats in maximizing their utility. William Niskanen suggested that bureaucrats had an interest in performing just well enough to ensure that the bureau would continue expanding (in order that legislatures would expand their budgets) while offering services of enough—but no more—quality than is necessary to gain continual funding.[74] Emanuel Savas was more direct. Savas's survey of private companies' and government bureaucracies' provision of municipal services led him to postulate the following explanation for the inefficiency of government bureaucracies: "Since most city agencies are monopolies, their staffs are automatically in a position to exercise that monopoly power for their own parochial advantage—and efficiency is rarely seen as an advantage. In short, we have unwittingly built a system in which the public is at the

---

[71] Milton Friedman, "Gammon's Black Holes," *Newsweek*, November 1977.
[72] Friedman and Friedman, *Free to Choose*, 156.
[73] Gordon Tullock, *The Politics of Bureaucracy* (Washington, DC: Public Affairs Press, 1965), 177.
[74] William A. Niskanen Jr., *Bureaucracy and Representative Government* (Chicago: Aldine, Atherton, 1971).

mercy of its servants."[75] While not citing Gammon or Gammon's Law, many public choice economists shared both Max Gammon's and Milton Friedman's concern for, and explanation of, the correspondence between the growth of the government bureaucracies' size and the decrease in their efficiency.

Friedman applied this public-choice-tinged view of bureaucracy to analyzing the bureaucratic structure of public education. Government administration of education was a bad idea because it couldn't be justified by an appeal to neighborhood effects and because it suffered from the inefficiency that often plagues monopolies, both criticisms made in Friedman's earlier writing on education. In *Free to Choose*, the Friedmans also suggested that the bureaucratic interests within the public education system had a vested interest in maintaining their own monopoly status—avoiding reforms like their own voucher proposal that might introduce competition, threaten existing public school budgets, or pressure those in public education to become more efficient. The far reach of the education bureaucracy may even temper the public enthusiasm for school choices if a great many parents are also teachers and administrators who have an interest in maintaining the current public system of education.

> There may be parents, too, sincerely desiring a fine school system. However, their interests as teachers, as administrators, as union officials are different from their interest as parents and from the interests of parents whose children they teach. Their interests may be served by greater centralization and bureaucratization even if the interests of the parents are not—indeed, one way in which those interest are served is precisely by reducing the power of parents.[76]

The Friedmans were able to use this appeal to bureaucratic self-interest as a way to explain the resistance of teachers' unions and public education bureaucracies to then-existing voucher proposals, from the short-lived and contentious voucher experiment in Alum Rock, California, to failed attempts in the late 1970s to introduce vouchers in Michigan and New

---

[75]Emanuel S. Savas, "Municipal Monopolies Versus Competition in Delivering Urban Services," in *Improving the Quality of Urban Management* (Beverly Hills, CA: Sage, 1974), 474.
[76]Friedman and Friedman, *Free to Choose*, 157.

Hampshire. Citing E. G. West's research, the Friedmans explained that the "perceived self-interest of the education bureaucracy is the key obstacle to the introduction of market competition in schooling. This interest group … has adamantly opposed every attempt to study, explore, or experiment with voucher plans."[77] One voucher plan that captured the Friedmans' interest took place in 1972 in the Alum Rock Elementary School District in San Jose, CA. It owed less to Milton Friedman's voucher proposal than to Christopher Jencks and his colleagues at the Center for the Study of Public Policy.[78] The program, organized in conjunction with the Office of Educational Opportunity, set up mini-schools within six participating public schools, allowing parents to choose between competing schools and paying with "compensatory vouchers" (where poor parents received a higher voucher so that schools had incentive to accept poor students). By most accounts, the Alum Rock voucher experiment did not work as planned—it did not boost test scores as expected, nor did it produce vigorous competition or significant exercise of consumer choice; thus, five years after its introduction, it was discontinued.[79] The Friedmans, believing the experiment to be a moderate success despite being more limited in scope than Milton's own universal voucher proposal, suggested that the Alum Rock voucher experiment was "ended by the educational establishment."[80] (There may be some truth to this; a Rand Corporation study examining the Alum Rock experiment lists several reasons for the experiment's failure.) While the report notes that "there was limited opposition from groups within the system," and that "the district staff was competent and open to the idea of vouchers," one reason for the failure was likely that "the suggested innovation was in conflict with the pre-existing authority structure of the school district." While the Rand study found that opposition within the district was less than it may have been elsewhere, "the beliefs in consumer sovereignty underlying a voucher system were not congruent with the beliefs underlying a public monopoly," pos-

---

[77] Friedman and Friedman, *Free to Choose*, 171.
[78] *Educational Vouchers: A Preliminary Report on Financing Education by Payment to Parents* (Cambridge, MA: Center for the Study of Public Policy, 1970); Areen and Jencks, "Educational Vouchers: A Proposal for Diversity and Choice."
[79] Eliot Levinson, *The Alum Rock Voucher Demonstration: Three Years of Implementation* (Santa Monica, CA: Rand Corporation, 1976).
[80] Friedman and Friedman, *Free to Choose*, 173.

sibly resulting in a quicker discontinuation of the program that may have been justified.[81]

The Friedmans also explained a failed attempt starting in 1973 to introduce vouchers into several New Hampshire districts by appealing to unions' and bureaucrats' self-interest in maintaining the public education bureaucracy. While historian Jim Carl later explained the failure by pointing to legal and political concerns over the exclusion of sectarian schools from the voucher plan and (somewhat paradoxically) the plan's potential to increase federal oversight of the state's education system,[82] the Friedmans chalked up the proposal's failure to organized opposition by special interests:

> The conditions seemed excellent, funds were granted by the federal government, detailed plans were drawn up, experimental communities were selected, preliminary agreements from parents and administrators were obtained. When all seemed ready to go, one community after another was persuaded by the local superintendent of schools or other leading figures in the educational establishment to withdraw from the proposed experiment, and the whole venture collapsed.[83]

In 2005, Milton Friedman was just as direct. "Centralization, bureaucratization, and unionization" was to blame for several failed attempts in different states to introduce and sustain voucher programs.

> The union leaders and educational administrators rightly regard extended parental choice through vouchers and tax-funded scholarships as the major threat to their monopolistic control. So far, they have been extremely successful in blocking any significant change in the structure of elementary and secondary education in the United States.[84]

---

[81] Levinson, *The Alum Rock Voucher Demonstration: Three Years of Implementation*, 33.
[82] Jim Carl, "Free Marketeers, Policy Wonks, and Yankee Democracy: School Vouchers in New Hampshire, 1973–1976," *Harvard Educational Review* 78, no. 4 (2008): 589–614.
[83] Friedman and Friedman, *Free to Choose*, 172–73.
[84] Milton Friedman, "School Vouchers Turn 50, But the Fight Is Just Beginning," in *Liberty and Learning: Milton Friedman's Voucher Ideas at Fifty* (Washington, DC: Cato Institute, 2006), 157.

Friedman was still optimistic that voucher programs like those he and his wife proposed could be enacted and would prove superior to existing public school systems. But his familiarity with the developing field of public choice theory, and its focus on how entrenched interest groups could wield substantial political power, left Friedman concerned that teachers' unions and the public education bureaucracy could thwart voucher policies even if those policies could benefit the general public. This conclusion, and the public choice economic analysis that led to it, was also a concern of fellow voucher supporter and (as chances had it) lifetime member of the National Education Association Myron Lieberman.

7

Myron Lieberman: Education Without Romance, Public Choice Economics, and Markets in Education

In a blurb on its book cover, Milton Friedman wrote that Myron Lieberman's 2000 book, *Teachers Unions: How They Sabotage Educational Reform and Why*, was a "must read for supporters of radical education reform."[1] The book argued that while teachers' unions had value in promoting the economic interests of teachers, they have thwarted many potentially fruitful reforms in education, including market-based school choice. Eleven years prior, Lieberman credited Friedman (then at Stanford University's Hoover Institution) as one of many colleagues who provided "various courtesies, criticisms, and suggestions related to the manuscript" of his book *Privatization and Educational Choice*, which used public choice economics to argue not only that public education was beyond the possibility of meaningful reform but also that it should be replaced by a market that included for-profit schools.[2] (Friedman is also listed in the acknowledgments of Lieberman's 1986 book, *Beyond Public Education*.[3])

---

[1] Myron Lieberman, *Teachers Unions: How They Sabotage Educational Reform and Why* (San Francisco: Encounter Books, 2000), back cover.
[2] Myron Lieberman, *Privatization and Educational Choice* (New York: St. Martin's Press, 1989), xiii.
[3] Myron Lieberman, *Beyond Public Education* (New York: Praeger, 1986), viii.

For his part, Lieberman contributed an essay to a collection honoring and expanding on Friedman's voucher proposals sponsored by the libertarian CATO Institute think-tank in 2006. Lieberman's essay, discussing ways that Friedman's school choice arguments could be most intelligently discussed in the twenty-first century, Lieberman proclaimed that "over 50 years ago, Milton Friedman wrote one of the most interesting and insightful articles on the union movement that I ever read."[4] (While Lieberman doesn't mention the article by name, he was almost certainly referring to an article Friedman published in 1951, arguing that trade unions had less positive economic impact than commonly assumed, and often functioned as dangerous monopolies.[5]) Lieberman opened his essay with an allusion to Friedman's essay in order to remind readers that the power of the largest teachers' unions, National Education Association, and American Federation of Teachers, "is reason enough to review our strategies and tactics carefully" in defending markets in education.[6]

For much of his career, Myron Lieberman argued that the American education system should be replaced by market competition between private schools (including for-profit schools). Yet Lieberman's advocacy of markets in education and his skepticism of teachers' unions (for their tendency to block major reforms in education, including the introduction of markets) were not beliefs Lieberman started his career with. Lieberman started his career in 1948, as a public school teacher in St. Paul Minnesota. After receiving a Ph.D. in education from the University of Illinois, Lieberman became a professor in their College of Education. He went on to teach at several more universities and serve as a collective bargaining negotiator in six states, helping to negotiate contract disputes between teachers' unions and public school districts.[7]

In 1956 Lieberman wrote his first book, *Education as a Profession*. The book was an economic and sociological argument exploring the bene-

---

[4] Myron Lieberman, "Free Market Strategy and Tactics in K–12 Education," in *Liberty and Learning: Milton Friedman's Voucher Ideas at Fifty*, ed. Robert C. Enlow and Lenore T. Ealy (Washington, DC: Cato Institute, 2006), 81.
[5] Milton Friedman, "Some Comments on the Significance of Labor Unions for Economic Policy," in *The Impact of the Union*, ed. David M. Wright (New York: Harcourt Brace, 1951).
[6] Lieberman, "Free Market Strategy and Tactics in K–12 Education," 82.
[7] Frederik Ohles, Shirley M. Ohles, and John G. Ramsay, *Biographical Dictionary of Modern American Educators* (Westport, CT: Greenwood Press, 1997), 204.

fits and difficulties of the "professionalization" of education, Lieberman's overall argument was that, difficulties notwithstanding, "strong teacher organizations are required to prevent arbitrary, irresponsible, action by school boards and officials."[8]

> The only way, that is, that teacher could ensure that decisions made by school boards, school districts, and politicians took sufficient account of teachers' interests was to create and sustain strong teachers' unions. A teaching group which had the power to resist the imposition of unprofessional, undemocratic, and socially wasteful functions might well be on the road to helping the public and the profession discover a feasible solution to the problem of what the public schools are supposed to accomplish.[9]

While Lieberman would later criticize teachers' unions' strong opposition to school choice and markets in education (for self-interested reasons, he argued), there is no mention of issues of school choice in Education as a Profession. Whether Lieberman thought about the issue at all, it is clear from the book (and the above passage) that Lieberman very much believed in the public school system, and that strengthening the collective voice of teachers through unionization could help school systems actualize "what the public schools are supposed to accomplish."

As Lieberman later described it, "my viewpoint changed as a result of my service as a labor negotiator," and in 1987, Lieberman "moved to Washington, where [he] enjoyed excellent opportunities to meet conservative educational policy leaders."[10] While talking with conservative intellectuals "convinced [him] that conservatives cannot bring about significant improvements in K–12 education without basic changes in their agenda and strategy," Lieberman would go on to argue that those changes should be in a more truly market-friendly direction, not less.[11] For instance, in books like *Public Education: An Autopsy* and, his final book, *The Educational Morass*, Lieberman would argue that conservatives' support for

---

[8] Myron Lieberman, *Education as a Profession* (Englewood Cliffs, NJ: Prentice-Hall, 1956), 12.
[9] Lieberman, *Education as a Profession*, 482.
[10] Lieberman defined "conservative' as those with a "conviction that school choice and much greater utilization of private schools would be in the public interest." Myron Lieberman, *The Educational Morass* (Lanham, MD: Rowman & Littlefield Education, 2007), xv.
[11] Lieberman, *The Educational Morass*, xix.

charter schools and small, targeted voucher programs that prohibited the participation of for-profit schools would likely fail for their failure to set up truly competitive market environments. Moreover, Lieberman was concerned that conservative support for such measures would give anti-market advocates the ability to use the (probably bad) results from (in truth) nonmarket reforms as proof of markets' futility in education.

There is no direct evidence of Lieberman referring to his views as "market libertarian," (or even "libertarian" in any sense) and since Lieberman only published on the subject of education (unlike other figures profiled in this book), we might not call him a libertarian in the same way we would call Murray Rothbard or Milton Friedman libertarians. Yet there is much indirect evidence suggesting that Lieberman is best situated as a market libertarian. First, he published one book (*Privatization and Educational Choice*) and several policy reports with the libertarian Cato Institute think tank.[12] In his final book, *The Educational Morass*, Lieberman distinguishes between two "wings" of the pro-school-choice movement, the "equalitarians" and the "libertarian wing." While Lieberman doesn't explicitly as part of the "libertarian wing," the arguments in the book align nicely with this wing's arguments (and suggestions) for school choice.[13]

Myron Lieberman and Public Choice Economics

In 1989, two years after Lieberman recalls beginning his ideological shift after moving to Washington, he wrote about the importance of public choice economics in making the case for markets in education. The growth of the "privatization movement," Lieberman ascertains, "has an intellectual base in the 'public choice' approach to government decision making. Simply stated, public choice theory asserts that behavior of politicians and bureaucrats can be explained by the same principles that govern behavior

---

[12] Myron Lieberman, "Market Solutions to the Education Crisis," *CATO Policy Analysis* 75 (1986); Lieberman, *Privatization and Educational Choice*; and Myron Lieberman, "Liberating Teachers: Toward Market Competition in Teacher Representation," *CATO Policy Analysis* 450 (2002).
[13] Lieberman, *The Educational Morass*, 208–12.

in private economic affairs."[14] Instead of modeling public institutions as populated with individuals who faithfully carry out the public good, public choice analysis modeled public institutions the same way as private, profit-making ones: consisting of people pursuing their own self-interest, whether that was to remain elected so that they could continue doing good or personal career advancement. "The public choice framework has its critics, but it is widely recognized as an important perspective from which to analyze the conduct of public officials."[15]

While Lieberman did not directly say so, his analyses of everything from teachers' unions and school boards to public and private schools are steeped in the public choice approach to economics. Lieberman's work from the late 1980s on (unlike his previous work) modeled public and private institutions as peopled with generally self-interested actors, or at least those who desired to do what was in the public interest only when it did not conflict with their own self-interest.

This is the same "economic theory of democracy" approach that E. G. West used in 1967 to argue that American and British public education grew less because citizens demanded it, and more because reformers and state bureaucrats had a vested interest in such growth.[16] By the time Lieberman discovered it, this "economic theory of democracy" had grown from a small subfield of economics into a robust research program with its own academic journals and textbooks—an approach to economics that appealed largely to conservatives and libertarians because of its general pessimism toward governments' abilities to correct for market failures.

In 1986—three years before Lieberman mentioned public choice economics as an influence in the school privatization movement—James Buchanan won the Nobel Prize in Economics for his pioneering work in public choice economics.[17] Buchanan described public choice economics as "politics without romance":

---
[14] Lieberman, *Privatization and Educational Choice*, 11.
[15] Lieberman, *Privatization and Educational Choice*, 11–12.
[16] E. G. West, "The Political Economy of American Public School Legislation," *Journal of Law and Economics* 10 (1967): 101–28; E. G. West, *Education and the State: A Study in Political Economy* (Indianapolis: Liberty Fund, 1994).
[17] James Buchanan is listed in Lieberman's acknowledgments in *Public Education: An Autopsy* as one of several scholars who provided "valuable suggestions or assistance on earlier versions of the manuscript." Anthony Downs, another economist working in the public choice tradition, was also

The avenue through which a romantic and illusory notion about the workings of governments and the behavior of persons who govern has been replaced by a set of notions that embody more skepticism about what governments can do and what governors will do, notions that are surely more consistent with political reality that we may all observe around us.[18]

Another pioneer of public choice economics, Gordon Tullock, described the public choice approach to the study of bureaucracy this way:

The problem faced by any designer of a bureaucracy is that he must employ human beings to act as his bureaucrats and they have individual objectives that are not necessarily those that would be desired by the organizer of the bureaucracy.[19]

In 2017, James Buchanan and public choice economics would become the subject of a cultural history by Duke historian Nancy MacLean, where she suggested that the movement of being a right-wing strategy to, among other things, maintain white supremacy in the Jim Crow South. Of particular note for our purposes, MacLean suggests that Buchanan used his public choice analysis to call for school privatization as a way to stave off *Brown v. Board of Education*'s call for state-enforced school integration.[20]

In so arguing, MacLean points to a position paper Buchanan and his fellow public choice economist Warren Nutter circulated privately to the Perrow commission, who was working on a possible statewide educational voucher plan designed to contain the effects of the *Brown v. Board* decision. The paper, "The Economics of Universal Education," suggested several reasons why the state should be involved in funding citizens' purchase of private education without maintaining its own public schools.

---

on this list. Myron Lieberman, *Public Education: An Autopsy*, 4th ed. (Cambridge, MA: Harvard University Press, 1993), ix.

[18] James M. Buchanan, "Politics Without Romance: A Sketch of Positive Public Choice Theory and Its Normative Implications," in *The Logical Foundations of Constitutional Liberty* (Indianapolis: Liberty Fund, 1999), 46.

[19] Gordon Tullock, *Private Wants, Public Means: An Economic Analysis of the Desirable Scope of Government* (New York: Basic Books, 1970), 124.

[20] Nancy MacLean, *Democracy in Chains: The Deep History of the Radical Right's Stealth Plan for America* (New York: Penguin, 2017).

While MacLean suggests that Buchanan and Nutter "made their case in the race-neutral, value-free language of their discipline, offering what they depicted as a strictly economic argument," she suspects that their neutral language masked a segregationist intent, "offer[ing] a plan they believed could salvage what remained of massive resistance while surviving court review."[21]

MacLean's *Democracy in Chains* became a surprise best-seller, even mentioned on Oprah Winfrey's list of twenty must-read books for the summer of 2017. The book was and is controversial, however, among those in the libertarian and public choice traditions. Several scholars with libertarian or public choice sympathies have charged MacLean with inaccuracies, most often having to do with her alleged misunderstandings of the public choice economics that underlies Buchanan's thought in these matters. Historian Jennifer Burns, who wrote a well-regarded intellectual biography of Ayn Rand, suggests that MacLean's history is "rife with distortions and inaccuracies."[22] Political scientist and former President of the Public Choice Society Mike Munger goes as far as to write that "*Democracy in Chains* is a work of speculative historical fiction."[23] Particularly at issue in these and other criticisms were MacLean's alleged misunderstandings of Buchanan's employment of ideas like *methodological individualism* and *self-interest*, and the general public choice critique of public institutions. Buchanan, as others working in public choice economics, believed that economic analysis should employ methodological individualism, by which he did not mean moral individualism (as MacLean seems to think) but the idea that one should assume that preferences are an individual matter; any talk of group preferences should "reduce" to preferences by individuals within the group. Similarly, when Buchanan suggests that public and private are equally likely to act in their own self-interest, Buchanan and other public choice economists take a broad view of what that means: self-interest is not per se selfishness, but whatever one might be interested in (including

---

[21] Maclean, *Democracy in Chains*, 66.
[22] Jennifer Burns, "Democracy in Chains: The Deep History of the Radical Right's Stealth Plan for America by Nancy MacLean," *History of Political Economy*, 50, no. 3 (September 1, 2018): 640–48, 640.
[23] Michael C. Munger, "On the Origins and Goals of Public Choice: Constitutional Conspiracy?" *Independent Review* 22, no. 3 (2018): 359–82, 368.

altruistic interests). Most egregiously, suggest the critics, Buchanan did not critique governments in order to stealthily dismantle democratic society, but with an eye toward ensuring that democratic society operated within appropriate limits of what governments could and ought to do while safeguarding people's liberties. Given this context, it is at least arguable that Buchanan and Nutter's advocacy of statewide school choice after *Brown v. Board* was motivated by a sincere belief in the efficacy of privately administered education funded by the state through tuition vouchers—a belief shared with Friedman and, as we will see, several reformers traditionally aligned with the political left.

Like James Buchanan, public choice economists did not see their brand of economic analysis as attributing particularly bad or devious motive to government (or other nonmarket) actors. Rather, they sought to analyze those actors using only the same set of assumptions of self-interest that economists had long used when analyzing the behavior of private actors in markets, a potentially useful corrective to orthodox economic methods that viewed private actors, but generally not government actors, with suspicion. The task, then, of public choice analyses of institutions is to describe how the outcomes of (public or private) organizations can be explained by looking at how individuals respond to incentives within the organization and the social arena it operates in. This is important particularly when institutions generate outcomes that seem at odds with the institution's stated mission or "the public good." Thus, for example, E. G. West's concern in "The Political Economy of American Public School Legislation" was to find out why the public school bureaucracy continued to grow despite evidence showing that New Yorkers were largely being educated in private schools. West explains this discrepancy between "the public good" (possibly the addition by government only of more funds to supplement the tuition of New Yorkers who couldn't afford private school) and the political outcome (the quick expansion of public schooling) by appealing to the self-interest of reformers and public school employees. Particularly, reformers and public school employees were likely driven by a desire to avoid competition from private schools. Reformers and public school employees "can afford to bring greater than average influence to bear upon government policy since their incomes will be particularly responsive to it" than consumers who may each only be mildly affected by such legislation. Thus, West argued that a minority whose members had strong vested interests in bureaucratic expansion were able to trump a minority who may not have desired such expansion, but whose individual members had weak incentive to oppose the expansion.[24]

We can see a similar approach to Lieberman's explanations of teachers' unions behaviors, and why teachers' unions often use the rhetoric of doing what is in the public interest while generating results seemingly, as he saw them, at odds with the public interest (such as creating impossibly strict rules governing the firing process of teachers and the filing of grievances by parents). As Lieberman put it:

> A union is an organization chosen by teachers to advance the interests of teachers. In doing so, it will try to equate teacher interests with the public interest, or with the interests of students. But just as what is good for General Motors (GM) is not necessarily good for the nation, what is good for teachers and teacher unions is not necessarily in the public interest or the interest of students.[25]

Using the same "concentrated benefits, dispersed costs" reasoning as E. G. West, Lieberman explained that the vested interests of teachers' unions induced their members to be much more active in advocating policies that benefit teachers' interests than the average citizen (who may or may not benefit from such policies).

> For example, proposals to increase the teacher workday would immediately affect teachers adversely if implemented. In contrast, the benefit to any particular student (or parent) is highly speculative. It is therefore understandable why teachers would oppose the reform while parents are unlikely to devote much time or energy to achieving it.[26]

---

[24] West, "The Political Economy of American Public School Legislation," 114. The theory that minorities' preferences can trump majorities when the benefits to the minority are concentrated but the costs borne by the majority are dispersed was originally laid out by public choice economist Mancur Olsen. See Mancur Olson, *The Logic of Collective Action: Public Goods and the Theory of Groups* (Cambridge: Harvard University Press, 1971).
[25] Lieberman, *Privatization and Educational Choice*, 35.
[26] Lieberman, *Privatization and Educational Choice*, 35.

While public choice economics has never been an explicitly libertarian or even pro-market theory, economists in the tradition have often preferred market solutions to governmental ones. While Gordon Tullock and William Niskanen's well-known public choice analyses of bureaucratic inefficiency did not specifically criticize government bureaucracies harder than private ones,[27] other economists argued that the differences in incentives faced by for-profit and government organizations led the former to perform in more socially beneficial ways than the latter.

James Buchanan wrote:

> The behavior of persons in trying to maximize returns on their own capture can be socially beneficial in an ordered market structure, behavior that we may here describe as "profit seeking." The same behavior under a different set of institutions, however, may not produce socially beneficial consequences. The unintended results of individual efforts at maximizing returns may be "bad" rather than "good."[28]

Since the for-profit firm's ultimate goal is to maximize profit, and profit is generally achieved by doing what consumers will voluntarily pay for, those in a for-profit firm will likely find that their self-interest aligns with the firm's larger goal of making a profit and, thus, providing benefit to consumers. Comparatively, governmental institutions "maximize profits" by political, not economic, channels—petitioning legislatures and the like—decoupling the well-being of organization members from generating value for consumers.

Other public choice economists took a more empirical approach—comparing delivery of certain services (from garbage delivery and fire protection to airline services), finding and arguing that, because of the difference in incentive structure, for-profit firms tend to operate at less

---

[27] Gordon Tullock, *The Politics of Bureaucracy* (Washington, DC: Public Affairs Press, 1965); William A. Niskanen Jr., *Bureaucracy and Representative Government* (Chicago: Aldine, Atherton, 1971). Tullock did write, however, that "the larger the bureaucracy *and the less it is possible to reduce its objectives to some single numerical measure such as profit*, the more likely it is that the individual bureaucrats will be able to follow their individual preferences rather than the preferences of the 'organization.'" Tullock, *Private Wants, Public Means: An Economic Analysis of the Desirable Scope of Government*, 124, my italics.

[28] James M. Buchanan, "Rent Seeking Versus Profit Seeking," in *The Logical Foundations of Constitutional Liberty* (Indianapolis: Liberty Fund, 1999), 104.

cost and in ways more consistent with consumer preference. Reviewing studies of the electrical power industry (under government and private ownership), Louis de Alessi concluded, "Government firms, particularly those endowed with a politically influential clientele, can survive for long periods, and their managers prosper, in the presence of persistent deficits (let alone economic losses) and grossly inefficient management."[29] Reviewing five different industries where both public and private provision exist in various services, Robert Spann concluded, "For the majority of activities, private producers can provide the same service at the same or lower costs than can public producers. In some cases, the costs of private firms are half that of government agencies for producing the same goods or services."[30] Public choice economists may never have set out to attach the approach to a philosophy of small government and active markets (and several public choice theorists, like the aforementioned Mancur Olsen, produced policy recommendations running deeply against this grain).[31] Yet public choice's treatment of all actors (public and private) as predominantly self-interested—and its focus on the power of incentives to determine whether the self-interested will act in socially beneficial or socially wasteful ways—led many public choice theorists to prefer market over government solutions to social problems.

We can see the same ideas (that a for-profit framework will likely ensure that organization members pursue self-interest by satisfying consumers rather than resorting to political means) at work in Lieberman's analysis of teachers' unions. It was Lieberman's hope that opening public education to competition from for-profit schools would correct for excesses in unions' power. Since public schools "depend largely on state and federal aid that is independent of client satisfaction," private schools that are "directly dependent on their ability to satisfy clients" will be less willing to cede to union demands that might decrease the company's ability to

---

[29] Louis De Alessi, "An Economic Analysis of Government Ownership and Regulation," *Public Choice* 19, no. 1 (1974): 7.

[30] Robert M. Spann, "Public Versus Private Provision of Government Services," in *Budgets and Bureaucrats: The Sources of Government Growth*, ed. Thomas Borcherding (Durham, NC: Duke University Press, 1979), 88.

[31] Jack C. Heckelman and Dennis Coates, "On the Shoulders of a Giant: The Legacy of Mancur Olsen," in *Collective Choice: Essays in Honor of Mancur Olsen*, ed. Mancur Olson, Jac C. Heckelman, and Dennis Coates (Berlin, Germany: Springer-Verlag, 2003), 7.

satisfy customers and maintain profits. And since teachers' employment and salaries in private schools are contingent on their schools' ability to be profitable, "union appeals that may be successful in public schools will be correctly perceived as a threat to teacher well-being in entrepreneurial [for-profit] schools."[32]

Lieberman's public-choice-influenced approach to institutional analysis didn't stop with explaining why teachers' unions often results in tension with public interest, and why private schools might weaken those union excesses. Lieberman used such analysis to explain not only why the public education bureaucracy was likely beyond any radical (and meaningful) change, but also why genuine markets, where profit schools compete alongside nonprofits (and maybe public) would almost certainly produce socially beneficial results.

A Public Choice Autopsy of Public Schools

Myron Lieberman's advocacy of markets in education (and the importance of for-profit schools in them) was coupled with a deep pessimism that the public school system could introduce meaningful reforms. By 1993, the former collective-bargaining negotiator declared that the rationale for public schooling was "beyond life-sustaining measures" because school systems persistently failed to enact measures that would help them achieve their stated or proper objectives of fostering widespread literacy, civic virtue, and basic knowledge in students.[33] According to Lieberman, the problem had everything to do with well-meaning reformers' failure to fully appreciate that attempting reforms within the current public system (and its incentive structures) was to try and change a system that had evolved to resist change. Paraphrasing a like-minded education reformer Ted Kolderie, Lieberman wrote that "the basic issue is no how to improve the educational system; it is how to develop a system that seeks improvement."[34] Before looking at Lieberman's arguments that introducing competitive markets would help bring about the latter, it is crucial to understand Lieberman's reasons for

---

[32] Lieberman, *Beyond Public Education*, 44.
[33] Lieberman, *Public Education: An Autopsy*, 1.
[34] Lieberman, *Privatization and Educational Choice*, 21.

believing the current public system to be unsalvageable enough that a new system was in order.

To start, Lieberman suggested that public school systems are doomed to be unresponsive to parent preference because the very process of figuring out who is accountable for what school policies, let alone lobbying to get them changed, is complex enough to discourage all but the most determined parents. "Because of the plethora of interrelated local, state, and federal, legislation, it may not be clear what legislative or executive body or officials should be held accountable for what happens at the school or district level." Because it is difficult for citizens to accurately glean the political rules regarding to whom particular grievances should be brought (and easy for officials to adopt an "our hands are tied" approach), Lieberman argued that all but the most determined citizens are able to voice concerns over public school practices.[35]

Elsewhere, Lieberman wrote that of all the "functions that have been added to government since our nation was founded … few if any of the others impose such a heavy informational burden on citizens or officials" than deciding education policy.[36] Lieberman appealed to Anthony Downs's theory of "rational ignorance"—that it was often rational for voters to remain ignorant when acquiring necessary information is costly compared to the likelihood of their vote influencing an election's outcome.

> Putting aside the great folklore of education, it would be irrational for most parents to devote a great deal of time to getting educational information, either for voting purposes or to influence educational policy. The information required is not just about education; it must also include information about how others think or can be persuaded to think on the educational issues. After all, being well informed on educational policy is futile unless many others are also well informed and motivated to act in concert.[37]

For these reasons, teachers, administrators, and their unions likely had a disproportionate effect on education policy. Not only were they likely to understand policy intricacies better than parents, but they were already

---

[35] Lieberman, *The Educational Morass*, 273.
[36] Lieberman, *Public Education: An Autopsy*, 101.
[37] Lieberman, *Public Education: An Autopsy*, 101.

organized into an interest group. Using the aforementioned "concentrated benefits and dispersed costs" argument first used by Anthony Downs, Lieberman also argued that teachers likely had more motivation than parents to affect public school legislation. "Teacher and support personnel unions have a larger stake in who is elected to the board than any other group. Parents may be interested, but it is practically impossible or prohibitively expensive for most to try to change school district policies or practices."[38] If this is true, then teachers' unions are more likely to be involved in school board elections (and other elections involving issues affecting education) than parent groups. As long as school board members "have the same needs for support as other candidates for public office," then, teachers' unions will have a disproportionate sway over school boards.[39] And while it sometimes happened that teachers' collective interests aligned with the interests of parents and students, "a panoply of statutory and contractual provisions protect school district personnel, but only at an enormous cost to consumers."[40]

Lieberman also mentioned the lack of incentives in the public education system to produce exploratory research and adopt changes based on it. First, there is what economists refer to as a free-rider problem preventing local school districts and even states from engaging in their own research and development. "School districts have no reason to fund R&D when the benefits would go largely to pupils outside the district. This is especially true when the district contribution does not affect the viability of the project" because each district may be tempted to "free ride" on research done—and funded—by other districts.[41]

Even though federal expenditures for research and development might alleviate this free-rider problem, "as it happens, political clout, not technical expertise, becomes the dominant factor in awarding federal R&D

---

[38] Lieberman, *Privatization and Educational Choice*, 64.
[39] Lieberman, *Privatization and Educational Choice*, 64.
[40] Lieberman, *Public Education: An Autopsy*, 63. In various writings, Lieberman mentioned examples ranging from the uniformity of teacher pay irrespective of subject (which perpetuates shortages in "critical need" areas), creation of strict "due process" rules for dismissal of ineffective teachers and parental grievances against teachers, and other instances of potential conflict between teachers' and "consumers'" interests. See particularly Lieberman, *Beyond Public Education*, chap. 2.
[41] Lieberman, *Public Education: An Autopsy*, 252.

contracts and grants."[42] Sometimes, this means that a disproportionate share of federal grants go to research that potentially validates or mildly tinkers with existing (politically popular) practices. Other times, it means the research funds go to those who have political connections.

Just as the political process affects who receive federal research funds (and what gets researched), so the political process affects whether particular research results get implemented into public school systems. Policymakers—from congresspeople to school board members—use research results "primarily to legitimize what they are doing."[43] Rather than funding and utilizing the results of research as a means of genuinely figuring out what policies and practices carry the most potential for positive change, research is used to validate moves the policymakers already want to make. "Research also tends to be ignored, unfunded, or even defunded if it points in politically unpopular directions."[44] Essentially, Lieberman argued that the public school system doesn't adopt potentially beneficial changes because no one has great incentive to do research or implement changes based on its results. Districts and states don't have incentive to conduct research owing to the free-rider problem (ultimately owing to the nonproprietary nature of the research). College professors who conduct the majority of educational research have incentive to conduct research on politically favorable projects rather than more potentially impactful (but politically unpopular) research. Politicians have incentive to use research primarily to validate current programs or politically popular changes, and do not bear any costs of ignoring potentially useful research or implementing changes that turn out badly.

---

[42] Lieberman, *Public Education: An Autopsy*, 263.
[43] Lieberman, *Public Education: An Autopsy*, 259.
[44] Lieberman, *Public Education: An Autopsy*, 259. Elsewhere, Lieberman made the same point by reference to the then-recent debate over language arts instruction being grounded either in a phonics or whole-word approach. The issue, he suggested, was divided largely by political bias—those on the conservative right supporting a more traditional phonics approach and those on the liberal left supporting a more "progressive" whole-word approach, each using academic research to bolster their positions. "Politics comes into play when it is essential to adjust competing interests; it is not supposed to be the environment in which we resolve empirical research. In fact, it is remarkable that how to teach reading is still a controversial matter. What private for-profit enterprise would still be debating the issue after it has been addressed by thousands of researchers and expenditures in the billions?" Lieberman, *The Educational Morass*, 57.

Lastly, Lieberman argued that "taxpayers may think they know how much education costs, but they do not know how much they pay personally for public education."[45] Years earlier, economist James Buchanan similarly argued that taxpayers' lack of knowledge about their share of the nation's tax burden and national debt often led them to a "fiscal illusion" where they may vote for spending programs they otherwise would not vote for.[46] Lieberman argued that the public school system's ability to keep service costs hidden from consumers might lead them to prefer costly improvements they might otherwise abjure, and forgo cost-cutting reforms they might otherwise choose. Thus, consumer preferences are ascertained by political processes (votes, speeches made at school board meetings) that "cannot isolate preferences or measure their intensity," unlike when individual choices are made in markets with explicit knowledge of opportunity costs.[47]

A Voucher System with Emphasis on For-Profit Schools

In a 2002 C-SPAN interview, Myron Lieberman described the type of voucher system he believed was necessary as a replacement for the existing public education system:

> What I think we need is a voucher that's available to everybody; I wouldn't target it to lower income groups or any ethnic groups. And the reason is that I think what we need education is a significant for-profit sector... You can't think of an industry that hasn't improved tremendously—a for-profit industry, because there is competition. We don't have any competition in education, and the denominational schools that make up most of the private schools, they're getting students not because they say they are introducing new technology. They're saying, "Choose us because we're doing what we've always done." ... In my view, if you really want a significant improvement

---

[45] Lieberman, *Public Education: An Autopsy*, 71.
[46] James M. Buchanan, *Public Finance in Democratic Process: Fiscal Institutions and Individual Choice* (Chapel Hill: University of North Carolina Press, 1967), chap. 10.
[47] Lieberman, *Public Education: An Autopsy*, 71.

in education, we need more for-profit schools. Maybe if just 10–15% of the student population was in for-profit schools, that would be a market big enough to get the advantages of for-profit schools.[48]

While Lieberman acknowledged the similarities between Milton Friedman's previous voucher proposals and his own, Lieberman's proposal differs from Friedman's in its specific emphasis on for-profits and their importance in education markets. While Friedman was in no way opposed to for-profit schools entering the education market, Lieberman specifically emphasized the necessity and importance of for-profit schools in any responsive and robust education market. Friedman only suggested in his voucher plan that many schools would be nonprofit, that others would be for-profit, and that "there is no way of predicting the ultimate composition of the school industry" except for competition.[49] As we will see, Lieberman went further and emphasized the potential superiority of for-profit schools (owing to the profit motive they had to offer superior service).

Also, while Friedman was committed to truly free market s in education—markets that were open to new for- and non-profit providers as well as the entire school-going population as consumers—his later career found him supporting more targeted voucher programs for pragmatic reasons. These programs were usually targeted programs that allowed voucher-enabled school choice only to low-income groups (Milwaukee's and Cleveland's voucher programs in the 1990s) and all banned for-profit schools from entering the market (California's failed "Proposition 38" initiative, for instance).

Lieberman, on the other hand, consistently supported only the idea of universal voucher programs that would be open to for-profit schools. While Lieberman acknowledged the legitimacy of Friedman's pragmatism in supporting more limited voucher programs, Lieberman was worried that limited voucher programs would fail because they did not carry the benefits of actual markets. Lieberman worried that "as long as the media and most of the professional literature do not draw any distinctions

---

[48]"Economic Forces and Education," *Washington Journal* (C-SPAN, August 26, 2002), www.c-spanvideo.org/program/Forcesan, accessed on December 15, 2013.
[49]Milton Friedman and Rose Friedman, *Free to Choose: A Personal Statement*, 1st ed. (New York: Harcourt Brace Jovanovich, 1980), 169.

between school choice plans, the acceptability of free-market plans will be dependent on the outcomes of plans that are basically contrary to the free-market positions on school-choice."[50] The failure of plans that do not harness the full power of markets—limited voucher plans, voucher plans that disallowed for-profit schools—would inadvertently serve to discredit the entire idea of school choice in the minds of many.

Of particular concern to Lieberman was that all voucher proposals in the United States to that point had disallowed for-profit schools from eligibility to receive voucher money. The exclusion of for-profit producers from school choice proposals significantly hampered these choice plans from functioning as actual markets. "It is an open question whether a voucher system utilizing only nonprofit schools, or an overwhelming preponderance of them, can achieve the benefits of competition in the for-profit sector."[51]

Lieberman's emphasis on the importance of the for-profit sector in fostering the benefits of competition points to a subtle difference between his main rationale for supporting choice programs and the rationale of others. Where others—like Chodorov and Friedman —stressed consumer choice between diverse options as the major benefit of markets in education, Lieberman tended to stress markets' ability to foster innovation and continually force service providers to raise their quality and efficiency in order to compete.

This is not to say that Lieberman denied the importance of consumers' ability to choose an appropriate school from an array of choices. Drawing on economist Albert Hirschman's comparison of "voice" and "exit" as ways to affect organizational change, Lieberman recognized the effectiveness of allowing consumers to move from service to service over having to voice complaints to a monopoly service provider. Given his deep pessimism that the public school system can effectively respond to criticism, Lieberman noted that "the parent who can exit enjoys a tremendous advantage over one who must organize a community or state campaign to change a policy." Displeased parents stand a better chance of attaining better service by shopping for a new producer rather than voicing complaints to the

---

[50] Lieberman, *The Educational Morass*, 207.
[51] Lieberman, *Privatization and Educational Choice*, 168.

subpar producer. Additionally, when producers are aware that dissatisfied consumers can exit (taking their money with them), they will be more likely to take complaints seriously than when producers know consumers cannot leave or when there is no financial penalty to them doing so. "Voice is much more effective when an exit option is also available."[52] The very presence of an exit option—irrespective of the kinds of schools consumers could choose from in the market—obviated the need to use voice options, making any market system likely more responsive to consumers than the existing public system.

Yet, for Lieberman, "to achieve the benefits of competition, schools must compete on common criteria."[53] Nonprofit schools tend to be relatively small and cater to niche markets (religious affiliations or particular groups, like those with low income). While nonprofit schools catering to niche markets certainly gave parents who fit those niches options, competition would be most robust when a wide variety of schools competed for a wide variety of customers and offered services that directly rivaled each other. To illustrate this point, Lieberman imagined two scenarios: in the first, consumers face an alternative between a public school and a denominational nonprofit school, where in the second, consumers face a choice between (presumably secular) schools competing solely on educational quality. In the former case, Lieberman suggests that there is no legitimate competition because "the parochial school provides something the public school cannot, no matter how effective it is educationally" rather than "striving for superiority on the basis of a common criterion." The second situation is more truly competitive because "the choice of school is made on the basis of such [common educational] criteria."[54] This belief that

---

[52] Lieberman, *Privatization and Educational Choice*, 151. Lieberman's analysis of "voice" and "exit" draws heavily on Hirschman's. Yet Lieberman does not address a criticism of the exit option particularly aimed at school choice. Hirschman believed that allowing parents to exit public schools and enter private schools would both discourage parents who would voice criticisms to use exit instead, and leave public schools with less-concerned parents by inducing the more savvy and involved parents to exit the public schools. This, Hirschman argued, risked weakening the already-weak public school system. Lieberman likely did not address this concern because he was already deeply pessimistic that the public school system was organized in a way that could be responsive to voice, even by relatively more attentive parents. Albert O. Hirschman, *Exit, Voice, and Loyalty* (Cambridge, MA: Harvard University Press, 1970), 45–47.
[53] Lieberman, *Beyond Public Education*, 213.
[54] Lieberman, *Beyond Public Education*, 212.

rivalry on common criteria was essential to a truly competitive market even led Lieberman to support the idea that "although a federally mandated curriculum is out of the question" (as a violation of the freedom of producers to determine what they will produce), "a nationally accepted one, especially in mathematics and science is not only possible but desirable."[55] As long as the curriculum is voluntary, Lieberman believed that the existence of a common "national" curriculum might induce producers to compete on similar educational criteria. (This argument, though, is difficult to square with Lieberman's belief that markets and the profit motive might bring about more innovation in education. It is plausible that if markets spur innovation, they will likely spur private schools to innovate curricula as well. In these cases, it is possible that innovation-inducing markets may undermine attempts to sustain a national curriculum.)

Compare this view of competition and the virtue of school choice to that of Frank Chodorov. Chodorov envisioned an educational landscape where

> every pedagogue who takes pride in his profession would be tempted to start on his own, to ply his skill free from institutional restrictions. Every school of thought would offer its wares to the public. Every pedagogical theory would have a chance of proving itself. Every denomination would expand its parochial activities. There would be, so to speak, a private school on every city block.[56]

While Lieberman recognized the value of diversity insofar as students can find educational niches (Catholic schools, Montessori schools, etc.) that benefit them, Lieberman argued that such a landscape was not truly competitive. Systems of very diverse private schools that cater to a wide variety of needs will be less likely to find schools competing on the same metrics. Denominational schools will cater to those who value religiously focused schooling, schools dedicated to unique pedagogies (Montessori schools, for instance) will cater to those seeking those approaches, and schools catering to specific types of students (such as those with specific

---

[55] Lieberman, *Public Education: An Autopsy*, 275.
[56] Frank Chodorov, "Private Schools: The Solution to America's Educational Problems," in *Fugitive Essays: Selected Writings of Frank Chodorov*, ed. Charles H. Hamilton (Indianapolis: Liberty Fund, 1980), 131.

learning disabilities) will cater to students fitting that profile. Each school would differentiate itself from the others not by outperforming others on common metrics, but by targeting specific niches, and each will be more focused not on competing head-to-head with the other, but on tailoring their services to their specific niches.

Lieberman's suggestion that anything shy of producers "striving for superiority based on the basis of a common criterion" is "not 'competition' but the antithesis of it"[57] can be criticized as being unduly restrictive. In some way, the Chodorovian situation depicted above can be seen as non-competitive. (A deeply committed Catholic may not feel the benefits of choice if her options are between schools of different religious denominations, nor would most schools of most denominations really compete for her business.) But when we assume a world of diverse consumers with diverse preferences (and each customer likely having several potential criteria on which to form and change their preferences), it is no stretch to see this Chodorovian scenario as competitive. Not only does each school compete to ascertain and cater to some segment of consumer preference, but also it is possible that different kinds of schools could compete for the same customers. (For instance, a Montessori and a military school could compete by trying to convince customers that its pedagogical approach will produce the best results, or a Catholic and a secular school could compete for the same consumers, allowing each to decide what trade-offs they want to make between religiosity of instruction and other factors.)

Lieberman's big concern, though, was that if schools were not largely competing on the same criteria—and if the competing schools were not competing for-profit—the tendency of markets to lead to overall improvements in quality might not take shape. For instance, Lieberman wrote several times about how truly competitive markets in education would benefit the poor as much as any other economic group. This, because:

> The system brings higher-quality and lower-priced goods and services to an ever growing group of consumers. The evidence for this is overwhelming. Black-and-white (later color) television, automobiles, telephones, photo copiers, frozen foods, pharmaceuticals, travel, computers—the lit of goods and services that have risen in quality and declined in cost is too large to

---

[57] Lieberman, *Beyond Public Education*, 212.

require debate. The free-market position is that the poor have benefited the most from this system because they could not afford these things prior to the reduction in costs and improvement in quality that resulted from competition.[58]

But in order for this overall improvement of quality to occur, companies had to engage in the competitive process of trying to outdo each other on similar criteria. Each, competing for the same potential customers, had to pay attention to the other's innovations and do their best to offer a similar, but better, product. (While it may be possible to compete by offering product catering to different preferences, this is not the kind of competition Lieberman believed leads to industry-wide increases in quality over time that he cared about.)

And for this type of competition, the profit-motive was essential.

> The usual reasons for the greater efficiency of private enterprise is that its management incentives encourage getting the work done as efficiency as possible in order to maximize profits. The important point is that managers in the private sector share in the profits or gains resulting from increased productivity.[59]

Because, Lieberman argued, a great many nonprofit schools are funded by "tax exemptions, church budgets, charitable contributions, and other relatively invisible sources ... teachers and administrators are under less pressure to regard productivity as important."[60]

Another condition (that only for-profits were likely to provide) was necessary for competition to bring about overall improvements in educational quality: a good amount of productive research and development. In the previous section, we saw Lieberman's criticism of the incentive structure for research and development in public school systems. Those

---

[58] Lieberman, *The Educational Morass*, 201.
[59] Lieberman, *Beyond Public Education*, 216.
[60] Lieberman, *Beyond Public Education*, 215. While Lieberman's focus in this passage was on efficiency, the same rationale—that gain and loss in profit provide a valuable incentive to improve one's good and services, a motive that non-profits lack—can be applied to any area of innovation in education. And while some may want to dismiss Lieberman's focus on efficiency as a valid educational goal, Lieberman argued that "the naive idea that the concept of productivity does not apply to education results partly from the way it is funded," 215.

who produce the research (generally college professors) apply for research money through the political process, and the political process is also utilized to make changes to current practice based on the research's findings. Since education research is generally not proprietary, neither party stands to make a profit on research that affects education for the better when implemented; since the politicians and researchers do not work directly for the public school system, neither party is likely to experience negative consequences for either research that proves wasteful or potentially impactful research not being applied.

Lieberman compared this system with research and development conducted in the private sector and argued that the change in incentive structure alleviates all of these problems. "In the private sector, R&D is based on the anticipation that companies will eventually profit from it."[61] As companies "have entrepreneurial incentive to develop productive innovations," they will be judicious about what research gets done (with an eye toward what can help them improve their wares and maximize profit), and how much gets spent.[62] Since companies often employ their own research staff, researchers often have the potential to experience (good or bad) consequences of their research and its ultimate use in improving the companies' products and services.[63]

Lieberman doesn't seem to have addressed potential moral concerns about research on education being proprietary. In light of Lieberman's argument that competition led companies to try and outdo each other's developments, improving overall quality over time, Lieberman likely thought this would happen with proprietary education research as well. Thus, while one company might create a successful, but proprietary, curriculum, it would not be long before other companies would either emulate or improve upon the curriculum, being only a matter of time before

---

[61] Lieberman, *Public Education: An Autopsy*, 252.
[62] Lieberman, *Public Education: An Autopsy*, 259.
[63] As for potential conflicts of interest arising from companies paying researchers to come to conclusions desired by the company, Lieberman suggests that "bias of any kind in … research is much more likely to be exposed [by the market process of competition] and it runs the risk of career- and company-ending liabilities." While Lieberman doesn't say so directly, his worry seems to be that, as long as we assume an equal potential for bias in governmentally funded research, researchers face much more accountability in a market system than through the political process. Lieberman, *The Educational Morass*, 53.

most or all schools' curricula improve accordingly. It could also be that, in light of the incentive problems Lieberman saw in the public education system, he believed that the improvement in research in a for-profit system would yield enough benefit to outweigh any moral downside of allowing propriety in education research.

For-profit education companies would have sufficient incentive to maintain active research and development owing to the competitive pressures to innovate and compete. Also, though, for-profit producers "constantly seek larger markets. Their incentive is that larger markets bring them larger financial rewards."[64] To expand market share, companies need to continuously seek ways to cater to new markets and new clientele. While this would certainly not be true of all businesses—some would be content to cater to smaller niches than large customer bases—Lieberman feared that nonprofit schools were usually small institutions organized around a particular mission and may well have incentive not to expand into new markets. "Denominational schools that make up most of the private schools, they're getting students not because they say they are introducing new technology. They're saying, 'Choose us because we're doing what we've always done.' … In my view, if you really want a significant improvement in education, we need more for-profit schools."[65]

For Lieberman, the Chodorovian picture of a "private school on every city block," each catering to a different kind of consumer preference, was not the likely way to harness the most important benefit of competition: gradual improvements in quality and efficiency of schools. And while Friedman suggested that markets would be the ultimate arbiter of whether for-profit or nonprofit schools satisfied customers, Myron Lieberman was quite willing to spell out, in a way Friedman never did, the particular advantages of for-profit participation in education markets.

---

[64] Lieberman, *Public Education: An Autopsy*, 222.
[65] C-Span, "Economic Forces and Education."

Conclusion

Myron Lieberman's approach to performing an "autopsy" on public education and pointing to private markets as its replacement can be boiled down to a public-choice-infused study of the different incentive structures that affect how people act within each system. Individuals in the public and private sectors are modeled as, by and large, pursuers of their own self-interest, rather than treating private actors as self-interested and public actors as altruistic. The problem, for Lieberman, is figuring out what system allows individuals to pursue their own self-interest (however they conceive it) in ways that produce social value (or minimize social waste).

To quote Buchanan again regarding the difference between rent-seeking (pursuing some benefit in some way other than voluntary trade, like through the political process) and profit seeking:

> The behavior of persons in trying to maximize returns on their own capture can be socially beneficial in an ordered market structure, behavior that we may here describe as "profit seeking." The same behavior under a different set of institutions, however, may not produce socially beneficial consequences. The unintended results of individual efforts at maximizing returns may be "bad" rather than "good."[66]

The public system, and its dependence on the political process, is a system set up to benefit the interests of producers (particularly teachers and administrators). Funding is allocated by the political process, and individuals' success (consumers, teachers, professors seeking grant money for education research) is primarily based on how effectively one can navigate the political process, rather than providing something of value in exchange for what one values.

The market process, on the other hand, allows individuals to pursue self-interest only to the extent they can induce others to trade. This generally means that self-interest in ordered markets is best pursued by providing something of enough value to others that they will engage in exchange. While Lieberman was not averse to nonprofit schools, unlike other figures in this book, he argued explicitly that for-profit businesses had the most

---

[66] Buchanan, "Rent Seeking Versus Profit Seeking," 104.

incentive to create the kinds of educational improvements that should occur in education markets—the kinds of improvements public schools had no incentive to provide, and that nonprofits had little incentive (or capacity) to provide.

Also, unlike other figures in this work, Lieberman put less emphasis on the benefits of pluralism and diversity of choice in markets, and more emphasis on the qualitative benefits of competition. Thus, the markets Lieberman preferred were those with a strong for-profit sector and less reliance on small nonprofits who might cater to small niche markets.

Lieberman, though, was pessimistic about whether this vision of truly free markets in education would ever be realized—a pessimism slightly different from Albert Jay Nock's a generation before. Nock, no friend of state-administered education, was pessimistic that for-profit companies could offer any real alternative aside from educational services diluted in quality to reach the widest—and lowest—customer base. Lieberman's pessimism was not about the potential of for-profit companies to improve education; in fact, he thought that the profit motive was the appropriate catalyst for such improvements.

Instead, Lieberman's pessimism was about whether the current public education system's inertia was reversible and whether pro-market advocates could marshal enough support to steer it in the direction of free markets. Given the system's change-resistant design and the vested interests of teachers' unions, Lieberman saw several reasons for pessimism on this score.

First, "the American people support public education partly because they have little understanding of how market systems function."[67] Not only was this because people often feared the potential downsides of markets (i.e., producers duping misled customers into buying subpar service) without appreciating the potential upside of markets (i.e., that such producers are more quickly weeded out by market competition than the political process). This is also because—contra Lieberman's public-choice-inspired approach—people often think of workers (in this case, teachers and school administrators) in for-profit companies as driven by different motives than those in government. "While the basest motives are

---

[67] Lieberman, *Public Education: An Autopsy*, 295.

attributed to private-sector producers, the pursuit of teacher welfare is treated as a concern for pupil welfare."[68]

Even if education markets would lead to improvements in education, finding groups willing to support such markets against the current public school system would still be difficult. First, invoking Anthony Downs's "concentrated benefits, dispersed costs" argument, teachers and administrators are well-organized and have acute interests in maintaining the system they operate in. Yet, like in other industries where regulation reflects a pro-producer bias, "the problem is that it is extremely difficult to organize consumers, especially if they are geographically dispersed, pay different amounts, and have different criticisms of what they are getting for what they pay."[69]

While private schools may seem an obvious advocacy group to support markets for private schools, this may be more tenuous than it first seems. Existing private schools are often denominational schools that frequently support religious freedom in education but whose "support for a market system is highly problematical, or otherwise enjoy a privileged place in a small market that might be threatened if widened." Support for private schools, or for parents who wish to send their children to private schools, is not necessarily supported for a market system of education.[70]

Lastly, Lieberman laments what he thought was a misguided strategy on the part of many advocates of free markets in education, Milton Friedman included. With misguided pragmatism, organizations like Milton and Rose Friedman's Friedman Foundation (started in 1986 to promote universal school choice) "bless[ed] every expansion of school choice, without an reservation or mention of its noncompetitive or anti-competitive features, and without pointing out that the outcomes under such school choice plans cannot reasonably be attributed to a free market in education and may even be antithetical to it."[71]

"Public school choice" (giving families the choice to choose between public schools) was inadequate to harness the benefits of markets for several reasons; at the top of the list were the lack of price competition and

---

[68] Lieberman, *Public Education: An Autopsy*, 287.
[69] Lieberman, *The Educational Morass*, 224.
[70] Lieberman, *Public Education: An Autopsy*, 283.
[71] Lieberman, "Free Market Strategy and Tactics in K–12 Education," 83.

the lack of financial penalties for failing schools.[72] Other choice programs offered targeted vouchers (which meant that choice was largely limited to a particular demographic—usually low income—meaning that sizable markets could not develop), and all banned for-profit schools from eligibility to receive voucher money. Support for such programs (without stipulating the degrees to which they were "compromises" that did not resemble the end goal of truly free markets) was counterproductive for two reasons. First, it ensures that in the public consciousness, "the acceptability of free-market plans will be dependent on the outcomes of plans that are basically contrary to free-market positions on school choice."[73] Second, Lieberman suspected that legislatures and school boards who would be resistant to truly free markets in education could use highly compromised "market" plans as a way to placate the disaffected (especially over-eager advocates of choice), forestalling genuine reform and by "propping up the system they are supposed to replace."[74]

Myron Lieberman's public-choice-steeped "autopsy" of public education left no optimism that U.S. public education could be reformed from the inside. The system had the inefficiency of public bureaucracies functioning by the political, rather than a market, process—no competition, no pressure to maximize efficiency, personal advancement contingent on politics rather than market exchange. Yet Lieberman believed that the very inefficiencies that rendered his "autopsy" necessary left the system impervious to the dismantling and replacing it sorely needed. Perhaps the best that could be done was to call attention to why public education failed, why markets offered a promising replacement, and point out the various obstacles to anyone brave enough to take up the fight.

---

[72] Lieberman, *The Educational Morass*, 237–238.
[73] Lieberman, *The Educational Morass*, 207.
[74] Lieberman, *The Educational Morass*, 210.

8

"Other Conceptions, Both Powerful and Exotic": School Choice Visions from Voices from the Political Left

In a 2006 essay, law professor and school-choice advocate John Coons assessed the state of the school choice movement and Milton Friedman's role in it. After some perfunctory niceties about Friedman, Coons suggested that despite the movement's modest successes, Friedman's free-market libertarian focus might have hampered what could have been a more successful movement with broader appeal:

> The champion of school choice who intends the outcome to be something more than an academic exercise eventually comes to terms with the reality that the central ideas of market individualism bear obscurely on the complex of relationships that we call school. To the enthusiast, that can come as a surprise. Embarked on his historic mission to pulverize yet another bloated monopoly, the economist-liberator sails straight into a Bermuda triangle of confounding ideologies. The classical images of economics are not unwelcome here, but, in the context of schooling, they find themselves

confronting other conceptions, both powerful and exotic, that lurk within the equally enigmatic triangle of parent, child, and state.[1]

As much as Friedman's "Role of Government in Education" got policy analysts and politicians talking about school choice, Coons was concerned that Friedman assumed that one could apply the same fixes to education that one could to any other market good or service, ignoring complexities that might make education distinct from those services. As examples, Coons points out that unlike most other markets, who the consumer is (the child, the parent, or the family as a whole) is not clear. Similarly, concerns about equitable access and whether schools should be able to select customers using discriminatory standards are issues in education in a way they might not be in other markets. Choice programs that didn't address such issues (or addressed them with "Let the market decide!") might satisfy libertarians, but probably few others.

Coons and Sugarman were two of several academics and activists to formulate school choice plans on non-market libertarian grounds during the 1970s and 1980s. Folks like Coons, Sugarman, legal scholar Stephen Aarons, and education reformers Theodore Sizer and John Holt were different from market libertarians in their advocacy for school choice and markets in education. They did not, like Friedman, simply extend an existing belief in the superiority of markets into education. For them, markets in education were a perceived solution to other problems. For some (like Coons and Sugarman), it was a concern about persisting inequalities in the public education system and a belief that decentralized markets might get more equitable results. For others (like Sizer and colleague Deborah Meier), it was a concern with excessive bureaucratization and centralization in the public school system and a hope that markets would lead to more autonomy for schools in determining how to educate. For still others (like John Holt), it was a "small 'l' libertarian" concern that people be free to choose the educational forms that work best for them

These school choice advocates differed from the market libertarians in their motivations and rationales, and thus, their proposed plans are

---

[1] John E. Coons, "Give Us Liberty and Give Us Depth," in *Liberty & Learning: Milton Friedman's Voucher Idea at Fifty*, ed. Robert Enlow and Lenore T. Ealy (Washington, DC: Cato Institute, 2006), 63.

accordingly different from those of market libertarians. Those who defend school choice from a belief that markets are morally or economically superior to govern mentally controlled systems will understandably be reluctant to allow much or any regulation into their plans. On the other hand, those for whom markets are an instrument toward a desired goal (like increased equity or school autonomy) will likely support regulations that might help toward those goals. Coons's point, then, is that Friedman and other "enthusiasts" of "market individualism" might advocate school choice plans that focus too much on uniquely libertarian concerns (like reducing the scope of government) that leave other legitimate concerns unaddressed (like how to craft government regulation that ensures equitable access for all to education).

Here, I have chosen diverse arguments and plans for school choice coming from voices we can fairly say are situated on the political left. There were, of course, voucher plans advocated by more conservative right-wing voices, but I have chosen to focus on voices from the left largely for three reasons. First, several histories have already explored voucher plans coming from the conservative right.[2] Secondly, since market libertarians arguably share more in common with the conservative right than the liberal or progressive left (via their mutual desire to reduce the scope of government), examining school choice advocacy and proposals from the left might give a more interesting counterpoint to the market libertarian figures in previous chapters. Lastly, because school choice has largely acquired a reputation as a right-wing project, looking closely at several choice advocates of the left (who supported choice for fairly different reasons) might serve as an interesting and necessary counterpoint.[3]

The previous chapters each focused on one market libertarian figure and what they had to say about school choice. For contrast, it might be useful to end with a chapter examining several school choice plans crafted by non-market libertarians, emphasizing their similarities with and differences from market libertarian plans, as well.

---

[2] See, for instance, Molly Townes O'Brien, "Private School Tuition Vouchers and the Realities of Racial Politics," *Tennessee Law Review* 64 (1996): 359–98; Jim Carl, *Freedom of Choice: Vouchers in American Education* (Santa Barbara, CA: Praeger, 2011).

[3] For a more comprehensive overview of the history of progressive support for school choice, see: James Forman, "The Secret History of School Choice: How Progressives Got There First," *Georgetown Law Journal* 93, no. 4 (2005).

Theodore Sizer (and Deborah Meier): Advocating Small Autonomous Schools of Choice

In 1968, Theodore Sizer, then the Dean of the Harvard Graduate School of Education, and colleague Phillip Whitten wrote an article in *Psychology Today* called "A Proposal for a Poor Children's Bill of Rights." Their chief concern was that poor children be guaranteed access to a good education. Social and economic inequality, they argued, had remained persistent despite the best attempts of the courts, legislatures, and social programs like Lyndon Johnson's "War on Poverty." The key, they argued, may be largely in empowering poor families to choose how their children are educated from the marketplace of competing firms.

> Ours is a simple proposal: to use education—vastly improved and powerful education—as the principle vehicle for upward mobility. While a complex of strategies must be designed to accomplish this, we wish here to stress one: a program to give money directly to the poor children (through their parents) to assist in paying for their education. By doing so, we might create both significant competition among schools serving the poor (and thus improve the schools) and meet in an equitable way the extra costs of teaching the children of the poor.[4]

Sizer and Whitten proposed a voucher system that would "give money in the form of a coupon to a poor child who would carry the coupon to the school of his choice," whereupon "the school could use the sum as it saw fit."[5] While they were aware that a similar voucher system had been proposed "recently from Milton Friedman, the conservative University of Chicago economist," they point out that other such voucher systems had been proposed by liberals like John Stuart Mill and Thomas Paine, and that the "appeal" of such programs "bridges ideological differences."[6]

---

[4] Theodore Sizer and Phillip Whitten, "A Proposal for a Poor Children's Bill of Rights," *Psychology Today*, August 1968, 59.
[5] Sizer and Whitten, "A Proposal for a Poor Children's Bill of Rights," 61.
[6] Sizer and Whitten, "A Proposal for a Poor Children's Bill of Rights," 59.

Their proposal, while broad in detail, differed in several ways from most market libertarian proposals. First, because redress of economic inequity was the goal of this Poor Children's Bill of Rights, Sizer and Whitten unabashedly offered a plan that will "frankly discriminate in favor of poor children."[7] Speaking in broad terms, their "research suggests several alternative patterns which provide sliding scales—allowing for the allocation of different amounts of money proportional to family income and number of school-aged children."[8] Children whose families made less money, and particularly those who lived under the poverty line, would receive more tuition money.

Another crucial area where they disagreed with Friedman was on his "emphasis on private enterprise." Sizer and Whitten envisioned a system that would allow *private* schools to compete for voucher money but also allowed "competition between *public* school systems or even between public schools within a system."[9] Additionally, while Sizer and Whitten wanted children to have access to a plurality of educational models, they shared none of Friedman's reluctance in granting the state a significant role in accrediting schools, as long as governments accredited on a plurality of metrics that were not too standardized.

Lastly, Sizer and Whitten envisioned this voucher system as "part of a package" governments make available to the poor as part of the Poor Children's Bill of Rights, a package that would include such things as "some form of guaranteed annual income and the provision of health and welfare services at a level of accommodation much higher than at present."[10]

Sizer was not a politician or economist, but an educator and educational reformer. By the time he and Whitten penned the "Proposal for a Poor Children's Bill of Rights," Sizer had been a high school history teacher in private schools, and had worked for several years as a professor in Harvard's Graduate School of Education (where he was colleagues with Jams Coleman and Christopher Jencks, who also wrote influential papers supporting school choice).

---

[7] Sizer and Whitten, "A Proposal for a Poor Children's Bill of Rights," 60.
[8] Sizer and Whitten, "A Proposal for a Poor Children's Bill of Rights," 61.
[9] Sizer and Whitten, "A Proposal for a Poor Children's Bill of Rights," 62.
[10] Sizer and Whitten, "A Proposal for a Poor Children's Bill of Rights," 6.

While Sizer doesn't appear to have written anything specifically on school choice prior to his article with Whitten, he showed a very consistent concern for the related issue of school autonomy. In an introductory essay he wrote for a collection of writings about the role of academies in early American education, Sizer suggested that one advantage academies had was in their "relatively private form of control." Sizer argued that academies offered a curriculum that generally "was broader and more 'practical' than that of their predecessor, the Latin grammar school,"[11] arguing that this was likely because their private structure allowed them more flexibility to build curricula that served the needs of its customers. "The founders were ambitious in their plans, organizing the academies as relatively independent institutions, usually tied closely to the local community."[12]

This concern for school autonomy followed Sizer throughout his career. In 1981, Sizer, then a Headmaster at Philips Academy, would lead a study of American high schools (cosponsored by the National Association of Independent Schools) that would lead both to his influential book *Horace's Compromise*, and to start the Coalition of Essential Schools, a consortium of public and private high schools based on Sizer's educational philosophy. At the heart of this philosophy was the idea that schools should be both small enough to allow a unique culture to form among those who inhabit it, and autonomous, so that the choices governing the school are made by those within and close to the school. When, in later years, Sizer was asked why he objected to plans for national curricular standards (and conversely, supported school choice), he suggested that:

> One … has to do with the importance of making sure that the politics of the community are brought to bear [on the school]. Say I'm a parent. If I really don't like what's being taught, I want to be able to look in the eye of the administrator who has the ability to change the curriculum. That's not going to happen if decisions are made by a committee of people far away from the community.[13]

---

[11] Theodore Sizer, "The Academies: An Interpretation," in *The Age of the Academy*, 1–49 (New York: Teachers College Press, 1964), 2.

[12] Sizer, "The Academies," 3.

[13] John O'Neil, "On Lasting School Reform: A Conversation with Ted Sizer," *Educational Leadership* (February 1995): 4–9, 6.

The Coalition of Essential Schools, then, was just that: a *coalition* of autonomous schools that agreed on the same core principles (such as valuing curricular depth over breadth, and student exhibition of work in lieu of traditional tests) but beyond that, made their own decisions based on their own unique cultures. Sizer and the Coalition's founders "started from the assumption that schools are unique. In order to be good, a school has to reflect its own community. And therefore, we offer no model."[14]

For that and other reasons, the Coalition of Essential Schools "have disproportionately been schools of choice. Because no one has to go there. Choice encourages people to experiment."[15] Alluding to his time at Philips Academy, Sizer was also affected by his time as "a principal at a school of choice. And it changed my whole relationship with parents. I had to be much more attentive to the parents, because my budget depended on their support."[16] Choice is valuable in large part because it meant that everyone involved in a school—parents, students, teachers, staff—were there because they chose to be and could choose differently if another school fit their needs better.

Like Frank Chodorov, Sizer was a pluralist who opposed all attempts to standardize education for all students. Students, families, and cultures (even within the very plural United States) differ. Not only do schools need the ability to differ in reflection of the communities they serve, but individuals need the ability to choose from a plurality of educational institutions. In a 1976 article pleading for an "educational smorgasbord," Sizer takes aim at the very idea of "the common school," that in such a diverse nation in fact "never was and clearly will never be."[17] Like Chodorov, Sizer recognizes that education is irreducibly value-laden and "there will inevitably be a powerful, if small, group of political 'ins' who will persistently argue for the existence of a school system to hammer kids into their molds."[18] Sizer does not argue against assimilation to a broad American culture, but he recognizes two things that make it possible or desirable to

---

[14] O'Neil, "Lasting School Reform," 4.
[15] O'Neil, "Lasting School Reform," 7.
[16] O'Neil, "Lasting School Reform," 7.
[17] Theodore Sizer, "Education and Assimilation: A Fresh Plea for Pluralism," *Phi Delta Kappan* 58, no. 1 (1976): 31–35, 34.
[18] Sizer, "Education and Assimilation," 34.

put the educational focus more on diversity. First, Sizer recognizes that at the time he wrote, the news and entertainment media and other outlets had taken over some of the assimilation role. Second, putting the primary educational emphasis on assimilation means that swaths of people will be forced to attend public schools where they do not see the values of their culture(s) reflected.

Sizer's pluralism ran so deep that he suggested that a program of educational choice might extend beyond the idea of one child attending one school at a time. It may be that some families choose for their child to attend one school that meets all that child's educational needs, but others might choose different schools throughout the child's educational career or even complementary educational institutions at the same time.

> What we need instead is a smorgasbord of schools, all of high quality (that is, accredited and all open and accessible to those who would choose among them). ... Diversity in schooling need not be divisive; schools can collaborate, not only compete; schools can be complimentary, not only alternatives to one another.[19]

Throughout his career as an educational reformer, Sizer remained committed to the values of school autonomy, the value of small schools that reflect the culture of their stakeholders, and school choice. While Sizer's body of work reflects increasing disenchantment with growing calls for centralization, bureaucratization, and standardization within public education, he remained optimistic that school choice was gaining champions of diverse political stripes. In 1997, perhaps thinking about President Bill Clinton's stated support for school choice,[20] Sizer was able to write:

> This fascinating and politically diverse cacophony reflects the growing—and sensible—acceptance of the notion that schools should not necessarily be alike and that families should have far greater control over the particular

---

[19] Sizer, "Education and Assimilation," 35.
[20] "We should reward the best schools, and we should shut down or redesign those that fail, and especially those that are unsafe. That's one reason why I have supported expanding school choice and charter schools-creative new schools started by parents and teachers and licensed by school systems." Bill Clinton, *Between Hope and History: Meeting America's Challenges for the Twentieth Century* (New York: Crown, 1996), 44.

schools that their children attend than they have had. Choice is on the banners of many influential groups. It is now a deeply entrenched idea.[21]

While Sizer never doubted that school choice was desirable as public policy, it was perhaps the gradual rightward tilt of this "politically diverse cacophony" that soured one of Sizer's closest colleagues away from school choice after Sizer's death of colon cancer in 2009. Deborah Meier, once an advocate of school choice alongside Sizer, would come to it as an idea used increasingly by the conservative right wing to serve ends at odds with those she and Sizer supported.

Meier met Sizer in the 1983, as he was getting ready to publish *Horace's Compromise* and was a central player in the founding of the Coalition for Essential Schools. Before that, she had founded the Central Park East elementary school, a small public school of choice in New York that became a school within the Coalition. Like Sizer, Meier advocated that to best fulfill their educational missions, schools should be small and autonomously run within a system of school choice. Like Sizer, though, she was quite ambivalent about whether schools of choice should be public or private. In a 1991 article, she warns that education reformers do not cede the idea of school choice to those on the political right. Central Park East and the district of "small, largely self-governing and pedagogically innovative" schools it existed in would not have been possible had District 4 not allowed school choice in the form of open public school enrollment. "It would have been impossible to carry out this ambitious agenda without choice. Choice was the prerequisite."[22] Like Sizer, Meier argues that "There's something galling about the idea that you're stuck in a particular school that's not working for you unless you are rich enough to buy yourself out of it."[23] Yet, Meier argues that choice supporters need not buy into the libertarian "rhetoric that too often surrounds choice: about the rigors of the marketplace, the virtues of private schooling and the Inherent mediocrity of public places and public spaces."[24]

---

[21] Theodore Sizer, *Horace's Hope: What Works for the American High School* (New York: Houghton Mifflin, 1996), 40.
[22] Deborah Meier, "Choice Can Save Public Education," *The Nation*, March 4, 1991, 253–71, 266.
[23] Meier, "Choice Can Save Public Education," 271.
[24] Meier, "Choice Can Save Public Education," 271.

To Meier and Sizer, choice was a vehicle for improving education that serves the public (whether or not the schools that did so were public or private). In addition to its ability to empower families by allowing them to choose the schools that fit them, Meier, believed, as Sizer had, that school choice would allow the flourishing of small, innovative, and autonomously controlled schools that a bureaucratic public school system would not allow. As time went on, however, Meier believed that the increasingly conservative visions of school choice did not share the same vision, and often favored privatization regardless of whether the schools were small and autonomous. By 2017, Meier had largely abandoned the idea of school choice, which "has taken a divisive and often destructive direction" in the hands of conservatives who were, she argued, using it as a rallying cry for corporate privatization; she now only "recommends its use with some significant caveats."[25]

"For better or worse," Meier wrote, "my message [of school choice] resonated with educators and reformers from across the political spectrum." But unlike Sizer, who saw the ideological diversity of school choice supporters as a sign of the idea's strength, Meier came to believe that the core vision of small, autonomous, schools of choice that she and Theodore Sizer had long championed had become hopelessly co-opted by folks whose primary goal was privatization and the withering away of the public sphere.

> Their aim: to demonstrate that education would work better, as would other public and private institutions, if the followed a free-market business model, with financial incentives in place, while starving out democratic voices and purposes. Schools that serve to educate a democracy increasingly seem like a luxury we can't afford.[26]

---

[25] Deborah Meier, "What Happens to Public Education Deferred," in *These Schools Belong to You and Me: Why We Can't Afford to Examine Our Public Schools* (Boston, MA: Beacon Press, 2017), 139.
[26] Meier, "What Happens to Public Education Deferred," 151.

Coons and Sugarman: Education for Subsidiarity

John Coons met Steve Sugarman when Coons was a law professor at Northwestern and Stephen was a student trying to decide where to go to law school. The two began an intellectual relationship that led to the 1970 publication, with colleague William Klune III, of the book *Private Wealth, Public Education*. The book reflected a shared concern with addressing the inequities of education funding that was tied primarily to the school district. Such funding schemes meant that districts would vary wildly in what they could spend on public education, leaving the educational quality children receive largely up to what district they lived in.

Rather than argue for a "true egalitarian" position held by some of their colleagues, where the state would take over school funding and districts would receive a certain dollar amount per child,[27] Coons, Sugarman, and Klune argued a more moderate position that they called "district power equalizing." As they wrote, "Power equalizing is a commitment by the state to the principle that the relationship between effort and offering of every district will be the same irrespective of wealth and that the district is to determine the effort (within appropriate limits if the state so desires)."[28]

This was a middle position between leaving districts to fund their own education and the state financing education by apportioning money to districts per child. It may be, the authors argue, that districts might want to spend different percentages of their budget on education. The problem is less that districts spend different amounts, but that poorer districts have to tax themselves at high rates to keep up with what more affluent districts can easily afford.

---

[27] Martin Meeker, *Jack Coons: Law, Ethics, and Educational Finance Reform* (Oral History Center, Bancroft Library, University of California, 2015), 89, http://digitalassets.lib.berkeley.edu/roho/ucb/text/coons_jack_2016.pdf.
[28] John E. Coons, William H. Klune III, and Stephen D. Sugarman, *Private Wealth and Public Education* (Cambridge, MA: Belknap Press, 1970), 202.

To preserve a balance between district autonomy over school spending and equity between districts, the authors suggested an intricate formula (replete with pages of diagrams). Their formula allows each district to determine what percentage of their tax revenue will go toward operating the district's public schools. The state will determine some amount of money that each percentage of districts' tax spending toward public schools will be "worth," and then pay the difference to each district between what their tax revenue raises and what the formula determines that level of tax should yield in spending. One reviewer of the book used the following example to illustrate:

> The state will contribute to each local district funds sufficient to provide $100 per pupil for each mill of education tax imposed on itself by the local district. Thus a 10 mill tax will produce $1,000 per pupil; a 15 mill tax will produce $1,500 per pupil—regardless of the wealth of the district or the amount per pupil actually produced at these rates. The poorer the district, the more the state will contribute at any given tax rate in order to reach the state-determined amount for the given tax rate; the wealthier the district, the less the state will need to contribute.[29]

In this way, Coons, Sugarman, and Klune sought to provide a balance between equality and what the authors called subsidiarity, "the power of localities to decide (a) how much education they desire (perhaps within minimums and maximums set by the state) and (b) how much they are willing to spend to reach their goals."[30] District power equalizing was, they argued, a way to ensure a level of equity while preserving district autonomy to make choices about education spending.

This model of district power equalizing, in fact, became a key part of a case that was headed to the California Supreme Court. Coons and Sugarman were asked to write briefs in support of the plaintiffs in, who (successfully) challenged the state's existing structure for school funding. It's "substantial dependence on local property taxes and resultant wide disparities in school revenue," they successfully argued, violated the Equal

---

[29] Hershel Shanks and William H. Clune, *Review of Private Wealth and Public Education*, by John E. Coons and Stephen D. Sugarman, *Harvard Law Review* 84, no. 1 (1970): 259–60, https://doi.org/10.2307/1339586.
[30] Klune Coons and Sugarman, *Private Wealth and Public Education*, 16.

Protection Clause of the Fourteenth Amendment.[31] (The state adopted a more equitable funding system, but not the district equalizing power model.)

Toward the end of their book, the authors also argued that if subsidiarity was the goal, it might be that district equalizing power was a step in the right direction but didn't get to the destination. Perhaps subsidiarity could be extended down to the family level. Fiscal control can be placed directly in the hands of the family, in the manner in which we have previously conceived it in the district.

In other words, subsidiarity can be maximized insofar as it remains consistent with the elimination of wealth determinants of equality. In order to prevent wealth discrimination, ultimate state financial responsibility, of course, would be maintained; the shift from district to family decision-making regarding effort, therefore, would mean that each family now would have the same financial backing as any other for purposes of public education. We call this notion family power equalizing.[32]

Coons and Sugarman were intrigued by the idea of achieving subsidiarity through family choice, and explored the issue in subsequent essays culminating in the 1978 book *Education by Choice*. What they had previously called a family *power equalizing model* was now labeled the *quality choice model* of school funding, though the plan was largely the same as what they'd proposed in *Private Wealth and Public Education*. The state would set a range of acceptable tuition rates, largely to ensure that school tuition could not gradually creep up to put some choices out of reach of the poorest families. From there, "each family would select from the various priced schools the one it thought best for its child and pay a portion of its income towards tuition; the state would subsidize the rest."[33]

Of the choice advocates in this chapter, Coons and Sugarman did the most sparring with their libertarian counterpart, Milton Friedman. Prior to Coons's scholarship on school choice, Friedman had been an occasional guest on his Chicago radio show Problems of the City and had occasionally

---

[31] Raymond L. Sullivan, *Serrano v. Priest*, No. L.A. 29820 (California Supreme Court August 30, 1971).

[32] Klune Coons and Sugarman, *Private Wealth and Public Education*, 259.

[33] John E. Coons and Stephen D. Sugarman, *Education by Choice: The Case for Family Control* (Berkeley: University of California Press, 1978), 198.

discussed school choice, agreeing on its desirability but not on specifics, such things as who the customer (or primary beneficiary) of education was (child? parents? the government?).[34] Those disagreements only intensified once Coons and Sugarman articulated a school choice plan that differed from Friedman's.

In Education by Choice, Coons and Sugarman not only outline a school choice plan much different from Friedman's, but differentiate their plan, and those of other non-market libertarian choice advocates like Theodore Sizer, as being designed to "compensate for the discrimination inherent in the unregulated Friedman model."[35] They criticize Friedman for viewing "education through the lens of laissez-faire economics," not because there isn't merit to the pro-market argument, but because, in the authors' view, Friedman misses some key complexities, such as how "standard theories of consumer sovereignty" "merely raise, and do … nothing to answer, the crucial question of the child's own welfare under a family regime."[36] For these and other reasons—such as the potential inequities of giving all families regardless of financial ability the same sized voucher—Coons and Sugarman write that "if the Friedman scheme were the only politically viable experiment with choice, we would not be enthusiastic."[37]

We can already get an idea of some of the differences between the plans of Friedman and Sugarman and Coons. As we've seen, Coons and Sugarman's plan allows families to spend different amounts on their children's education (and schools to compete with different price points) in the way Friedman's plan does. But Coons and Sugarman's plan differs from Friedman's by establishing not only a range of price points above and below which schools cannot charge, but significant subsidies that essentially vary with income bracket.

Beyond this, like Sizer, Coons and Sugarman were not as eager as Friedman to get rid of or minimize the presence of public schools. "Under Milton Friedman's plan," the authors warn, "the public sector would begin to withdraw from the business of providing education," a goal Coons and Sugarman believe does not logically follow from support for school choice

---

[34] Meeker, *Jack Coons: Law, Ethics, and Educational Finance Reform*, 55.
[35] Coons and Sugarman, *Education by Choice*, 195.
[36] Coons and Sugarman, *Education by Choice*, 21–22.
[37] Coons and Sugarman, *Education by Choice*, 191.

and could produce ill effects. While Coons and Sugarman are noncommittal regarding what public school options would look like in a choice system, they suggest such possibilities as putting a cap on the "market share" private schools can have among educational choices in an area and "establish[ing] each public school as an individual nonprofit corporation" that, while having "independent power and duties" might still be subject to certain regulations that public, but not private, entities must comply with.

Coons and Sugarman's plan also differs from Friedman's in several other areas involving the role of the government. The authors of *Education by Choice*, for instance, advocate a quota system for admissions similar to that advocated by Christopher Jencks and the Office of Equal Opportunity (OEO), where schools might be allowed a certain portion of their seats to be filled by whatever selection criteria the school wants to use, where other seats have to be filled by lottery or some other random method. Where Friedman probably assumes that, as with other markets, companies will work hard to advertise and consumers, to inform themselves before making choices, Coons and Sugarman also suggest that government has a role to play to "ensure effective dissemination to all classes of families," a proposal also similar to that of the OEO.[38] Unlike the OEO's proposal, Coons and Sugarman recognize the potential danger of government demanding that schools report only particular metrics. Accordingly, they suggest that beyond data like average class sizes, dropout rates, and similar data, "schools would also be invited to set their own criteria of success" and report on factors they believe encapsulate their school.[39]

As with their work with William Klune on school finance Coons and Sugarman's voucher proposal made an appearance in the public sector when it attracted the attention of Democratic Senator Leo Ryan who, in 1978, met Coons and Sugarman and was intrigued by the possibility of putting the authors' recent voucher plan onto the California ballot in 1980. In 1976, the California Supreme Court heard a continuation of the aforementioned *Serrano v. Priest*, finding that while the state had taken some steps to reduce inequity in school funding (via "Proposition 13"), the

---

[38] Coons and Sugarman, *Education by Choice*, 149.
[39] Coons and Sugarman, *Education by Choice*, 148.

persisting inequities were sufficient to remain unconstitutional.[40] Coons, Sugarman, and Ryan all thought that a plan for school choice might stand the best chance of leading to constitutionally equitable outcomes.

The law professors and Senator were aiming to get their school voucher proposal (now called the Initiative for Family Choice) on the 1980 California state ballot. Even with the political capital of Senator Ryan behind them, however, there was considerable pushback against the proposal. The executive secretary of the California state teacher's union called the Coons–Sugarman plan "social dynamite," and the teacher's union president in San Diego predicted that the proposal would invite "all the racist scumbags" to create and attend schools to indoctrinate youth "and the public will [financially have to] support them."[41]

While those on the political left were reluctant to support any proposal that could introduce private competition to the public schools, several libertarians introduced their own competing ballot proposals that went in a more libertarian direction, introducing many fewer government regulations into their plan. One proposal was drawn up by Jack Hickey, an electrical engineer and many time Libertarian candidate for governor and Congress.

Both Coons and Sugarman, and Hickey, sought to get Milton Friedman's public endorsement of their favored proposals, and in the end, Friedman chose to endorse Hickey's plan. Jack Coons later told an interviewer that he suspects the ultimate failure of his and Sugarman's plan also had to do with Friedman talked several donors out of backing the Family Choice in Education proposal. "Well, they all sort of drifted away and we wondered what was wrong. Milton had, in fact, dissuaded them. He thought this [our plan] was not a good idea."[42]

On top of those obstacles, Coons and Ryan lost their key ally in the Democratic party, Leo Ryan, when Ryan was shot and killed in November 1978 by members of the People's Temple of the Disciples of Christ in

---

[40] Raymond L. Sullivan, *Serrano v. Priest*, No. 557 P. 2d 929 (California Supreme Court, December 30, 1976).
[41] Ron Matus, "California Dreamin': How the Left Almost Pulled off School Choice Revolution," redefinED, December 16, 2015, https://www.redefinedonline.org/2015/12/how-the-left-almost-pulled-off-school-choice-revolution/.
[42] Meeker, "Jack Coons," 123.

Guyana. As Coons later recalled, Ryan's tragic death was not only tragic but spelled "the end of our democratic supporter with political power."[43] Coons went on to recall that by that time.

> We had already, I think, gotten the initiative into official status, where we had so many days to get the signatures. And we tried. It cost me a lot of money. In the end, we made every possible mistake, I think, imaginable.[44]

In the end, Coons and Sugarman were not able to muster the financial, political, or popular support to get their Family Choice in Education proposal on the ballot. They created other voucher proposals in subsequent years, ones they believed might be more streamlined so that they were easier to explain to politicians and the public. But an environment that was becoming increasingly polarized on the issue of school choice, and a cause most often championed by the political right, none of these proposals met with political success.

John Holt: Turning S-chools into s-chools Through Educational Choice

In John Holt's ideal world, schools would not exist. At least that is what he wrote in his 1972 book *Freedom and Beyond*. In a chapter called "Beyond Schooling," Holt offers an imagined dialogue, where he travels five hundred years into the future to a civilization that is more advanced than ours. He asks someone from that culture a question:

> 'But where are your schools?'
> 'Schools? What are schools?' he replies.
> 'Schools are places where people go to learn things.'
> 'I do not understand,' he says. 'People learn things everywhere, in all places.'
> 'I know that,' I say. 'But a school is a special place where there are special people who teach you things, help you learn things.'

---

[43] Meeker, "Jack Coons," 123.
[44] Meeker, "Jack Coons," 123.

'I am sorry, but I still do not understand. Everyone helps other people learn things. Anyone who knows something or can do something can help someone else who wants to learn more about it. Why should there be special people to do this?'
And try as I will, I cannot make clear to him why we think that education should be, must be, separate from the rest of life.[45]

Strictly speaking, Holt was not primarily concerned with school choice. He did not, as other figures in this chapter, develop anything like a formal proposal of what school choice should look like. His primary concern was to lessen the legal and cultural grip formal schooling had in the United States. Since his days as a private school teacher, he'd gradually become disenchanted with the idea that formal schooling—with its curriculum, grading, and other structures that systematically inhibited students' freedom and curiosity—was conducive to good learning.

Holt, however, was an advocate of school choice, and even, as we shall see, hinted at some different proposals he thought might bring it about. For Holt, though, school choice was something he entertained largely as a means to reduce the compulsory nature of conventional schooling (both legal compulsion by way of compulsory education laws, and cultural compulsion via that assumption that school is the only way kids can learn). While Holt's ideal was that schools would not exist at all, the more achievable goal was to lessen schools' legal and cultural monopoly on learning and to ensure that, to exist, schools had to persuade rather than force. That would require some sort of school choice.

Holt started teaching in the early 1950s, first at a "progressive" private school in Colorado, and then at several private schools in Boston, Massachusetts. Hold was previously in the military, and teaching had never been his intended career. He took up teaching at the behest of his sister, who recognized his talent for interacting with children. During his teaching career, Holt became gradually disenchanted with what he saw as a mismatch between how he believed children naturally learned and the regimented way schools expected them to learn. As his concerns grew, Holt "was fired from several schools for his refusal to accommodate

---

[45] John Holt, *Freedom and Beyond* (New York: Dutton, 1972), 117.

administrative needs" like accommodating to what Holt believed to be rigid pedagogical methods or administering required tests to students.[46]

During his teaching career, Holt kept journals about what he saw, and this felt contrast between how children seem to learn naturally and how schools expect children to learn. In 1964, these journals would be published as *How Children Fail*, a book which became wildly successful and gained Holt a reputation as an important education critic. Holt's second book, *How Children Learn*, consisted of a similar set of journals, this time recounting various children he had known learning things outside of the confines of school.

As Holt increasingly thought, wrote, and gave invited lectures, he became less convinced that schools could simply be reformed to be better places of learning. He came gradually to believe that, for various reasons, reforming schools was less likely to produce good results than finding ways to bypass schools and lessen their legal and cultural grip. In an essay called "Not So Golden Rule Days," Holt flatly suggests, in what he says is a change of mind, that "compulsory education laws of good education," that "they should be relaxed, repealed, or overturned in the courts."[47] His reasoning was both that having to learn under the threat of compulsion violated children's liberty, and also that it created a prison-like atmosphere bad for both teacher and student. Schools were forced to teach students whether or not they wanted to be there, and schools and the authorities in them would feel no necessary pressure to earn—because they could force—student attention.

While Holt increasingly became pessimistic that reform of conventional schooling was possible, generally owing to their political and cultural inertia, his first mention of school choice as an idea was in 1970's *What Do I Do Monday?* There, he expressed hope that more parents sending their children to "free schools" (schools that afforded children more freedom than conventional schools) might "rouse public support for the voucher plan, in which parents are given money directly for their children's education, to spend as they wish," or "bring closer a time when independent

---

[46] Mel Allen, "The Education of John Holt," *Yankee Magazine*, December 1981; Milton Gaither, *Homeschool: An American History* (New York: Palgrave Macmillan, 2008), 123–24.
[47] John Holt, "Not So Golden Rule Days," in *The Under-Achieving School* (New York: Pitman, 1969), 71.

schools with no tuition and non-selective policies, no weeding out of children ... will be considered 'public' and supported by tax funds on the basis of the number of students attending."[48] All of these would serve to loosen the legal and cultural grip schools have on students and families, and hopefully, introduce more pressure on conventional schools to serve rather than compel.

> Only when all parents, not just rich ones, have a truly free choice in education, when they can take their children out of a school they don't like and have a choice of many others to send them to, or the possibility of starting their own, or of educating their children outside of school altogether—only then will we teachers begin to stop being what most of us still are, and if we are honest know we are, which is jailers, baby-sitters, cops without uniforms, and begin to be professionals, freely exercising an important, valued, and honored skill and art.[49]

Several years later, in his 1976 book *Instead of Education*, Holt proposed more several more ways to expand learner choice and, in so doing, weaken the monopoly of formal education on learning. The book itself is devoted to articulating a vision of what educational institutions might look like if not schools in the conventional sense, the difference between what Holt called "S-chools" (conventional Institutions of Learning that we now call "school") and "s-chools," places where anyone of any age could go to learn things on their own or with asked-for help.

Holt, of course, was pessimistic—even fatalistic—that such s-chools could replace S-chools without both a shift in cultural attitudes about education and a reduction in the ways government vests schools with power. (Holt believed very much that the latter perpetrated the former.) As he had in earlier works, Holt argued against compulsory education, that any education should be voluntary, on the part of the learner, not just the parent. He also argued that one reason for S-schools' ascendance was that they, by state mandate, were both educative institutions and issuers of credentials like diplomas, and insofar as certain professions require these credentials, S-chools retain their cultural dominance. Holt suggested that

---

[48] John Holt, *What Do I Do Monday?* (New York: Dutton, 1970), 299.
[49] Holt, *What Do I Do Monday?* 265.

we could "do away with the near monopoly of S-chools over credentials," by governments "pass[ing] laws saying that whenever a credential was needed to do a given kind of work, there would have to be ways to get this credential without going to or through a S-chool."[50]

Holt also continued the defense of some type of voucher-like system of school choice, reiterating that "It seems only fair that if the state can force young people to go to school it should at least allow them to pick the school."[51] Holt's idea of school choice, however, was more granular than most proposals, less *school* choice and more *educational* choice. Holt, for instance, argued that we might allow a learner to "get some of his schooling in one school, some in another" and issue "school credit for a much wider variety of activities, including work."[52] Holt envisioned a world where learners (of all ages) would have a bevy of options to choose from far beyond S-chools: "Thus we might have small neighborhood tutoring centers, or the kind of storefront mini-schools … that were often so successful in New York, or neighborhood versions of the Beacon Hill Free School or the Learning Exchange, or something like the Storefront Learning Center we had in Boston for some time, or other inventions."

Beyond sketches like these, Holt was quite noncommittal on details. As suggested in a previous quote, Holt believed that to accept state voucher money, a school must have "non-selective policies"; though what he meant by that was not clear, it is reasonable to suppose he meant that schools not be allowed to introduce selection criteria for admittance.[53] If students "need transportation to do this [attend the institution of their choice], the state and/or their home district should pay for it," though, again, Holt did not offer specifics of how transportation funding might be determined.

This lack of committal to any specific school choice plan may be because for Holt, school choice was a tertiary issue, important, but as a means toward weakening the cultural and legal monopoly of S-chools. It could also be because, as historian Milton Gaither notes, "One of Holt's most appealing qualities was his willingness to listen to and make common

---

[50] John Caldwell Holt, *Instead of Education: Ways to Help People Do Things Better* (New York: Dutton, 1976), 192.
[51] Holt, *Instead of Education*, 197.
[52] Holt, *Instead of Education*, 196.
[53] Holt, *What Do I Do Monday?* 229.

cause with people from a wide range of ideological perspectives."[54] Holt's mission was to open people's eyes to the idea that S-chools were not the only ways to educate people (largely turning his attention toward homeschooling and what he later called "unschooling" as a result of suggestions in *Instead of Education*). It could be that Holt was more concerned with building support for this broader mission and feared that advocating for one specific school choice vision would alienate potential allies.

Whatever the reason for his lack of specificity when sketching a vision for school choice, Holt's ability to make common cause with diverse groups may have been what led to some contact with the market libertarian movement. Certainly, Holt had some things in common with market libertarians: they both wanted to repeal compulsory education laws, give people more choice about how they receive education, and both had a philosophy that put freedom at its center. There were, of course, differences: Holt never explicitly embraced markets the way market libertarians did. Nor was he as reluctant as they to suggest government involvement in the form of some type of welfare state. (Holt's 1974 book on children's rights, *Escape from Childhood*, advocated that children and potentially adults be able to receive a guaranteed minimum income from the state.)[55]

Nonetheless, in 1978, Holt found himself a "surprise guest" on a panel at that year's libertarian convention after walking over to the convention from his Boston office to see "his old friend" Karl Hess, a libertarian activist and author. The panel consisted of conservative author Samuel Blumenfeld, and a staff member and student from the private Sudbury Valley School. Jeff Riggenbach, a reporter for Libertarian Review magazine, reported Holt as saying that he thought of himself as "a small 'l' libertarian." "The opposite of liberty is coercion. I'm interested in minimizing the amount of coercion in human affairs." (Holt did issue the caveat that from the child's perspective, a private school is just as compulsory as a public one.)[56] Later, the Libertarian Review ran the full transcript of the panel, where Holt reiterated his contempt for compulsory education laws ("It's a terrible

---

[54] Milton Gaither, *Homeschool: An American History* (New York: Palgrave Macmillan, 2008), 127.
[55] John Holt, *Escape from Childhood* (New York: Dutton, 1974).
[56] Jeff Riggenbach, "Convention Diary 1978," *Libertarian Review* 7, no. 9 (October 1978): 31.

situation, and I think it's only going to get worse"[57]), and got a chance to plug a project that would make up a large part of his work until his death in 1985: a magazine devoted to homeschooling called *Growing Without Schooling*.

Theodore Sizer, Deborah Meier, John Coons, Stephen Sugarman, and John Holt advocated for school choice on grounds that were not particularly grounded in pro-market libertarianism. None were particularly hostile toward government as a matter of principle, and each was willing to give the government some substantive role in education beyond funding tuition.

Each of these figures argued that market forces should be brought into education not because markets were inherently superior to government or out of any belief that individuals had rights against government coercion, but because markets might be an effective means toward educational goals existing governments seemed unable to reach. For Sizer and Meier, the goal was to achieve educational equity and the types of small, autonomous schools that would empower all stakeholders. For Coons and Sugarman, the issue was to redress persisting economic and racial inequality. For Holt, the goal was to lessen the cultural and legal monopoly of public education and formal schooling generally, to allow a variety of educational forms to emerge.

I offer these non-market libertarian visions of school choice to serve as points of comparison to the market libertarian plans advocated by the subjects of previous chapters. These figures were writing at a time when the idea of school choice could attract, as Sizer suggested, a "fascinating and politically diverse cacophony" of voices from across the political spectrum. In subsequent years, the landscape would become more polarized, school choice largely associated with the conservative right wing and resistance to it, the politically liberal position. This polarization, perhaps, is well-illustrated by the differing but equally firm positions on school choice taken in the concluding chapter, by former Republican Congressman Ron Paul and former Assistant Secretary of Education and one-time school choice supporter Diane Ravitch.

---

[57]"The Crisis in Schooling: An LR Colloquium," *Libertarian Review* 7, no. 11 (December 1978): 25–28, 27.

9

Conclusion

On September 17, 2013, two books were released taking very different positions on school choice and markets in education. In *School Revolution*, former U.S. congressman and three-time presidential candidate Ron Paul called for an end to a federal and state role in funding or administering education, and for its replacement with a laissez-faire market in education services. In *Reign of Error*, historian of education and former assistant secretary of education Diane Ravitch argued that school choice movements not only would not improve the U.S. education system but would subject education to a morally dubious profit motive.

Paul released *School Revolution* shortly after ending his third presidential candidacy and retiring from Congress, where he served as a Republican but often took libertarian positions advocating free markets (in things like health care) and personal liberty (on issues like drug legalization and gun-ownership rights). Like Chodorov a generation before, the issue of education was, for Paul, important primarily because state education breaches the natural right and authority Paul argued that parents had to raise their children as they see fit:

A free society acknowledges that authority over education begins with the family. I am not saying that a free society grants that authority. I do not believe that such authority is delegated by society. But a free society acknowledges that families have that authority. To the extent that any society substitutes a source of authority over education other than the family, it departs from liberty.[1]

Because parents have a natural authority over their children, they have a right and "are in a position to teach children about what they believe matters most in life."[2] Professional educators, on the other hand, want to "reduce the influence of the parent" and are "thoroughly convinced that there are better ways to educate a child than the traditional ways" where parents choose what education is best for their children. "It is now a matter of political power, and the professional educators have succeeded in gaining a near-monopolistic control over the structure and content of education during the first dozen years of school."[3]

This near-monopoly on content gained by professional educators is bad for two reasons, Paul argued. First, in an argument similar to Rand's and Rothbard's, state education is very likely to turn out students taught a collectivistic pro-government doctrine that will leave them ill-prepared for a life of individual responsibility. "The government does not have to burn books in order to persuade the next generation of voters to favor the government. The government needs only screen out books and materials that are hostile to the expansion of the state."[4]

The second reason Paul argued that it is important to get the state out of education is that opening markets in education will lead to the kind of pluralism Chodorov cared about. When families are free to make their own educational choices, each may choose the curriculum that reflects what they are most comfortable with. And rather than the "near-monopolistic control" government exercised over education's content and methodology, the market will provide a range of options for parents and families.

---

[1] Ron Paul, *The School Revolution: A New Answer to Our Broken Education System* (New York: Grand Central Publishing, 2013), 5–6.
[2] Paul, *The School Revolution*, 14.
[3] Paul, *The School Revolution*, 12.
[4] Paul, *The School Revolution*, 94.

Producers can specialize. They can target specific groups within the society. Entrepreneurs can provide education at a competitive price. The range of choices available to parents increases. There will be competing systems with respect to educational methodology. There will also be competing systems with respect to the content of education.[5]

Unlike the voucher proponents, Paul believed that any government funding of education was a potential threat to liberty because whoever funds education controls that education. "Consistent tax-funded education does not look like family-funded education," because when the state funds education, it stipulates the terms under which it will fund education; thus, even a state-funded voucher system will find the state creating accreditation criteria, limiting the sphere of available choices.[6]

Paul suggested that for families to regain control of education from the state, they would have to retake the responsibility for funding education. Paul envisioned particularly that new technologies, particularly internet technologies, would create new models of lower-cost education, and market competition between all models of schooling would gradually reduce prices to make private education more affordable. "When the costs begin to fall, the institutional reforms become not merely possible, but inevitable."[7] Paul hoped that, as with the U.S. Post Office, the advent of rivals (like UPS and Federal Express in the case of postal service), as well as rival technologies (like e-mail alternatives to letter delivery), would reopen discussions about whether to reduce public education services and, potentially, abolish it altogether, leaving customers with a variety of private options.

In *Reign of Error*, Diane Ravitch, historian of education and former Assistant Secretary of Education (under President George H. W. Bush), moved away from her previous but measured support of market reforms in education. Ravitch argued both that years of market-based experimentation (primarily via targeted voucher plans and charter school additions to public school systems) yielded troubling results. She also claimed that the

---

[5] Paul, *The School Revolution*, 87.
[6] Paul, *The School Revolution*, 6.
[7] Paul, *The School Revolution*, 75.

privatization movement threatened to undermine the democratic potential of the American public school system.

Ravitch's change of mind was remarkable largely because she had long supported (if a bit tepidly) market-based choice in education. Yet Ravitch's support for these reforms owed little to appeals about the natural rights of parents to direct their children's education or school choice as a way to achieve cultural pluralism. Rather, Ravitch's support for markets in education employed a similar rationale to Myron Lieberman's (even though her enthusiasm for markets was decidedly more tempered): Ravitch believed that competition and choice could raise the overall quality of education in a way that spread through the private sector and eventually found its way to the public sector. Ravitch described her measured enthusiasm for markets in education before and during her stint as assistant secretary of education thus:

> For many years, I too agreed that our public schools were in crisis. I wanted them to be better. I worried about the content of the curriculum. I worried about the low standards for students and for teachers. ... I was an ambivalent supporter of school choice and certainly had no desire to replace public education with a voucherized, privately managed system of schools.[8]

Elsewhere, Ravitch clarified the extent to which her support for markets in education was based on a belief that competition might improve the overall quality of American education rather than an allegiance to any sort of pluralism that markets might usher in. Using language very similar to Lieberman's, Ravitch suggested that for markets to bring about the desired result of better education for all, private schools competing against each other would have to compete on the same metrics, and "standards would be even more necessary in a society that used public dollars to promote school choice. The more varied the schools, the more important it would be to have common standards to judge whether students were learning."[9] Otherwise, the fight between public and private schools—likely compet-

---

[8] Diane Ravitch, *Reign of Error: The Hoax of the Privatization Movement and the Danger to America's Public Schools* (New York: Alfred A. Knopf, 2013), 12.
[9] Diane Ravitch, *The Death and Life of the Great American School System: How Testing and Choice Are Undermining Education* (New York: Basic books, 2010), 19.

ing on different metrics—would be unfair and educational results for students would be unequal.

Ravitch had a testable hypothesis: the introduction of market-based reforms in education—whether targeted voucher programs or allowing students to choose privately maintained charter schools—will bring about schools that outperform public schools in terms of setting and reaching high standards of learning. It was the perceived failure of market reforms to consistently produce schools that outperformed public schools on such metrics that led Ravitch to become "increasingly skeptical about these reforms, reforms that I had supported enthusiastically."[10]

While Ravitch acknowledged that "the academic result of charter schools are inconsistent, which is unsurprising because the sector itself is so variable," she ultimately concluded that "most studies consistently conclude that the on average the academic results of charters are no better than those of traditional public schools."[11] As for the online schools that Ron Paul believed had the potential to revolutionize education by delivering more personalized and responsive education while lowering costs, Ravitch had a more pessimistic conclusion: qualitative data so far showed that "incentives to grow enrollments are much larger than the incentive to provide high-quality education."[12]

Like Albert Jay Nock generations before and in marked contrast to Myron Lieberman, Ravitch was skeptical that the profit motive could or would spawn high-quality education; instead, she surmised, it was more likely to create and reward schools that promised more than they produced. For instance, Ravitch suggested that some products of market reforms in education—particularly some charter schools—"have potential if the profit motive were removed, and if the concept were redesigned to meet the needs of the communities served rather than the plans of entrepreneurs."[13] Unless strict checks were put on allowing the profit motive into education—the kind of checks Lieberman specifically warned *against*—Ravitch warned that "the transfer of public funds to private management and creation of thousands of deregulated, unsupervised, and

---

[10] Ravitch, *Death and Life*, 12.
[11] Ravitch, *Reign of Error*, 205.
[12] Ravitch, *Reign of Error*, 241.
[13] Ravitch, *Reign of Error*, 13.

unaccountable schools [will] open … the public coffers to profiteering, fraud, and exploitation by large and small entrepreneurs."[14]

Ravitch's previous support and subsequent skepticism—at times, hostility—toward markets in education were largely evidence-based. Her original support for markets in education was contingent on their ability to introduce a bevy of schools that outperformed public schools by particular educational outcomes, and was retracted when data called this ability into question. As such, Ravitch distrusted the kind of "conservatives with a fervent belief in free market solutions" for reasons that were philosophical and resisted empirical testing.

> They believe in choice as a matter of principle. The results of vouchers don't matter to them. They cling to any tidbit of data to argue on behalf of vouchers. If there is evidence of parental satisfaction, that's good enough for them. But even if there were no evidence of success, they would still promote vouchers. They want to create a free market in schooling with multiple providers and competition. The true reward of vouchers is that they will end government control, supervision, and regulation of schooling. They let parents decide where their children should enroll in school, without regarding the quality of the school. Those schools that enroll the most students will thrive; those that do not attract enough students will not survive. Let the markets decide.[15]

Ravitch surely meant this as a negative depiction—the "believe[rs] in choice as a matter of principle" who support markets for ideological reasons (disdain for the state, deep-seated faith in markets) that are impervious to any empirical falsification. If we read this passage in a more neutral tone, though, Ravitch might easily have been talking about any defender of markets in education reviewed in this book. To greater or lesser degrees, each supported markets in education for reasons of principle.

Ravitch depicts "believe[rs] in choice as a matter of principle" as a fairly homogeneous group, driven by an unwavering faith in market competition and obstinate distrust in government. While the figures that make up this book (save Albert Jay Nock and the market advocates "on the left"

---

[14] Ravitch, *Reign of Error*, 11.
[15] Ravitch, *Reign of Error*, 261.

of the previous chapter) fit that depiction only in a very broad sense. As we've seen, each also had fairly different reasons for wanting the government out of, and markets into, education. For Chodorov, it was largely an appeal to educational pluralism that he believed markets, but not government, could (or would) provide. For Rand, it was an appeal to natural rights that she believed flowed from reason, which disallowed the state any authority to coerce people into paying for and sending their children to public schools. Lieberman's concern was less a desire to reduce the role of government and more a concern over the counterproductive effects of a public quasi-monopoly on educational quality. While Friedman's impetus for supporting markets in education might match Ravitch's depiction of the "believer in choice as a matter of principle," the other figures in this book have a more varied relationship to markets in education and what makes them desirable.

It may be a bit ironic that the only figure reviewed in this book who might ultimately share Ravitch's pessimism is Albert Jay Nock. Unlike Diane Ravitch, a "registered Democrat,"[16] Albert Jay Nock was a champion of *laissez-faire* capitalism and skeptic of government action in most areas of life, a position he came to out of appreciation for philosophers like Herbert Spencer. It was his skepticism both that people would choose good quality education on the market and that businesses would not give people the watered-down education they wanted (rather than the superior education that some needed) that made him distrust markets for schooling, a skepticism Nock drew from "conservative" social critic Matthew Arnold. In some ways, Nock's skeptical position mirrored Ravitch's own suspicion: that markets in education would not enhance educational excellence and, because of the profit motive, may lead to proprietary schools more interested in enrolling students than educating them.

For Frank Chodorov, the overarching principle in his support for markets in education was markets' promotion of consumer sovereignty. Versed as he was with economists like Ludwig von Mises, for whom consumer sovereignty was a virtue of markets, Chodorov argued that markets can and should allow different individuals (with different religions, worldviews, and values) to be the ultimate arbiter of what education was appropriate

---

[16] Ravitch, *Death and Life*, 18.

for them and their family, especially if the other option was the state as arbiter. The difference between Chodorov and his intellectual predecessor Nock was that, unlike Nock, Chodorov was uncomfortable suggesting that he was highly uncomfortable opining about the merits of others people's educational choices. Where Nock saw an objective standard on which to judge the merits of different models of education, Chodorov thought that individuals were the best judges of what has merit for their own situations. In this, Chodorov can be seen in Ravitch's above depiction of the principle-reliant supporter of school choice as he who would "let parents decide where their children should enroll in school, without regarding the quality of the school"[17] (though Chodorov might have preferred to say that parents, not the state, are in the best position to determine what "quality" is in their familial situation.)

Both Rand and Rothbard may be the type of supporter of school choice and markets for whom Ravitch suggested "the true reward of vouchers is that they will end government control, supervision, and regulation of schooling."[18] For both, whether or not markets in education produce empirical results superior to public schooling is largely beside the point. The larger point is that they get the state out of education. For Rand, influenced as she seems to have been by her friend Isabel Paterson's writing on education, this was important because the irreducibly collectivist state, would teach collectivist doctrines, the kind that would not be compatible with a free (and free market) society. Rothbard's reasons were similar: his concern—like those of his peers within the New Left like Paul Goodman—was that, as the state governs us, education produced by the state will aim at making us more governable and blindly patriotic, rather than to teach us to be autonomous individuals.

For Friedman—one of the less purely ideological libertarians in this study—the principle that grounded his support for markets in education was the economic idea that private organizations were better equipped than governments to create schools that operated efficiently and responded to consumer preference. Unlike Chodorov, Rand, and Rothbard, Friedman was more open to the idea that government's function need not be relegated

---

[17] Ravitch, *Reign of Error*, 261.
[18] Ravitch, *Reign of Error*, 261.

to a strictly minimal state; a less doctrinaire libertarianism of his Chicago School teachers like Henry Simons and Frank Knight. Friedman believed the state had a role to play in guaranteeing that all citizens had adequate funding for education and needed to provide education funding either to all or to those who could not afford it otherwise. Friedman's concern was that there was no good economic justification for states to administer, rather than just fund, schools, and that there were economic reasons why educational services were better left to private organizations from which families could choose in competitive markets. This was not because Friedman distrusted the state in the same way Rothbard did, but because Friedman believed both that markets allowed more diversity and choice to consumers and that competitive pressures would force companies to be more responsive to consumers than would government quasi-monopoly.

Myron Lieberman's support for vouchers in education owed an allegiance to public choice economic theory; his believed that free markets—where multiple producers could enter and exit, and for-profits were allowed—would respond to a better set of incentives than political actors working in government bureaucracies.

While both Friedman and Lieberman supported choice for semi-ideological reasons—Friedman's belief that freedom of choice and liberty had some intrinsic value, and Lieberman's defense of the exit option that markets in education would provide that public education didn't—neither Friedman nor Lieberman resemble Ravitch's depiction of the "believe[r] in choice as a matter of principle" as much as other figures.[19] Their economic approaches at least left open the possibility that empirical evidence—either that markets produce schools no more responsive or efficient than public schools, or that competition does not lead to improved educational quality over time—could have led either Friedman or Lieberman to reevaluate their defenses of markets in education.

Sizer, Coons, Sugarman, and Holt—the market proponents "of the left"—each had similar concerns as Ravitch about equity and equality. Like Ravitch earlier in her career, they were all concerned that, despite aspirations for the public schools, the existing public schools could not or would not produce equitable results. For Sizer as for Coons and Sug-

---

[19] Ravitch, *Reign of Error*, 261.

arman, market systems could be crafted in such a way that allow the benefits of markets to accrue primarily to the poor and vulnerable who needed them most. Holt, driven by a concern that contemporary public schools do not educate in productive ways, welcomed any plan—market or otherwise—that could undermine the cultural monopoly of conventional K–12 schooling.

While Ravitch's book *Reign of Error* focuses its attention on the issue of charter schools and voucher programs as the vehicles of school choice—because these have recently been the most visible vehicles for school choice in the United States—the advocates for markets in education we've seen in this book came to very different conclusions about the desirable scope for government involvement in education. Murray Rothbard (and, for different reasons, Ron Paul) supported a complete *laissez-faire* separation of school and state. Rothbard, an anarchist, argued that any service currently provided by government either was immoral (redistribution by taxation) or could be provided better by private organizations (roads and other "public goods"); education was no exception, and any state involvement in education—even funding it—would likely mean ultimate state control of education. Frank Chodorov and Ayn Rand both argued—similarly to Rothbard—that the state should not provide "social services" like education and that any state should limit itself to basic police functions (national defense, maintain a legal system). Yet they both ultimately believed that, for matters of expediency, a completely *laissez-faire* approach would leave some unable to afford private education, and, therefore, some sort of tuition tax-credit system would more easily allow the poor to afford education while minimizing the state's role in education to allowing tax exemptions on educational expenses or donations to private schools. Milton Friedman and Myron Lieberman were much less ideologically opposed to state involvement in education, and while they criticized state administration of schooling on economic grounds, neither was averse to state funding of education. Lieberman supported a universal voucher program where the state would distribute money to all parents such that each school-aged student had an equal voucher that parents would use to purchase their education (that could be augmented with private money). Friedman argued for a similar universal program early in his career, but was subsequently persuaded by historical data that government funding of education was only necessary (and hence, justified) in cases of poverty. Friedman ended his career favoring not universal but targeted vouchers. Sizer, Coons, Sugarman, and Holt, of course, had no ideological objection to state involvement in shaping an equitable system of markets in education, one that would even, as Sizer and Whitten wrote, "discriminate in favor of poor children."[20]

While released on the same day, Ron Paul's and Diane Ravitch's very different books are illustrative of the impassioned argument around the issue of school choice. Diane Ravitch and many advocates of public schooling worry that introducing markets and privatization in education result in "debates about the role of schooling in a democratic society, the lives of children and families, and the relationship between schools and society" being "relegated to the margins as no longer relevant to the business plan to reinvent American education."[21] Tax-supported, government-administered, and compulsory education become part of the American landscape largely because these debates have been won by those who favor a strong government role in education and are skeptical leaving education to private industry. To Ravitch, the privatization and pro-market movements in education threaten to discontinue this tradition of striving for more inclusive, democratic, and egalitarian education.

Perhaps the only thing on which Diane Ravitch and Ron Paul agree is that the battle between public education and markets in education must continue. Paul reminds pro-market advocates that "we are fighting a 180 year war" over "who will maintain control of the system of education"—the current system of increasing governmental monopoly and control or a dynamic system of private providers that will return control of educational decisions back to the family.[22]

In this book, I have told the story of a very loud minority in Paul's "war" and Ravitch's "debates." For these market libertarians, the very idea of governmentally administered education was as objectionable as the governmentally administered news media of Murray Rothbard's thought experiment. For differing reasons—from desire to return sovereignty to

---

[20] Theodore Sizer and Phillip Whitten, "A Proposal for a Poor Children's Bill of Rights," *Psychology Today*, August 1968, 60.
[21] Ravitch, *Reign of Error*, 28–29.
[22] Paul, *The School Revolution*, 11.

education's consumers, to distrust of government instruction, to economic arguments about the benefits of markets—these figures looked forward to a day when government's role in education was either curtailed or extinguished. They imagined a day when educational services were purchased from private producers competing in markets with the same (beneficial, they argued) results as any other industry where services are bought and sold. Where advocates of public education saw public schools as a valuable component of American democracy, these market libertarians saw a dangerous constraint on freedom of choice and individual liberty. To market libertarians, the replacement of a public school system with private markets in educational services was not to be feared as a loss of a vital public service, but was to be seen as an opportunity to extend dynamic markets into an area where they were sorely needed. In the idea of replacement of public schools with markets of private providers, advocates of public schools saw inequality and a disastrous return to unbridled individualism. Market libertarians saw liberty.

Bibliography

Alessi, Louis de. "An Economic Analysis of Government Ownership and Regulation." *Public Choice* 19, no. 1 (1974): 1–42.
Allen, Mel. "The Education of John Holt." *Yankee Magazine*, December 1981.
Areen, Judith, and Christopher Jencks. "Educational Vouchers: A Proposal for Diversity and Choice." *The Teachers College Record* 72, no. 3 (1971): 327–36.
Army Times Publishing Company. *The GI Bill of Rights and How It Works*. Washington, DC: Army Times, 1945.
Arnold, Matthew. *A French Eton, or, Middle Class Education and the State*. London: Macmillan, 1864.
———. *Culture and Anarchy: An Essay in Political and Social Criticism*. London: Smith, Elder, and Co., 1869. https://books.google.com/books?id=gVgJAAAAQAAJ&printsec=frontcover&dq=culture+anarchy+arnold&hl=en&sa=X&ved=0ahUKEwj2tYOFoK_hAhXtqFkKHSjoAoMQ6AEIKjAA#v=onepage&q=culture%20anarchy%20arnold&f=false.
Bagley, William C. *Education and Emergent Man*. New York: T. Nelson & Sons, 1934.
Berlin, Isaiah. "Two Concepts of Liberty." In *The Proper Study of Mankind*, edited by Henry Hardy, 191–42. New York: Farrar, Strauss and Giroux, 1997.
Berry, Christopher. "School Inflation: Did the 20th-Century Growth in School Size Improve Education?" *Education Next* 4, no. 4 (2004): 56–62.

Bode, Boyd Henry. *Progressive Education at the Crossroads*. New York: Newson & Co., 1938.

Bonastia, Christopher. *Southern Stalemate: Five Years Without Public Education in Prince Edward County, Virginia*. Chicago: University of Chicago Press, 2012.

Bowles, Samuel, and Herbert Gintis. *Schooling in Capitalist America: Educational Reform and the Contradictions of Economic Life*. New York: Basic Books, 1977.

Brameld, Theodore. *Education for the Emerging Age: Newer Ends and Stronger Means*. New York: Harper & Row, 1965.

———. *Patterns of Educational Philosophy*. New York: Holt, Reinhart, and Winston, 1971.

Brennan, Jason. *Libertarianism: What Everyone Needs to Know*. New York: Oxford University Press, 2012.

Buchanan, James M. *Cost and Choice: An Inquiry in Economic Theory*. Chicago: Markham, 1969.

———. "Politics Without Romance: A Sketch of Positive Public Choice Theory and Its Normative Implications." In *The Logical Foundations of Constitutional Liberty*, 45–59. Indianapolis: Liberty Fund, 1999.

———. *Public Finance in Democratic Process: Fiscal Institutions and Individual Choice*. Chapel Hill: University of North Carolina Press, 1967.

———. "Rent Seeking Versus Profit Seeking." In *The Logical Foundations of Constitutional Liberty*, 103–15. Indianapolis: Liberty Fund, 1999.

Buchanan, James M., and Gordon Tullock. *The Calculus of Consent*. Ann Arbor: University of Michigan Press, 1962.

Buckley, William. "Murray Rothbard, RIP." *The National Review*, February 6, 1995.

Burgin, Angus. *The Great Persuasion: Reinventing Free Markets Since the Depression*. Cambridge: Harvard University Press, 2012.

Burns, Jennifer. "Democracy in Chains: The Deep History of the Radical Right's Stealth Plan for America by Nancy MacLean." *History of Political Economy* 50, no. 3 (September 1, 2018): 640–48.

Carl, Jim. "Free Marketeers, Policy Wonks, and Yankee Democracy: School Vouchers in New Hampshire, 1973–1976." *Harvard Educational Review* 78, no. 4 (2008): 589–614.

———. *Freedom of Choice: Vouchers in American Education*. Santa Barbara, CA: Praeger, 2011.

Chodorov, Frank. "A Really Free School System." *The Freeman*, July 1954.

———. "About Me: An Editorial." *The Freeman*, July 1954.

———. "Education and Freedom: My Friend's Education." In *Fugitive Essays: Selected Writings of Frank Chodorov*, edited by Charles H. Hamilton, 119–21. Indianapolis: Liberty Fund, 1980.

———. "How to Curb the Commies." In *Fugitive Essays: Selected Writings of Frank Chodorov*, edited by Charles H. Hamilton, 95–98. Indianapolis: Liberty Fund, 1980.

———. *Out of Step*. Ludwig von Mises Institute EPUB edition. Auburn, AL: Ludwig von Mises Institute, 2007.

———. "Private Schools: The Solution to America's Educational Problems." In *Fugitive Essays: Selected Writings of Frank Chodorov*, edited by Charles H. Hamilton, 127–33. Indianapolis: Liberty Fund, 1980.

———. *The Rise and Fall of Society*. Auburn, AL: Ludwig von Mises Institute, 2007.

———. "What Individualism Is Not." In *Fugitive Essays: Selected Writings of Frank Chodorov*, edited by Charles H. Hamilton, 108–12. Indianapolis: Liberty Fund, 1980.

———. "Why Free Schools Are Not Free." In *Fugitive Essays: Selected Writings of Frank Chodorov*, edited by Charles H. Hamilton, 122–26. Indianapolis: Liberty Fund, 1980.

———. "Why Teach Freedom?" In *Fugitive Essays: Selected Writings of Frank Chodorov*, edited by Charles H. Hamilton, 115–17. Indianapolis: Liberty Fund, 1980.

Chubb, John E., and Terry M. Moe. *Politics Markets and Americas Schools*. Washington, DC: Brookings Institution Press, 1990.

Clinton, Bill. *Between Hope and History: Meeting America's Challenges for the Twentieth Century*. New York: Crown, 1996.

Coons, John E. "Give Us Liberty and Give Us Depth." In *Liberty & Learning: Milton Friedman's Voucher Idea at Fifty*, edited by Robert Enlow and Lenore T. Ealy, 57–65. Washington, DC: Cato Institute, 2006.

Coons, John E., and Stephen D. Sugarman. *Education by Choice: The Case for Family Control*. Berkeley: University of California Press, 1978.

Coons, John E., William H. Klune III, and Stephen D. Sugarman. *Private Wealth and Public Education*. Cambridge, MA: Belknap Press, 1970. http://hdl.handle.net/2027/mdp.39015035328874.

Cox, Stephen. "Merely Metaphorical? Ayn Rand, Isabel Paterson, and the Language of Theory." *Journal of Ayn Rand Studies* 8 (n.d.): 237–60.

Crunden, Robert M. *The Mind and Art of Albert Jay Nock*. Chicago: Henry Regnery, 1964.

Cubberley, Elwood P. *Changing Conceptions of Education*. Cambridge, MA: Houghton Mifflin, 1909.

"Democratic Party Platform of 1960." The American Presidency Project, 1960. http://www.presidency.ucsb.edu/ws/index.php?pid=29602.

Dewey, John. *Experience and Education*. New York: Macmillan, 1938.

———. "How Much Freedom in New Schools?" Greenwich, CT: Information Age Publishing, 2006.

Doherty, Brian. "Best of Both Worlds." *Reason Magazine*, June 1996. http://reason.com/archives/1995/06/01/best-of-both-worlds.

———. *Radicals for Capitalism: A Freewheeling History of the Modern American Libertarian Movement*. 1st ed. New York: PublicAffairs, 2007.

Downs, Anthony. *An Economic Theory of Democracy*. New York: Harper, 1957.

"Economic Forces and Education." *Washington Journal*. C-SPAN, August 26, 2002. http://www.c-spanvideo.org/program/Forcesan.

Eisenhower, Dwight. "Transcript of President Dwight D. Eisenhower's Farewell Address (1961)." *www.ourdocuments.gov*, January 17, 1961. http://www.ourdocuments.gov/doc.php?flash=true&doc=90&page=transcript.

Eow, Gregory T. "Fighting a New Deal: Intellectual Origins of the Reagan Revolution, 1932–1952." PhD dissertation, Rice University, 2007. https://scholarship.rice.edu/handle/1911/75005.

Everson v. Board of Education, No. 330 U.S. 1 (Supreme Court of the United States of America 1947).

Flynn, John T. *The Decline of the American Republic*. Auburn, AL: Ludwig von Mises Institute, 2007.

Forman, James. "The Secret History of School Choice: How Progressives Got There First." *Georgetown Law Journal* 93, no. 4 (2005): 1287–319.

Friedman, Milton. *Capitalism and Freedom*. 40th anniversary edition. Chicago: University of Chicago Press, 2002.

———. "Gammon's Black Holes." *Newsweek*, November 1977.

———. "George Stigler: A Personal Reminiscence." *Journal of Political Economy* 101, no. 5 (October 1, 1993): 768–73.

———. "Liberalism, Old Style." In *The Indispensable Milton Friedman*, edited by Larry Ebenstein, 11–24. Washington, DC: Regnery, 2012.

———. "My Five Favorite Libertarian Books." In *The Indispensable Milton Friedman*, edited by Larry Ebenstein, 122–24. Washington, DC: Regnery, 2012.

———. "Neoliberalism and Its Prospects." In *The Indispensable Milton Friedman*, edited by Larry Ebenstein, 17–24. Washington, DC: Regnery, 2012.

———. "Public Education." *Newsweek*, March 1967.

―――. "School Choice: A Personal Retrospective." In *The Indispensable Milton Friedman*, edited by Larry Ebenstein, 125–29. Washington, DC: Regnery, 2012.

―――. "School Vouchers Turn 50, But the Fight Is Just Beginning." In *Liberty and Learning: Milton Friedman's Voucher Ideas at Fifty*, 155–58. Washington, DC: Cato Institute, 2006.

―――. "Selling Schools Like Groceries: The Voucher Idea." *New York Times Magazine*, September 1973.

―――. "Some Comments on the Significance of Labor Unions for Economic Policy." In *The Impact of the Union*, edited by David M. Wright. New York: Harcourt Brace, 1951.

―――. "The Role of Government in Education." In *Economics and the Public Interest*, edited by Robert A. Solo, 123–44. New Brunswick, NJ: Rutgers University Press, 1955.

―――. "The Solution to the Public School Crisis." *San Francisco Chronicle*, March 20, 1979.

Friedman, Milton, and Rose Friedman. *Free to Choose: A Personal Statement*. 1st ed. New York: Harcourt Brace Jovanovich, 1980.

Friedman, Milton, and George Stigler. *Roofs or Ceilings?: The Current Housing Problem*. Irvington-on-Hudson, NY: Foundation for Economic Education, n.d.

Gammon, Max. *Health and Security: Report on the Public Provision for Medical Care in Great Britain*. London: St. Michael's Organization, 1976.

Glenn, Charles L. *The American Model of State and School: An Historical Inquiry*. New York: Continuum, 2012.

Goodman, Paul. "A Touchstone for the Libertarian Program." In *American Radical Thought: The Libertarian Tradition*, 308–11. Lexington, MA: D.C. Heath and Company, 1970.

―――. *Compulsory Mis-education, and The Community of Scholars*. New York: Vintage Books, 1964.

―――. *Growing Up Absurd: Problems of Youth in the Organized System*. New York: Random House, 1960.

Goodway, David. *Anarchist Seeds Beneath the Snow: Left-Libertarian Thought and British Writers from William Morris to Colin Ward*. Liverpool, UK: Liverpool University Press, 2006.

Griffin v. School Board of Prince Edward County, No. 218 (U.S. May 25, 1964).

Harvey, David. *A Brief History of Neoliberalism*. New York: Oxford University Press, 2005.

Heckelman, Jac C., and Dennis Coates. "On the Shoulders of a Giant: The Legacy of Mancur Olsen." In *Collective Choice: Essays in Honor of Mancur Olsen*, edited by Mancur Olson, Jac C. Heckelman, and Dennis Coates, 1–8. Berlin, Germany: Springer-Verlag, 2003.

Heller, Anne Conover. *Ayn Rand and the World She Made*. EPUB edition. New York: Anchor, 2010.

Herbert, Auberon. "State Education: A Help or Hindrance?" In *The Right and Wrong of Compulsion by the State, and Other Essays*, edited by Eric Mack, 53–80. Indianapolis: Liberty Fund, 1978.

Hirschman, Albert O. *Exit, Voice, and Loyalty*. Cambridge: Harvard University Press, 1970.

Holt, John. *Escape from Childhood*. New York: Dutton, 1974.

———. *Freedom and Beyond*. New York: Dutton, 1972.

———. *Instead of Education: Ways to Help People Do Things Better*. New York: Dutton, 1976.

———. "Not So Golden Rule Days." In *The Under-Achieving School*, 71–79. New York: Pitman, 1969.

———. *What Do I Do Monday?* New York: Dutton, 1970.

Hülsmann, Jörg Guido. *Mises: The Last Knight of Liberalism*. Auburn, AL: Ludwig von Mises Institute, 2007.

Hutt, Ethan L. "Formalism Over Function: Compulsion, Courts, and the Rise of Educational Formalism in America, 1870–1930." *Teachers College Record* 114, no. 1 (January 1, 2012): 1–27.

Hutt, W. H. *Economists and the Public: A Study of Competition and Opinion*. New Brunswick, NJ: Transaction Publishers, 1990.

———. *Politically Impossible …?* London: Institute of Economic Affairs, 1971.

———. "The Concept of Consumers' Sovereignty." *The Economic Journal* 50, no. 197 (March 1, 1940): 66–77.

Illich, Ivan. *Deschooling Society*. New York: Harper & Row, 1971.

Jefferson, Thomas. "First Inaugural Address," 1801. http://avalon.law.yale.edu/19th_century/jefinau1.asp.

Jones, David Stedman. *Masters of the Universe: Hayek, Friedman, and the Birth of Neoliberal Politics*. Princeton, NJ: Princeton University Press, 2012.

Kaestle, Carl. *Pillars of the Republic: Common Schools and American Society, 1780–1860*. New York: Hill and Wang, 1983.

Kandel, Isaac Leon. *American Education in the Twentieth Century*. Cambridge: Harvard University Press, 1957.

Katz, Michael B. "A History of Compulsory Education Laws." *Phi Delta Kappan*. Fastback Series, no. 75 (1976).

———. "From Voluntarism to Bureaucracy in American Education." *Sociology of Education* 44, no. 3 (July 1, 1971): 297–332.

———. *The Irony of Early School Reform: Educational Innovation in Mid-Nineteenth Century Massachusetts.* New York: Teachers College Press, 2001.

Kenny, Lawrence W., and Amy B. Schmidt. "The Decline in the Number of School Districts in the U.S.: 1950–1980." *Public Choice* 79 (1994): 1–18.

Kirkpatrick, David W. *Choice in Schooling: A Case for Tuition Vouchers.* Chicago: Loyola University Press, 1990.

Kirzner, Israel. "Mises and His Understanding of the Capitalist System." *Cato Journal* 19, no. 2 (1999): 215–32.

Kolko, Gabriel. *The Triumph of Conservatism; a Re-interpretation of American History, 1900–1916.* New York: Free Press of Glencoe, 1963.

Lane, Rose Wilder. *The Discovery of Freedom: Man's Struggle Against Authority.* New York: The John Day Company, 1943.

Lens, Sidney. *The Futile Crusade.* Chicago: Quadrangle Press, 1964.

Levinson, Eliot. *The Alum Rock Voucher Demonstration: Three Years of Implementation.* Santa Monica, CA: Rand Corporation, 1976.

Lieberman, Myron. *Education as a Profession.* Englewood Cliffs, NJ: Prentice-Hall, 1956.

———. "Free Market Strategy and Tactics in K–12 Education." In *Liberty and Learning: Milton Friedman's Voucher Ideas at Fifty*, edited by Robert C. Enlow and Lenore T. Ealy, 81–101. Washington, DC: Cato Institute, 2006.

———. "Market Solutions to the Education Crisis." *CATO Policy Analysis* 75 (1986).

———. *Privatization and Educational Choice.* New York: St. Martin's Press, 1989.

———. *Public Education: An Autopsy.* 4th ed. Cambridge: Harvard University Press, 1993.

———. *Teachers Unions: How They Sabotage Educational Reform and Why.* San Francisco: Encounter Books, 2000.

———. *The Educational Morass.* Lanham, MD: Rowman & Littlefield Education, 2007.

Lippmann, Walter. *Public Opinion.* New York: Harcourt Brace, 1922.

MacLean, Nancy. *Democracy in Chains: The Deep History of the Radical Right's Stealth Plan for America.* New York: Penguin, 2017.

Mann, Horace. *Lectures and Annual Reports on Education.* Cambridge, MA: M.T. Mann, 1867.

Marcuse, Herbert. *One-Dimensional Man: Studies in the Ideology of Advanced Industrial Society.* Boston: Beacon Press, 1964.

Marshall, Peter. *Demanding the Impossible: A History of Anarchism.* Oakland, CA: PM Press, 2010.

Matus, Ron. "California Dreamin': How the Left Almost Pulled Off School Choice Revolution." *redefinED*, December 16, 2015. https://www.redefinedonline.org/2015/12/how-the-left-almost-pulled-off-school-choice-revolution/.

McElroy, Wendy. "Albert Jay Nock on Education." *The Freeman.* January 1, 2000. http://www.independent.org/newsroom/article.asp?id=232.

Meeker, Martin. "Jack Coons: Law, Ethics, and Educational Finance Reform, 2015." Oral History Center, Bancroft Library, University of California. http://digitalassets.lib.berkeley.edu/roho/ucb/text/coons_jack_2016.pdf.

Mehta, Jal. *The Allure of Order: High Hopes, Dashed Expectations, and the Troubled Quest to Remake American Schooling.* New York: Oxford University Press, 2013. https://books.google.com/books?hl=en&lr=&id=tkQSDAAAQBAJ&oi=fnd&pg=PP1&dq=jal+mehta&ots=TlcNHXA3dG&sig=ZSMKjSCWOlWMRriy8fpKKk-_8ZQ#v=onepage&q=jal%20mehta&f=false.

Meier, Deborah. "Choice Can Save Public Education." *The Nation*, March 4, 1991.

Meier, Deborah, and Emily Gasoi. "What Happens to Public Education Deferred." In *These Schools Belong to You and Me: Why We Can't Afford to Examine Our Public Schools*, 137–60. Boston, MA: Beacon Press, 2017.

Meyer, Frank S. "In Defense of Freedom." In *In Defense of Freedom and Related Essays*, 33–151. Indianapolis: Liberty Fund, 1996.

———. "Libertarianism or Libertinism?" In *In Defense of Freedom and Related Essays*, 183–86. Indianapolis: Liberty Fund, 1996.

Mill, John Stuart. *On Liberty, and the Subjection of Women.* Henry Holt 1879 edition. Indianapolis: Liberty Fund, 2011.

Mills, C. Wright. *The Power Elite.* Oxford, UK: Oxford University Press, 1956.

Moe, Terry M. *Schools, Vouchers, and the American Public.* 1st ed. Washington, DC: Brookings Institute Press, 2001.

———. *Special Interest: Teachers Unions and America's Public Schools.* Washington, DC: Brookings Institution Press, 2011.

Munger, Michael C. "On the Origins and Goals of Public Choice: Constitutional Conspiracy?" *Independent Review* 22, no. 3 (2018): 359–82.

Nasaw, David. *Schooled to Order: A Social History of Public Schooling in the United States.* New York: Oxford University Press, 1979.

Nash, George H. *The Conservative Intellectual Movement in America Since 1945.* New York: Basic Books, 1979.

Neill, Alexander Sutherland. *Summerhill: A Radical Approach to Child Rearing.* New York: Hart Publishing, 1960.

Newport, Frank, and Joseph Carroll. "Iraq Versus Vietnam: A Comparison of Public Opinion." *www.gallup.com*, August 24, 2005. http://www.gallup.com/poll/18097/Iraq-Versus-Vietnam-Comparison-Public-Opinion.aspx.

Niskanen, William A., Jr. *Bureaucracy and Representative Government.* Chicago: Aldine, Atherton, 1971.

Nitsche, Charles Gerald. "Albert Jay Nock and Frank Chodorov: Case Studies in Recent American Individualist and Anti-statist Thought." University of Maryland College Park, 1981.

Nock, Albert Jay. "A Cultural Forecast." In *On Doing the Right Thing and Other Essays,* 72–96. New York: Harper & Brothers, 1928.

———. "Anarchist's Progress." In *On Doing the Right Thing and Other Essays,* 123–60. New York: Harper & Brothers, 1928.

———. *Henry George: An Essay.* New York: W. Morrow, 1939.

———. *Letters from Albert Jay Nock.* Edited by Frank W. Garrison. Caldwell, ID: Caxton Printers, 1949.

———. "Life, Liberty, and...." In *The Disadvantages of Being Educated and Other Essays,* 29–41. Tampa, FL: Hallberg, 1996.

———. *Memoirs of a Superfluous Man.* New York: Harper & Brothers, 1947.

———. "On Doing the Right Thing." In *On Doing the Right Thing and Other Essays,* 161–78. New York: Harper & Brothers, 1928.

———. *On Doing the Right Thing and Other Essays.* New York: Harper & Brothers, 1928.

———. *Our Enemy the State.* New York: William Morrow, 1935.

———. *The Theory of Education in the United States.* Auburn, AL: Ludwig von Mises Institute, 2008.

———. "The Value of Useless Knowledge." In *The Disadvantages of Being Educated and Other Essays,* 83–96. Tampa, FL: Hallberg, 1996.

———. "Towards a New Quality Product." In *On Doing the Right Thing and Other Essays,* 97–122. New York: Harper & Brothers, 1928.

O'Brien, Molly Townes. "Private School Tuition Vouchers and the Realities of Racial Politics." *Tennessee Law Review* 64 (1996): 359–98.

Oglesby, Carl. *Ravens in the Storm: A Personal History of the 1960s Anti-war Movement.* New York: Scribner, 2010.

Ohles, Frederik, Shirley M. Ohles, and John G. Ramsay. *Biographical Dictionary of Modern American Educators.* Westport, CT: Greenwood Press, 1997.

Olson, Mancur. *The Logic of Collective Action: Public Goods and the Theory of Groups.* Cambridge, MA: Harvard University Press, 1971.

O'Neil, John. "On Lasting School Reform: A Conversation with Ted Sizer." *Educational Leadership*, February 1995.
O'Neil, Patrick M. "Ayn Rand and the Is-Ought Problem." *Journal of Libertarian Studies* 7, no. 1 (n.d.): 81–99.
Ortega y Gasset, Jose. *The Revolt of the Masses*. New York: W. W. Norton, 1993.
Paterson, Isabel. *The God of the Machine*. Baltimore, MD: Laissez Faire Books, 2012.
Paul, Ron. *The School Revolution: A New Answer to Our Broken Education System*. New York: Grand Central, 2013.
Paxton, Bill. *What Did You Learn in School Today?* Ramblin' Boy. Elektra Records, 1964.
Perkinson, Henry J. *The Imperfect Panacea: American Faith in Education*. Boston: McGraw Hill, 1995.
Persky, Joseph. "Retrospectives: Consumer Sovereignty." *The Journal of Economic Perspectives* 7, no. 1 (1993): 183–91.
Pierce v. Society of Sisters, No. 268 U.S. 510 (Supreme Court of the United States June 1, 1925).
Radosh, Ronald. *Commies: A Journey Through the Old Left, the New Left and the Leftover Left*. San Francisco: Encounter Books, 2001.
Raimondo, Justin. *An Enemy of the State: The Life of Murray N. Rothbard*. Amherst, NY: Prometheus Books, 2000.
———. *Reclaiming the American Right: The Lost Legacy of the Conservative Movement*. 2nd ed. Wilmington, DE: Intercollegiate Studies Institute, 2008.
Rand, Ayn. *Atlas Shrugged*. 50th anniversary EPUB edition. New York: Signet, 2007.
———. *Ayn Rand Answers: The Best of Her Q & A*. Edited by Robert Mayhew. New York: Penguin, 2005.
———. "Doesn't Life Require Compromise?" In *The Virtue of Selfishness*, 68–70. New York: Signet, 1964.
———. *Letters of Ayn Rand*. New York: Dutton, 1995.
———. "Man's Rights." In *The Virtue of Selfishness*, 96–104. New York: Signet, 1964.
———. "Tax Credits for Education." In *The Voice of Reason: Essays in Objectivist Thought*, edited by Leonard Peikoff, 247–53. New York: New America Library, 1988.
———. "The Comprachinos." In *The New Left: The Anti-industrial Revolution*, 187–239. New York: Signet, 1975.
———. "The Nature of Government." In *The Virtue of Selfishness*, 111–19. New York: Signet, 1964.

———. *The New Left: The Anti-industrial Revolution*. New York: Plume, 1975.
———. "The Question of Scholarships." In *The Voice of Reason: Essays in Objectivist Thought*, edited by Leonard Peikoff, 40–45. New York: New America Library, 1988.
———. "What Is Capitalism?" In *Capitalism: The Unknown Ideal*, 15–34. New York: Signet, 1986.
Ravitch, Diane. *Reign of Error: The Hoax of the Privatization Movement and the Danger to America's Public Schools*. New York: Alfred A. Knopf, 2013.
———. *The Death and Life of the Great American School System: How Testing and Choice Are Undermining Education*. New York: Basic books, 2010.
———. *The Revisionists Revised: A Critique of the Radical Attack on Schools*. New York: Basic Books, 1978.
"Republican Party Platform of 1972." The American Presidency Project, 1972. http://www.presidency.ucsb.edu/ws/?pid=25842.
Riggenbach, Jeff. "Convention Diary 1978." *Libertarian Review* 7, no. 9 (October 1978) edition.
———. "John Holt: Libertarian Outsider." Text. Mises Institute, April 19, 2010. https://mises.org/library/john-holt-libertarian-outsider.
Rothbard, Murray. "Atlas Shrugged." *Commonweal*, December 20, 1957.
———. *Education: Free & Compulsory*. Auburn, AL: Ludwig von Mises Institute, 1999.
———. *For a New Liberty*. Auburn, AL: Ludwig von Mises Institute, 1973.
———. "Historical Origins." In *The Twelve Year Sentence: Radical Views on Compulsory Schooling*, edited by William F. Rickenbacker, 7–30. San Francisco: Fox & Wilkes, 1974.
———. "Kid Lib." In *Egalitarianism as a Revolt Against Nature*, 115–23. 2nd ed. Auburn, AL: Ludwig von Mises Institute, 2000.
———. "Milton Friedman Unraveled." *Journal of Libertarian Studies* 16, no. 4 (n.d.): 37–54.
———. *Power and Market: Government and the Economy*. EPUB edition. Auburn, AL: Ludwig von Mises Institute, 2004.
———. *The Betrayal of the American Right*. 1st ed. Auburn, AL: Ludwig von Mises Institute, 2007.
———. *The Ethics of Liberty*. New York: NYU Press, 2003.
Rothbard, Murray, and Ronald Radosh, eds. *A New History of Leviathan: Essays on the Rise of the American Corporate State*. New York: E. P. Dutton, 1972.
Ruger, William. *Milton Friedman*. New York: Continuum, 2011.

Savas, Emanuel S. "Municipal Monopolies Versus Competition in Delivering Urban Services." In *Improving the Quality of Urban Management*, 473–500. Beverly Hills, CA: Sage, 1974.

Schmidtz, David, and Jason Brennan. *A Brief History of Liberty*. 1st ed. Malden, MA: Wiley-Blackwell, 2010.

Schwartz, Peter. "Libertarianism: The Perversion of Liberty." In *The Voice of Reason: Essays in Objectivist Thought*, edited by Leonard Peikoff, 311–33. New York: New America Library, 1988.

Shanks, Hershel, and William H. Clune. Review of *Review of Private Wealth and Public Education*, by John E. Coons and Stephen D. Sugarman. *Harvard Law Review* 84, no. 1 (1970): 256–62.

Simons, Henry. "A Positive Program for Laissez Faire." In *Economic Policy for a Free Society*, 40–77. Chicago: University of Chicago Press, 1948.

Sizer, Theodore. "Education and Assimilation: A Fresh Plea for Pluralism." *Phi Delta Kappan* 58, no. 1 (1976): 31–35.

———. *Horace's Hope: What Works for the American High School*. New York: Houghton Mifflin, 1996.

———. "The Academies: An Interpretation." In *The Age of the Academy*, 1–49. New York: Teachers College Press, 1964.

———. "The Case for a Free Market." *Saturday Review* no. 11 (January 1969): 34–38, 42.

———. *The Red Pencil: Convictions from Experience in Education*. New Haven, CT: Yale University Press, 2006.

Sizer, Theodore, and Phillip Whitten. "A Proposal for a Poor Children's Bill of Rights." *Psychology Today*, August 1968.

Smith, George H. "Nineteenth Century Opponents of State Education: Prophets of Modern Revisionism." In *The Public School Monopoly*, 109–44. Cambridge, MA: Ballinger, 1982.

Smith, Michael. *The Libertarians and Education*. Boston: Allen & Unwin, 1983.

Spann, Robert M. "Public Versus Private Provision of Government Services." In *Budgets and Bureaucrats: The Sources of Government Growth*, edited by Thomas Borcherding, 71–89. Durham, NC: Duke University Press, 1979.

Spencer, Herbert. "From Freedom to Bondage." In *The Man Versus the State*, 235–48. Indianapolis: Liberty Fund, 2008.

———. *Social Statics*. Indianapolis: Liberty Fund, 1850.

Spring, Joel. *Education and the Rise of the Corporate State*. Boston: Beacon Press, 1972.

———. *Political Agendas for Education: From the Christian Coalition to the Green Party*. Mahwah, NJ: Psychology Press, 2005. https://www.worldcat.org/title/

political-agendas-for-education-from-the-religious-right-to-the-green-party/oclc/493204735&referer=brief_results.

Steelman, Aaron. "Frank Chodorov: Champion of Liberty." *The Freeman*, 1996. http://www.thefreemanonline.org/features/frank-chodorov-champion-of-liberty/.

Sullivan, Raymond L. *Serrano v. Priest*, No. L.A. 29820 (California Supreme Court, August 30, 1971).

———. *Serrano v. Priest*, No. 557 P. 2d 929 (California Supreme Court, December 30, 1976).

Szasz, Thomas. *Law, Liberty, and Psychiatry: An Inquiry into the Social Uses of Mental Health Practices.* New York: Macmillan, 1963.

"The Crisis in Schooling: An LR Colloquium." *Libertarian Review* 7, no. 11 (December 1978).

"The General Line." *Left and Right* 1, no. 1 (1965): 5.

Thorndike, E. L. *Human Nature and the Social Order.* New York: Macmillan, 1940.

Tooley, James. *Education Without the State.* London: Institute of Economic Affairs, 1998.

———. "From Universal to Targeted Vouchers: The Relevance of the Friedmans' Proposals for Developing Countries." In *Liberty and Learning: Milton Friedman's Voucher Ideas at Fifty*, edited by Robert C. Enlow and Lenore T. Ealy, 139–54. Washington, DC: Cato Institute, 2006.

Tullock, Gordon. *Private Wants, Public Means: An Economic Analysis of the Desirable Scope of Government.* New York: Basic Books, 1970.

———. *The Politics of Bureaucracy.* Washington DC: Public Affairs Press, 1965.

Tyack, David B. *The One Best System: A History of American Urban Education.* Cambridge: Harvard University Press, 1974.

———. "The Perils of Pluralism: The Background of the Pierce Case." *The American Historical Review* 74, no. 1 (October 1, 1968): 74–98.

Veerman, Philip E. *The Rights of the Child and the Changing Image of Childhood.* Boston: Martinus Nijhoff, 1992.

Vinovskis, Maris A. *The Origins of Public High Schools: A Reexamination of the Beverly High School Controversy.* Madison: University of Wisconsin Press, 1985.

von Mises, Ludwig. *Bureaucracy.* Indianapolis: Liberty Fund, 2007.

———. *Human Action: A Treatise on Economics.* Indianapolis: Liberty Fund, 2010.

———. *Liberalism: The Classical Tradition.* Indianapolis: Liberty Fund, 2008.

———. *Socialism: An Economic and Sociological Analysis.* New Haven: Yale University Press, 1951.

———. *The Anti-capitalist Mentality.* Auburn, AL: Ludwig von Mises Institute, 2008.

von Mises, Ludwig, and Murray N. Rothbard. "Mises and Rothbard Letters of Ayn Rand." *Journal of Libertarian Studies* 21, no. 4 (Winter 2007): 11–16.

Weingarten, Randi. "School Choice—Past and Present." American Federation of Teachers, July 22, 2017. https://www.aft.org/column/school-choice-past-and-present.

West, E. G. *Education and the State: A Study in Political Economy.* Indianapolis: Liberty Fund, 1994.

———. "Private Versus Public Education: A Classical Economic Dispute." *Journal of Political Economy* 72, no. 5 (October 1, 1964): 465–75.

———. "The Political Economy of American Public School Legislation." *Journal of Law and Economics* 10 (1967): 101–28.

Zellers v. Huff, No. 55 N.M. 501, 236 P.2d 949 (1951).

Index

A
abuse of power
  by the state 16, 18, 24
  by the wealthy 94
administrative progressivism 20
Alum Rock voucher experiment 124
anarchism 78, 97
  anarcho-capitalism 95
Arnold, Matthew 28, 37, 38, 51, 185
Austrian school of economics, the 78
authoritarianism 26
autonomy, school 156, 157, 160, 162, 166

B
Barnard, Henry 15, 17, 88
Bastiat, Frederic 41, 46

Bode, Boyd 67
Brameld, Theodore 67, 68
Brown v. Board of Education 5, 106, 109, 132
Brownson, Orastes 16, 17
Buchanan, James 6, 10, 30, 120, 121, 131–134, 136, 142, 151
Burke, Edmund 33

C
capitalism 7, 8, 24, 30, 37, 41, 60, 63, 67, 68, 70, 95–97, 100, 101, 103, 104, 107, 108, 110–116, 121, 185
Chicago School of economics, the 187
children's liberation 80–82
children's rights
  and exit rights 82–84

in a libertarian society 79, 81
Chodorov, Frank
  beliefs 6, 13, 38, 39, 43, 44, 49, 50, 102, 104
  influences 6, 10, 39, 44, 180
classical liberalism 101, 103, 114
Coalition of Essential Schools, the 160, 161
coercion
  and children's rights 79, 80, 176
  by the state 95
  unjustifiable 81
collectivist ideology 62
common school movement, the 19, 22
compulsory education
  and homogeneity 84, 88
  and paternalism 88, 118
  early European 87
  in France 107, 109
  in Prussia 87
  in the United States 19, 84, 87, 88, 172
  laws 19, 66, 88, 107, 113, 114, 117, 119, 172, 173, 176
  religious motivations for 87, 88
consumer sovereignty 7, 30, 37, 51–57, 124, 168, 185
  in education 7, 29, 51, 54, 56, 57, 125, 168, 185
Coons, John
  beliefs 156, 157, 168, 177
  influences 9, 155, 165–169, 171
corruption
  in government 20
  in public schools 20
Counts, George 67
Cubberley, Edward 32
cultural conservatism 30

D

democratic free schools 32, 35, 44, 52, 89, 90, 134, 164, 182, 189
dependence on the state 12, 25
Dewey, John 62, 67
district power equalizing model, the 166
distrust in government 184

E

economic theory of democracy 118–120, 131
economism 33, 34
education
  by the state 18, 20, 25, 36, 39, 47, 66, 88, 107, 134, 165, 166, 186
  different models of 186
  egalitarianism in 31, 35, 88, 189
  for upward mobility 33, 158
  markets in 2, 3, 6–8, 10–13, 16, 39, 45, 48–51, 54–57, 75, 97, 100, 102, 104, 108, 112, 119, 124, 127–130, 138, 143, 144, 146, 147, 150, 152–154, 156, 177, 179–190
  parents' role in 5, 10, 15, 19, 35, 45, 46, 48–50, 57, 61, 69, 71, 74, 79–81, 90, 105–107, 109, 119, 123, 124, 135, 139, 153, 158, 161, 173, 179, 180, 182, 184, 186, 188
  "tracks" in 32
  vs. training 7, 31–34, 38, 39, 44, 51
egalitarianism 31, 35, 80, 189
entrepreneurship 62

Equal Protection Clause, Fourteenth Amendment's 111, 167
Establishment Clause, First Amendment's 108
Everson v. Board of Education 47
exit costs 81
　in education 81
exit rights 82–84

Family Choice in Education proposal, the 170, 171
family *power equalizing model*, the 167
free-rider problem, the 140, 141
freedom of choice 5, 74, 79, 109–111, 157, 187, 190
　and children's rights 79
　in education 79
Friedman, Milton
　beliefs 102, 105, 116, 134, 156, 187
　influences 101, 102, 110, 113, 120, 121
Friedman, Rose 8, 109, 112, 153

Gammon, Max
　and Gammon's Law 121, 123
George, Henry 42
GI Bill of Rights 106, 108, 110
Goodman, Paul 10, 80, 83, 84, 86, 94–96, 116, 186

Hickey, Jack 170

Holt, John
　beliefs 173–175
　homeschooling 176, 177
Hutt, William H. 52, 53, 55, 56

Illich, Ivan 86, 94, 96
individualism
　economic 59
　intellectual 59, 60
individuality 46, 62, 66, 67, 75, 84, 86
indoctrination in education 67, 104
integration, forced 5, 110
intrinsic motivation
　definition 33
　in education 33, 34
　lack of 33

Jencks, Christopher 109, 124, 159, 169

Katz, Michael 66, 90, 96, 118
Kirk, Russell 38
Klune III, William 165
Knight, Frank 101, 187
Kolko, Gabriel 85

laissez-faire economics 6, 23, 38, 52, 168
Law of Equal Freedom (Herbert Spencer's) 26
Lens, Sidney 85

libertarianism
  in education 10, 97, 100, 177, 186, 187
  past trends in 14
libertarian movement in education 23
Libertarian Party, the 6, 74
Lieberman, Myron
  beliefs 146, 148, 154
  biography 133
  influences 131
Liggio, Leonard 93

M

MacLean, Nancy 132, 133
Mann, Horace 15, 16, 22, 87, 88
Marcuse, Herbert 85
marginalist (economics) tradition 54
marginalist revolution 30
market anarchism. *See* anarchism, anarcho-capitalism
market capitalism
  defense of 30
  definition of 100
  proponents of 187
market libertarianism 10, 78
  vs. "libertarian" (terminology) 130
markets
  criticism of 100, 127, 144, 153
  defense of 6, 8, 10, 11, 30, 51, 53, 96, 187
  virtues of 35
Marshall, Peter 95
Meier, Deborah
  beliefs 164
Menger, Carl 54, 78
Meyer, Frank 96, 97
Mill, John Stuart 46, 48, 50, 106, 107, 158

Mills, C. Wright 84
Mises, Ludwig von 1, 6, 24, 30, 31, 37, 41, 43, 44, 52–57, 59, 77, 78, 80, 87, 89, 185
monopolies
  in business 85
  in education 6, 11, 123
  in government 2, 6, 12, 85, 102, 122
Mont Pelerin Society, the 103
Murphy, Archibald 88

N

Nash, George H. 38
National Education Association 126, 128
natural rights 6, 35, 45, 75, 80, 89, 106, 179, 182, 185
negative liberties 42
neighborhood effects 105, 107, 114–116, 119, 123
Neill, A.S. 80
New Left, the 61, 79, 92–97, 186
New Psychology, the 44
Niskanen, William 122, 136
Nock, Albert Jay
  beliefs 26–28, 33, 35, 38, 51
  influences 26, 37, 39, 42

O

Objectivism (Ayn Rand) 7, 13, 59, 60, 70
Oglesby, Carl 96
Old Right, the 24, 79
Ortega y Gasset, Jose 27

parental values 84, 125
parents' role in education
  choosing irresponsibly 81, 83
paternalism 88
  and compulsory education 88
Paterson, Isabel 60, 63–66
Paul, Ron 177, 179–181, 183, 186, 188, 189
Paxton, Bill 86
personal responsibility 27
Pierce v. Society of Sisters 46
pluralism 9, 46, 49, 50, 152, 161, 162, 180, 182, 185
Poor Children's Bill of Rights, the (Sizer and Whitten's proposal) 158, 159, 189
private industry
  enterprising and innovative 25
  freedom of people in 16
  responsive to people's wants and needs 25
private schools
  distrust of 23, 27
  for-profit vs. nonprofit 109, 128, 137, 142, 143, 150
  problems with 53, 81, 95, 149, 153
  profit motive in 146
  receive state funding 188
  regulated by the state 47
  tuition fees deducted from taxes 48
processes of perversion 28, 30, 33
profit 11, 36, 38, 43, 103, 136, 138, 147–149, 151
  in education 9, 11, 27, 32, 94, 103, 128, 130, 131, 138, 142–144, 146, 148, 150–152, 154, 179, 183, 187
profit motive 118, 143, 146, 152, 179, 183, 185
public choice economics 11, 117, 120, 121, 126, 127, 130–133, 136, 187
public education
  dissatisfaction with 113, 145
  distrust of 190
  problems with 6, 150, 156
public good, the 8, 19, 131, 134, 135, 188
public school choice 153

Radosh, Ronald 93, 95, 96
Rand, Ayn
  beliefs 60, 62, 68–70, 75, 124
  biography 63, 133
  critiques of public education 60
  influences 60, 62, 63, 68, 186
rate bill system (in Early American public schools) 18, 19
rational egoism (Ayn Rand) 68
rational ignorance, theory of 139
Ravitch, Diane 4, 5, 32, 119, 177, 179, 181–189
Remnant, the 33, 34
Rothbard, Murray
  beliefs 8, 13, 80, 81
  biography 96
  influences 96
Ryan, Leo 169, 170

S

school choice 4–6, 8, 9, 103, 108, 123, 127–130, 134, 143–146, 153–157, 159, 160, 162–164, 167, 168, 170–173, 175–177, 179, 182, 186, 188, 189
  from the left 157
school privatization movement, the 131
segregation
  forced 5, 110
  racial 109, 110
self-discipline 26
self-ownership 69, 80
self-reliance 26, 44, 66
separation of church and state 47
separation of school and state 49, 50, 188
Serrano v. Priest 167, 169, 170
Simons, Henry 101, 102, 187
Sizer, Theodore
  beliefs 156, 177
Sklar, Martin J. 93
Spencer, Herbert 7, 18, 25, 26, 185
Spring, Joel 86, 96
Stigler, George 100, 101, 120, 121
subjective nature of value, the 78
Sugarman, Stephen
  beliefs 168
Summerhill 80
Szasz, Thomas 85

T

tax credits, educational 8, 11, 71–75, 102
Thorndike, Edward 32
training
  vs. education 7, 31, 32, 34, 35, 38, 44, 46, 51
  proper method of 32
Tullock, Gordon 120–122, 132, 136

U

uniformity of thought 46
unions, teachers'
  against education reform 127
  functioning as monopolies 128
  opposing school choice 129
  protecting teachers' interests 127, 135, 152
unschooling 10, 176

V

value subjectivism 30, 51
Viner, Jacob 101
voluntary exchange, principle of 25
vouchers, educational
  benefits of 113, 126
  distrust of 23, 184, 185
  in for-profit schools 9, 127, 130, 143, 154
  problems with 110
  targeted 119, 130, 143, 154, 181, 183, 189

W

welfare state 85, 176
West, E.G. 10, 15, 113–121, 124, 131, 134, 135
Williams, William Appleman 93

Z

Zellers v. Hoff 47